WOUNDED SOLDIER, HEALING WARRIOR

WOUNDED SOLDIER, HEALING WARRIOR

A Personal Story of a Vietnam
Veteran Who Lost His Legs
but Found His Soul

ALLEN CLARK

ZENITH PRESS

DEDICATION

To my daughters, Elizabeth and Christi—the joys
of fatherhood are cause enough for my survival in war.
To Linda, my wife, soul mate, ministry partner,
and faithful follower of Jesus.
To America's real First Team, the men and women
who have served and continue to serve the cause of freedom
in the uniforms of our nation's armed forces, the greatest
of each of their own generations.
To the caregivers of our nation's veterans in the Department
of Veterans Affairs of the United States of America.

First published in 2007 by Zenith Press, an imprint of MBI Publishing Company,
Galtier Plaza, Suite 200, 380 Jackson Street, St. Paul, MN 55101-3885 USA

Zenith Press titles are also available at discounts in bulk quantity for industrial
or sales-promotional use. For details write to Special Sales Manager at MBI
Publishing Company, Galtier Plaza, Suite 200, 380 Jackson Street, St. Paul,
MN 55101-3885 USA.

Library of Congress Cataloging-in-Publication Data

Clark, Allen B., 1942-
  Wounded soldier, healing warrior : a personal story of a Vietnam veteran who
lost his legs but found his soul / by Allen Clark.
    p. cm.
  Includes bibliographical references.
  ISBN-13: 978-0-7603-3113-2 (hardbound w/ jacket)
  ISBN-10: 0-7603-3113-8 (hardbound w/ jacket) 1. Clark, Allen B., 1942- 2.
Disabled veterans--Religious life. 3. Church work with veterans. 4. Combat
Faith (Organization) 5. Vietnam War, 1961-1975--Veterans--United States--
Biography. 6. Disabled veterans--United States--Biography. I. Title.
BV4589.C53 2007
277.3'0825092--dc22   .
[B]
                              2006032322

On the front cover: The author stands ready for an infiltration mission by
helicopter to the Tri-Border Point where South Vietnam, Cambodia, and
Laos touch, February 2, 1967. *Author's collection*

Cover design by Jennifer Bergstrom

Printed in the United States of America

TABLE OF CONTENTS

FOREWORD BY ROSS PEROT 6

INTRODUCTION 7

CHAPTER 1   "OH, GOD, I'M DEAD" 9

CHAPTER 2   HOME FOR HEALING 33

CHAPTER 3   PURSUING A LIFELONG DREAM 57

CHAPTER 4   MY QUEST FOR INDEPENDENCE 91

CHAPTER 5   THE BEGINNING OF MY OWN
PERSONAL WAR 109

CHAPTER 6   COVERT OPERATIONS IN B-57 121

CHAPTER 7   UP COUNTRY TO DAK TO 139

CHAPTER 8   HEALING OF BODY, SOUL, AND SPIRIT....163

CHAPTER 9   REBUILDING A LIFE ON EARTH
FOR ETERNITY 181

CHAPTER 10   THE SEDUCTION OF POLITICS.............211

CHAPTER 11   INFECTED WITH POTOMAC FEVER 251

CHAPTER 12   ARMOR FOR A HEALING WARRIOR 265

CHAPTER 13   "THANK YOU FOR BRINGING MY
DADDY HOME"..................................273

EPILOGUE 293

APPENDIX   BATTLE PLAN FOR VICTORY 302

BIBLIOGRAPHY 314

ACKNOWLEDGMENTS 316

INDEX 317

FOREWORD

BY ROSS PEROT

On a spring day in 1970 while he was finishing graduate business school at SMU in Dallas, Allen walked into my office on his two artificial legs. His legs were removed below the knee due to wounds from a mortar round in an attack at his Special Forces camp in Vietnam in 1967. It was a sight for this Annapolis graduate to be impressed by a West Point graduate!

Despite the severity of his injury, he was an up and enthusiastic guy. I hired him to be my personal financial assistant at my company, Electronic Data Systems (EDS). He was only in my employ for a short time because the fast-paced rigors of a growing entrepreneurial company were too taxing for this stage of his emotional healing process after his war, hospitalization, and graduate school.

He left to work at a large downtown bank in Dallas, and I told him I would hold the opportunity open for him for one year. He never came back to work for me, but we kept in touch and crossed paths several times through the years. Recently we had occasion to work together to help several military veterans in his role as public affairs officer at VA North Texas Health Care System.

Allen has been a thoroughly dedicated public servant and tremendous advocate for veterans, but as he related in his story, also a man of strong spiritual convictions. He knows God as his Creator and God's Son, Jesus Christ, as his Savior.

I know that Allen's story has the potential to touch many lives. It is a message of struggle, perseverance, courage, and hope. It is a message of never giving up on God, who never gives up on His children. It is a message of being lifted out of the pit of pain and discouragement into the light of hope, love, and victory. It is a message that Allen knows so well—and perhaps better than most—and he tells it with humor, honesty, and with the courage it takes to bare one's soul. It is a story one would want to read because it tells me that if Allen Clark can rise victorious from the ashes of defeat, then others can, too. I think that is how most readers will feel if they just have a chance to read this wonderful story of *Wounded Soldier, Healing Warrior.*

INTRODUCTION

My life has been one of both privilege and adversity. It has also been a pilgrimage that has taken me along many paths, paths that wound their way through Phillips Exeter Academy, West Point, the U.S. Army, and a seemingly insignificant Southeast Asian country where I would experience one of the greatest turning points in my life. My life's pilgrimage continued through Brooke Army Medical Center in San Antonio, rehabilitation, psychotherapy, and readjustment to a new way of life. My career path led into the military, came to an abrupt halt, and then continued in banking and investments and politics before it came full circle—right back to service to the men and women of the armed forces.

However, my spiritual pilgrimage turned out to be the greatest journey of all. My spiritual path has taken me through several churches and denominations, many seminars, countless discussions with ministers, extensive self-study, and the reading of hundreds of books. In my zeal to get to know my Lord and learn and understand about spiritual matters, I became a virtual sponge, taking in everything I could learn and asking questions along the way. This journey took me down a path of learning that has ultimately culminated in teaching others. In this book, I have related my life history interspersed with the spiritual elements I have experienced. It is my prayer that my experiences—the adversities, gifts, and blessings alike— will somehow be a source of encouragement and inspiration to my readers.

CHAPTER 1

"OH, GOD, I'M DEAD"

Dak To, Vietnam
4:30 a.m., June 17, 1967

Muffled sounds of distant mortar fire infiltrated the quiet stillness of the predawn darkness. This sounded so familiar by now that, even though we were expecting a ground attack, I barely took notice and only glanced up briefly from the letter I was writing to my wife. The sounds came increasingly closer, though, when suddenly, from just outside the inner perimeter, I heard the alarming shouts of a Vietnamese man employed in our camp at Dak To (pronounced "dahk toe"). I quickly pulled out my .38-caliber pistol and dove behind a nearby jeep for cover. I recall not understanding what he was saying, but soon realized that mortar fire had begun dropping into our camp.

In a Special Forces camp, an American Special Forces team member or attached personnel such as I were responsible for a two-hour shift inside the inner perimeter all night long. The morning of the attack I had the last shift, from 4 to 6 a.m. Our duty was to walk periodically the inner perimeter to ensure that none of our Montagnards nor Vietnamese did sneak in to spike our mortars or knife us in our bunkers prior to an attack. An American with a radio sat on duty inside an underground bunker situated just outside the mess hall. His super-secret SOG (Studies and Observation Group) unit monitored the US raiding parties in Laos and our radio relay site (code named Leghorn) across the border. Leghorn was a site up on a steep elevation in Laos and was used to receive radio messages from the SOG missions along the Ho Chi Minh Trail. If a team was in trouble, a message would go back for help to the SOG Reaction Force based in Kontum. Eventually, a North Vietnamese Army unit oversaw the position later in the war. In thinking about the enemy movement the previous evening, a ground attack was imminent. I shouted down to the SOG soldier to radio for flare/gun ships from Pleiku that would help us spot the enemy as they came at us from across the Dak Poko River or from any other direction. (*Dak* in Vietnamese means both "stream" and "village." Thus, *Dak Poko* refers to the Poko River and *Dak To* refers to the village of To.)

By that time the mortar rounds were hitting closer, and our soldiers popped out of bunkers and tents to scramble to battle positions. I ran to my bunk building just outside the inner perimeter. Smoke from exploding shells stung my nostrils as I grabbed my AR-15 rifle and strapped on ammo pouches and a grenade harness in preparation for battle. Hurrying back into the inner perimeter, I took it upon myself to get our three mortar positions manned so we could get flares up and deliver counter-battery fire on the suspected enemy firing positions. I collared a tall, blond Quartermaster Corps soldier and ordered him to one of our three mortar pits.

In the fog of war, mistakes are made and I will always regret one made the night before. Right at dusk we peered at the high ground across the river to our south and saw figures there. In the haze of the upcoming darkness, we must have decided they were perhaps a group of villagers rather than any of our people or a patrol from the Vietnamese army post at Tan Canh a few miles away. As a consequence no air strike was called on the enemy, who were obviously setting up their mortar positions for the next morning's barrage.

Amid the noise of exploding incoming mortars, I shouted to other soldiers to put flares on the south high ground where we had seen activity the previous night. They were to begin pumping in the flare canisters and rounds for our 81mm mortars. When I peered over the sandbags into a 4.2-inch mortar pit, A-team member Sergeant Cramer asked for someone to help him load. Rushing back to the center of camp, I found Sergeant Arturs Fisers, my B-57 team-mate, told him to help Cramer, and tried to grab soldiers for the other two mortar pits, while at the same time trying to spot enemy blasts through the smoky darkness so we could pinpoint return fire. I intently watched the area where we had seen movement seven hours earlier. Obviously, it was not distant guns attacking us; it was the enemy closing in—nearby and hiding in the cover of the dark night.

The camp executive officer (XO) came up beside me and handed me a small radio, but confusion, caused by the suddenness of the attack, made my communicating with the underground head-quarters bunker difficult. Why I remained unprotected in the open I will never know, but there I was.

"What's happening?" the XO's voice crackled on my radio. I assumed he was in an underground bunker.

With a rifle in my left hand and the radio in my right, I looked across the river to spot the enemy and started to respond to the com-mand bunker when a sudden jolting thud knocked me forward, and I landed flat on my stomach. There is no flash with mortar fire; it makes impact, and a splash of metal shoots out in a giant cone, hitting everything in its path. One had exploded about eighteen inches behind my left leg, knocking me to the ground.

"Oh, God, my legs, my legs! Help me!" I screamed. "Oh, God, I'm dead!"

Sergeant Leslie St. Lawrence, one of the Walter Reed Army Institute of Research medics assigned in my camp, heard my cries for help and ran to my side.

"I'll take care of you and get a litter," he shouted as he grabbed a soldier and ordered him to take care of me until he returned. However, confusion and fear for his own life caused that soldier to run for cover instead.

Our men returned fire, but the enemy's mortars fell ten to our one. With mortar shells raining down all around me, I began worry-ing that I might get a head wound in addition to the wounds in my legs. Knowing that a head wound would probably be fatal, I looked for possible cover. Spotting a nearby drainage ditch, I dragged myself through the dust then over concrete, inch by inch, on arms and elbows until I reached apparent and better safety in a small drainage ditch.

Sergeant St. Lawrence returned with Sergeant Cramer, a member of the A-team, and together they placed me on my stomach on a stretcher. Bent nearly double and dodging mortar blasts, they carried me through the camp toward the safety of the medics' bunker, which was nearby. As they slowed to make the 90-degree turn into the bunker, another mortar blast exploded nearby, wounding both sergeants. As they fell, my stretcher dropped to the ground with a jarring thud. An earlier blast had stunned Sergeant Jim Hill, the team medic, as he emerged from the bunker to help me. But, after regaining his composure, he managed to pull me inside to safety and much needed medical attention. Sergeant Hill quickly started an IV of dextran and placed pressure bandages on my legs.

"Don't waste your time with me," I mumbled. "Go outside and help the wounded. I know I'm going to die because I have no feeling in my legs."

My wife, Jackie, had occasionally pointed out what she called my overzealous sense of responsibility toward others. Perhaps she was right. As I lay wounded and in shock, I thought only of the other soldiers falling on the battlefield.

"No, sir," Sergeant Hill responded reassuringly. "You're not going to die. You have a shrapnel wound in your leg and a piece of it is putting pressure on a nerve. That's stopped the bleeding so don't worry about it. I'll check on the others when I'm through with you."

Hill turned, scrambled through the bunker entrance, and then disappeared through the barrage of mortar fire to get plasma, morphine, and bandages from the Vietnamese first-aid tent dispensary, which was outside the inner perimeter. While he was gone, I slowly surveyed the bunker. Sometime or other, I realized the body of an air force major sat slumped in the bunker corner with a mortar fin sticking out of his head, an instantaneous death for the pilot who had flown in the night before and was hit in an unprotected Quonset hut aboveground.

I could hear shrapnel from exploding mortar rounds falling on tin roofs like heavy rain. Eventually, through the sounds of those explosions came the sounds of the air force C-47, which we called

"Puff the Magic Dragon," firing at the North Vietnamese with three 7.62mm Gatling guns that rained terror on the enemy. I could envision the tension beneath the surrealistic effect caused by the shadows of the flarelight over the enemy positions.

Sergeant Hill returned and I was feeling no pain and took on a combative attitude by saying, "Kill those SOBs," knowing that the ship's Gatling guns would wreak misery and havoc upon the NVA (North Vietnamese Army) positions.

Thirteen years later, in 1980, I ran into Sergeant Jimmy Hill, and then again in 1992. I tried to contact him again in 2004 to no avail. Then, in December of that year, I received a surprise phone call from the man who knew more about my injuries than even I did at the time. It seems that he had been wondering all these years how I was doing. He has graciously provided the following account of what happened that day.

Sergeant Jimmy Hill

In the early morning hours, I was awakened by a series of loud explosions. I got out of my bunk, put on my pants, and heard another loud explosion—this time near my own bunker. I heard someone screaming, "My feet! My feet!" At the time, I thought that whoever had been on the 4.2 mortar had dropped a plate on his feet. As I exited my bunker and mounted the stairs, I saw a big flash. The next thing I knew, I had sandbags on my chest and pain in my right shoulder. After removing the sandbags, I started up the stairs where I met two men bringing a litter into my bunker. One may have been Sergeant St. Lawrence, but I don't remember. As I reached up to grab the foot end of the litter in order to assist them, blood poured off the litter and all over my chest.

We managed to get the litter into the bunker and placed it on a bunk. That's when I recognized Captain Clark. He had severe, traumatic wounds to his lower limbs and was in a state of shock. Another American, a member of the SOG, was with him. I had no plasma in my bunker, so I asked the SOG to stay with him while I ran to the dispensary where I retrieved the needed supplies— plasma and morphine. As I left the dispensary to return to my bunker, it took a direct hit from a rocket round. Fortunately, I was able to get back to Captain Clark and immediately started two IVs, administered morphine, and applied two loose tourniquets in the hopes that if he survived, his legs could be saved. The blood flow had subsided quite a bit.

At that time, Captain Clark told me that he couldn't feel his legs. I told him not to worry, that he had shrapnel wounds and quite possibly some shrapnel pressing on the nerves. In reality, I didn't think he would make it to be medevac'd. In confidence, he told me that he wanted me to contact his father and his wife because the name on his uniform was not his real name. He gave me his real name, as well as his father's and his wife's names, and asked me to write them and tell them what happened. His fear was that he didn't think they would be told. I assured him that I would write to them.

During this time, KIAs (killed in action) were being brought into the bunker, including the major with the tail fin between his eyes. As daylight started to appear, A-team Commander Larry Gossett summoned me to attend to the wounded Montagnards and South Vietnamese. About a day later, a medic showed up to treat my own wounds (shrapnel in the right shoulder) and assist me. It would be several years before I learned that Captain Clark had indeed made it after all.

Evacuation

Apparently, I never passed out in the bunker, but I did go into shock. Sometime in the early morning when the camp had grown strangely silent, two litter bearers carried me out facedown on my stretcher. I turned my head sideways to survey the aftermath of battle and saw confusing contradictions. The blue summer sky contained no clouds and stretched into eternity like a giant canvas awaiting the stroke of some unseen artist. Bright reflections from the rising sun bounced off the tin roofs of the camp buildings that were riddled with holes from mortar fire. Sandbags, ripped open by the shelling, reluctantly spilled their contents onto the battleground.

Captain Larry Gossett walked around, seemingly without purpose, grasping his rifle close to his chest as if it were some precious cargo. Wearing his black jumpsuit, the Vietnamese team sergeant just stood and stared into space, his face as blank as the cloudless sky above. The Vietnamese camp commander, Lieutenant Le Quang Nghia, had been killed in the battle. Stillness and silence replaced the shouts, screams, and mortar explosions of only a few minutes before and blanketed the camp with an eerie oppressiveness. I was so awestruck by this scene that I hardly noticed when the litter bearers gently placed my stretcher on the ground next to a waiting jeep.

I couldn't believe this was happening to me. I had tried not to think about it. I had tried to push the idea of being wounded, or worse, to the back of my mind. What I had always feared more was to have been captured. I had only forty-four days of duty left in Vietnam, and this was the day I should have flown out of Saigon for a week of rest and relaxation in either Australia or Thailand. After that, I would have returned to Dak To with my replacement, and then headed home to complete one more year of duty before my resignation would be effective. My war would have been over. Now it was over all right, but not the way I had planned or expected.

His face veiled in serious thought, Captain Gossett slowly approached me, looking sad, vulnerable, and pensive. "Sergeant Hill says I'm fine, Captain," I said reassuringly. "The medics will patch me up, and I'll be back in action this afternoon."

Obviously, the morphine had begun to influence my grasp on reality. Captain Gossett and I had been as close as soldiers become in a war. Now, he just stood there staring at me. Then, without saying a word, he slowly turned and walked away.

I learned from listening to conversations and from information gathered much later that on that day thirty-seven men were killed (including two Americans) and seventy wounded, nine of whom were Americans. The NVA had used launching tubes to fire captured U.S. Army 81mm mortar rounds into our camp. We had been attacked, wounded, and killed with our own ammunition!

As soon as my litter was shoved onto the chopper, the door gunner offered me a cigarette. I didn't smoke, but I will always remember that small gesture of kindness. I recall a C-130 landing on the Dak To airstrip as I was jeeped out to my medevac flight. The army is such a small world. I learned later the line companies of the

2nd Battalion, 503rd Regiment, 173rd Airborne Brigade, were being airlifted in to Dak To. The battalion commander was Lieutenant Colonel Edward A. Partain, with whom I had visited in our mess hall the day before.

I must have slept during the medevac flight, because I remember nothing after that until I was jarred back to consciousness by the thud and bounce of our landing. Although groggy from morphine, I could still hear the whirring of the helicopter's rotor blades overhead. Through heavy eyes, I looked through the open door to see two out-of-focus medics bent almost double as they ran through swirling clouds of dust toward the chopper. As they carefully slid my stretcher out of the helicopter, I learned we had landed at the 18th Surgical Hospital at Pleiku in the central highlands. This scene became forever ingrained in my memory. Years later, whenever I watched the popular television show *M.A.S.H.*, I winced each time the medics rushed to incoming choppers in that same bent-double position to offload the wounded of the Korean War.

The hospital staff placed me in a soft bed with crisp white sheets smelling of antiseptic. Everything around me looked white and peaceful—quite a contrast to the blood-soaked and body-strewn battlefield I had left that very morning. A young, light-haired Special Forces doctor from the Pleiku C-team approached my bed to check my chart. His familiar face and quiet demeanor took me back to the year before when I reported to B-57 in Saigon, and we had been roommates for one night. Would he remember me? The morphine administered on the battlefield that morning still shielded me from pain, and it again began its work, refusing to allow me more than a few minutes of consciousness at a time. As I slowly slipped back into its tenuous hold on my mind and body, I noticed a small grin spread across the lips of the young doctor, and I knew he had recognized me, too. When I told him I was working under an assumed name (due to my intelligence assignment), he responded that he knew who I was. He knew my real name.

I awakened approximately thirty hours later on Sunday afternoon, June 18, to be greeted by a domelike ceiling above me. At first I thought my eyes were playing tricks on me, but I just couldn't focus yet. I finally realized that the dome above me formed the ceiling of a Quonset hut that housed the hospital ward. I looked around slowly. The beds in the ward were positioned so close together I felt as if I could reach out and touch the men on either side of me. All the patients in the ward were covered with bandages or wearing casts or both. Did this obvious postsurgical recovery ward I lay in mean that I also had been through surgery?

In spite of the numbing effects of morphine and other medications, I slowly became aware of my physical condition and began to take inventory of my wounds. My right arm and hand felt numb. A needle emerged from the back of my left hand and connected to a tube that snaked its way up to a bottle hooked upside down on a rack above my head. My right leg and foot were in a cast, and my swollen, black-and-blue toes protruded like five proud sentries on duty. Although still groggy from anesthetic, as I surveyed my body, the reality of my condition not only rushed into my mind, but it also literally slammed into my very soul. Fear gripped every fiber of my being. I began to breathe rapidly, and my heart felt as if it would burst right out of my chest. Nothing protruded from the other side of my bed—no toes, no foot, NOTHING! My left leg was gone!

"Can you wiggle your toes, Captain?"

The voice of the young doctor sitting on my bed sounded like a distant whisper. Trying to take in and comprehend what I had just realized, while at the same time trying to follow his instructions, I tried and just barely felt sensation in my right leg and foot. He patiently proceeded to explain the extent of my wounds. I had sustained severe injuries in the mortar attack at Dak To, and as a result, doctors had amputated my left leg just below the knee. My right leg had sustained extensive shrapnel wounds and fractures of the tibia (shinbone) and fibula (a slender bone on the outside of the leg).

"We'll try to save your right leg," the doctor said reassuringly.

Try? The reality of that statement penetrated my mind like a knife, and I knew exactly what it meant. I guess he could see the worry on my face, so he tried to help me see the positive side of my situation.

"Captain, you needed eighteen pints of blood yesterday. We didn't have enough of your A-negative type, so we passed the word at the Green Beret camp and the air force base. A lot of men came and gave blood for you. I thought you'd like to know." (Years later when I visited with Sergeant Hill, he told me that I had looked so white from losing so much blood when he brought me into the bunker that he did not think I would make it.) I asked the doctor if I could have their names to thank them. He said it was not necessary. It was something we do for one another.

The young doctor went on to tell me what to expect. I would be sent to the Philippines in a couple of days, and then either to Japan or to the United States, depending on my condition. He told me I would be in a hospital for at least eight or nine months for further surgery and rehabilitation.

"You *will* walk again," he said. "There are wonderful artificial legs that you can be fitted with that will allow you to lead a normal life."

I had realized very quickly what had happened to me and found, to my surprise, that I wasn't depressed at all. In fact, I felt peace. I wondered later if that peaceful state was a result of shock or euphoria induced by the morphine, or perhaps both.

As the heavy sedation began to wear off, the slightest movement, even a cough, would cause excruciating pain to shoot through my legs. The doctors ordered shots of Demerol, a common substitute for morphine, every three hours. I soon begged the nurses to give it to me more often.

I had a lot of time to think that evening, and what concerned me most was how to notify my family. When I in-processed in Nha Trang, I signed a statement that no one was to be notified if I were wounded. The army overrode such requests when a soldier's wounds were severe. I knew that military officials would contact my family without my additional permission, so before they got the official notification, I had to find a way to let my family know I was really all right. I really believed that I was all right. After all, I was alive, wasn't I?

That evening, a wartime friend, an army intelligence officer from Pleiku, visited me. I explained to him that I wanted to write to my dad and my father-in-law and to explain the extent of my wounds before my mother and my wife were told. Someone needed to be with them when they found out. My friend agreed to take down dictated letters and see that they were mailed immediately.

Still under the influence of morphine, I dictated the first letter to my dad, Lieutenant Colonel Allen Clark Sr. (USA-Ret.), who by then worked as a civilian attorney in the Judge Advocate General's office at Fort Bliss in El Paso, Texas.

Pleiku, Vietnam
Sunday, June 18

Dear Dad,
   I wanted to (address) this letter (to) the office, so you could read it by yourself and then go home and tell Mother about it. Dak To had a mortar attack on June 17. I got caught out in the open and sustained serious damage to my legs. From my mid-thighs up, I'm all right. My face is all right, and my brain is all right. Nothing is wrong with my hands, except they're a little numb from all the shots I've had. So, I have a friend writing this letter for me.
   As it stands now, my left leg has been amputated just below the knee, and it's questionable at the present time about the right one. I will probably require more surgery in the States. It may be as long as eight or nine months before I'll be out of the hospital. As far as I'm concerned, everything will be the same in the future. The only difference is that I'll have to be fitted with a prosthesis. I don't know my schedule, but I'll send it to you when I do to let you know when I'm supposed to be back in the States and where I'm supposed to go.
   Really, Dad, I've accepted the situation. I'm over the difficult part, personally. Don't get all excited and call the DA (Department of the Army). And, don't worry. I'm getting excellent medical care.
   Love, Allen

Then my friend added the following personal note of his own.

Dear Lt. Col. Clark,
. . . I have only known Allen over here, but we have become friends, as men do in a war. He was not exactly "caught out in the open." Rather, he was trying to get illumination and counter-mortar fire started. His action during the attack, as now, clearly showed his courage. He is a young man with much happiness ahead of him. And it is my honor to be his friend and help him with these letters.
A friend

As I dictated letters home that carried news that would break the hearts of my loved ones, I couldn't help but reflect on my life and what had brought me to this place where my body was broken, my spirit depressed, and my emotions a jumble of fears, anxieties, and uncertainty about what the future held in store. My journey had begun innocently in 1949 as a young, idealistic wide-eyed boy listening to, watching, and admiring three army lieutenants. It had wound its way through the oath of office as a West Point cadet, graduation from the military academy, and a commitment to serve my country in the cause of freedom, only to end in a small South Vietnamese town that history and time would eventually forget forever. That innocent young patriot had become Captain Allen Clark, soldier, who had made the sacrifice that General MacArthur referred to in an eloquent speech that I had heard five years earlier. The toughest months of my life loomed before me like a long, dark tunnel, its end unseen and unknown. How had I come to this point where my life-long dream to serve my country had come to such an abrupt halt?

In the Beginning

The military had been a part of my life since birth because my father was a career army officer. Orphaned at age two, he had been raised by a very strict aunt and uncle, who had him in a Southern Baptist church several times a week. On the other hand, my mother, Amalia de la Fuente, had come from a very different background—devoutly Catholic with a rich Spanish heritage. Probably because my parents were products of incomplete families by typical standards (Mother's father had left his wife in Mother's early years), they were faithful in binding us together with love, caring, and time. They raised me by strict behavioral standards, but always with much attention and approval. Both parents were very strait-laced, moral, and ethical and taught me to follow a path decidedly marked by a high sense of faith, integrity, and a differentiation between right and wrong.

On my father's side, I am descended from Revolutionary War corporal Joseph Higdon, who fought in the battle of Yorktown. My maternal grandfather, Placido De la Fuente, emigrated from Asturias, Spain, around the turn of the century because economic times were hard in that coal-mining area. His adventures took him first to Mexico, where he met his wife and my maternal grandmother, Elizabeth Nielsen, a member of a merchant's family originally from Germany that had moved to Matamoros, Texas.

On June 20, 1942, I was born in the same hospital in which my mother received her nurse's training. Just two months after my birth, the army called Dad into active duty, and he remained in the U.S. Army until his retirement twenty years later. Dad had volunteered for overseas duty in World War II twice but was never sent overseas. (Perhaps volunteering for war was a genetic disorder I inherited!)

In 1948, Dad transferred to the Army of Occupation in Sendai, Japan. He had to leave the family behind in Texas until quarters in Japan became available for us. Eventually Dad wrote us, and we boarded a huge ship and left for Japan from Fort Lawton in Seattle, Washington, in February 1949. The voyage across the northern Pacific was an experience, to say the least. Stormy weather and rolling seas tossed the ship about like a toy in a bathtub, and the constant rolling of the large vessel made us all seasick. When Mother wasn't ill, she spent her time playing bridge with three 1948 West Point graduates who were newly commissioned Corps of Engineers officers. Needless to say, as a young, innocent, wide-eyed boy, they got my attention. I watched them in admiration through my six-year-old eyes as they walked stiffly around the ship in their neatly tailored uniforms. As long as those officers were within sight,

I couldn't take my eyes off them and imagined myself proudly wearing the same uniform someday. Recollections in the next few years of those young officers would bring the U.S. Military Academy at West Point into my life.

When we arrived in Tokyo, Dad drove us past the Dai Ichi building where General Douglas MacArthur, supreme commander of the allied powers, had his headquarters. The next day, we stood outside that same building at 5 p.m. just to watch the famous general walk down the steps. MacArthur's punctual departure every day had become a local tourist attraction. I stood in awe of the general knowing that he was the most important officer in the army in the Far East at that time.

I was eight years old when the Korean War began on June 25, 1950. Headlines in the official U.S. Army newspaper, *Stars and Stripes,* read of nothing but war. Grown-ups at the clubs talked endlessly about the atrocities inflicted by the communists. I listened intently as they spoke of how the communists tied the hands of American soldiers behind their backs and then shot them in the head. Those were not easy things for an eight-year-old boy to comprehend, much less understand. I soon became fascinated with every aspect of military life. I began collecting army shoulder patches at age six when most other boys my age collected baseball cards. Dad often showed me photographs of West Point, and I stared in awe at the snappy uniforms and shiny brass buttons. Even then I fantasized about attending West Point and becoming a soldier like my father and those shipboard lieutenants who had played bridge with my mother.

My dad's best friend, Lieutenant "Bud" Flook, and his wife, Bernice, played bridge with my parents, and he was there the night I pulled a loose tooth. A few days later, I waved good-bye to him, flashing my gaping smile as he boarded a troop train for the Korean War. He received a Silver Star and later died in combat at Chosin Reservoir. His death brought the war close to home. It was then that I saw my parents grieve for the first time. Now people I knew and loved were affected by it. This was no Saturday double-feature war movie. It was real, and it made a lasting impression on my young mind.

So great was that impression that during the third grade, I began to study with one goal in mind—to attend West Point when I graduated from high school. Every test I took and every grade I earned had to be good enough to enable me to be accepted by the academy. I had grown to hate communism, and my heart grieved when I heard about the atrocities our men had been subjected to in war. It so touched me that I wanted to do something about it when I grew up; I wanted to be an officer and defend the cause of freedom as my father had. From that point on, there was never any doubt in my mind about what I would be as an adult: I would be a professional soldier. Not many people can say that they knew exactly what they wanted to do with their lives at age eight, but I did.

We experienced our second move in Japan in 1951 when Dad transferred to Tokyo where he was a member of the 441st Counter Intelligence Corps Group. At the time, I never knew the nature of my father's military responsibilities in the Counter Intelligence Corps, but I read the definition of the corps mission by a former member, Dick Russell, in his book, *The Man Who Knew Too Much*, as the investigation of "...any matters relating to treason, subversion, espionage, disaffection, that might be taking place within the military establishment or that might be conducted by civilians which are employed by the corporations, factories, or concerns which are under military contract. That is their primary mission. When they are overseas, they have police powers.... In fact, overseas they are just like the FBI in some ways" (Russell: 97).

Once the Korean War started and the sixteen allied nations began sending troops to war, soldiers received leaves to go to Tokyo for rest and relaxation (R and R). I had no idea until my own war experience what soldiers actually did at night on R and R, but during the day, they were crawling all over the main PX (post exchange) in Tokyo, and I was able to add to my foreign patch collection by stationing myself at the front entrance and stopping men wearing unit patches I didn't have. When I asked if they had any extras on them, they of course did not. However, I exhibited an early enterprising nature when I produced my pocketknife each time, and many of those friendly, generous men actually cut off their patches and gave them to me.

In 1952, just before my family returned to the States, I contracted an intestinal disorder that landed me in the military hospital in Tokyo. A thin latticework screen separated the children's ward from the ward that cared for the head-wound soldiers from the Korean War. I held a strange and curious fascination for those wounded men whose moans and screams punctuated my nights. For two years, I had only heard about the war and about what they had suffered secondhand, and now I had an opportunity to see for myself. Now, for the first time, I became an eyewitness to its destructive forces. Our wards were L-shaped, and we could look out our windows into theirs. During my two-week hospitalization, I often stood by the screen and stared through the latticework at their bandaged and misshapen heads as they passed through the halls. To this day, their images are still vivid in my mind.

At the age of ten, war took on a new and very real meaning for me, and I became more determined than ever to strive toward my goal of becoming a military officer. It wasn't a romantic calling of drums, bugles, and bands, because now I knew what the aftermath of war could be like, and it wasn't glamorous. It was simply a conscious decision based on a desire to follow in the footsteps of my father and all his comrades in Japan and to do something about the atrocities I had heard of, read about, and saw the results of firsthand. I could not wait to grow up so I could be a soldier.

My family was happy wherever we moved, so I was happy, too. It was simply our way of life. Dad, forever the strong but fair man, and Mom, ever the sweet, caring, warm mother, provided a warm, secure youth for me and always encouraged me to care for others and broaden my world. Maybe that is partly why I aspired to make the military my life's work. I knew that would be a way to reach beyond myself to others and to satisfy my inner urgings to do meaningful things that were principled and idealistic.

In 1953 when I was eleven, Dad was reassigned to Korea. At the last of the Korean War, he had served as a commanding officer of the IX Corps Counter Intelligence Corps Detachment for sixteen months and was in Korea when the cease-fire was signed.

Surprise Attack
May/June 1967

On Mother's Day 1967, approximately one month before the attack at Dak To, I had written to my family, "I'm really getting close; only 87 days to go." Subsequent letters continued the countdown, "70 days to go," "65 days to go," and so forth. During those final remaining days, the North Vietnamese ring tightened like a noose around our necks at Dak To. Each of the other nine Green Beret camps in our area had been hit with mortar fire within the past few weeks, and we all feared that we were next. I had time on my side, or so I thought. On June 17, only three days shy of my twenty-fifth birthday, I was scheduled to go back to Saigon where I would perhaps serve the remaining few weeks of my tour before going home. My CO (commanding officer), Major George Nandor, wanted me out of there if there was to be major fighting. Had I left Dak To on June 17 as originally planned and the attack had been the next day, I probably would have been guilt-ridden my entire life. As it turns out, I was intimately involved in the attack begun hours before an originally planned safe exit. As an intelligence officer in a covert operation, I was aware that potential capture and inevitable torture would be devastating to the entire mission of my Detachment B-57.

Throughout June, the army chain of command and jungle grapevines both told us that the communists were moving major units into the area, and my agents refused to go back into the jungle at any price. I had already lost valuable time training new agents. It was terribly frustrating for me to try to get a job done under such adverse conditions. I shared my feelings with Tran, my smart and loyal twenty-year-old Vietnamese interpreter.

"Dai Uy" ("Captain"), he responded, "you need information. I will go for you up into the jungle." I marveled at his courage and loyalty, but I couldn't spare Tran.

Mid-June 1967 at Dak To was incomparably memorable and perilous. Tensions heightened as all evidence pointed toward the movement of the enemy toward an attack on our camp. While on patrol in a spotter plane earlier in the week before June 17, the pilot and I had seen movement near the old French fort in the Ben Het area about two miles from the Tri-Border point, the spot where the borders of Cambodia, South Vietnam, and Laos meet. At the time, we thought it was our own patrol, but now realized we were wrong—another "fog of war" example. Because of the NVA attacks on other camps and now on our own patrol, we were almost certain that Dak To had become the next enemy target.

On June 1, the 173rd Airborne Brigade was deployed into the upper Ia Drang Valley south and southwest of Pleiku. As the ambushes unfolded at Dak To, Captain Gossett asked for regular U.S. Army support, and the 173rd Task Force (named McQuarrie, after the deputy brigade commande,r Colonel Claude M. McQuarrie) was tasked into our area (Murphy).

Our Dak To patrol, which was attacked on June 14, tightened the noose around our necks. When the XO had come back into the camp alive, I witnessed a demonstrably shaken fellow soldier. The memory will never leave me. I will never be able to fathom how anyone back in the safe home of the United States can deny that the savage and horrifying effects of our warriors' experiences can cause post-traumatic stress disorder (PTSD). PTSD begins on battlefields as experienced by my fellow soldier, the XO.

In the early afternoon of Friday, June 16, 1967, Colonel McQuarrie entered our camp with three other officers for planning the move of his men the next day. I met him under a very strange set of circumstances that day. It is a given that we did not wear starched uniforms or steel helmets in Dak To. I recall leaving our mess hall to go to my quarters. With the sun its typically brilliant self, I wore sunglasses. With my green T-shirt outside my trousers, I was not the typical "sharp" paratrooper to which Colonel McQuarrie was accustomed. I guess I had been in the rather informal and non-military culture of a Special Forces camp so long that I did not salute the group of officers. The deputy brigade commander noticed my lack of military courtesy in not saluting him. That was a big mistake for this out-of-uniform and discourteous soldier who passed the officers. The colonel stopped me and asked, "Why did you not salute me?" I did so immediately and went on my way. A while later I returned to the mess hall and Lieutenant Colonel Ed Partain, who had taught me tactics at West Point and been G-1 company tactical officer was in there. I probably just ignored the salute reprimand but recall telling him I was undercover in the camp and asking him basically not to recognize me as the Cadet Clark he had known. So went my exposure to the hard-nosed discipline of the regular army. Never again after the next day would I personally experience it.

Sergeant Jimmy Hill

I was newly assigned in-country as a combat medic to the Dak To Special Forces camp in early June 1967. On June 8, I made my first combat patrol from Dak To accompanied by two Special Forces sergeants who carried radio signal intercept equipment. Their signals plotted two enemy columns, possibly an NVA battalion, moving toward Dak To. Eight miles from Dak To, our patrol came upon a wide trail cut through the jungle, which led to a mountain with well-used steps dug into its side.

We found recently occupied enemy foxholes, U.S. military jungle fatigues, C-rations, and one 81mm mortar crate indicating the enemy unit had been in contact with American troops in recent days.

I had studied maps of the area and wanted to further investigate Hill 875, six miles away, but the South Vietnamese Special Forces sergeant in command of the patrol began to make excuses why we could not further approach the hill due to high water in a river that would need to be crossed. So we turned away and returned to Dak To.

Upon my return on June 12, I could not get this hill 875 off my mind. When we reported the radio intercepts to higher headquarters, there apparently was much concern that heavy enemy activity was so close to Dak To. Another immediate patrol was ordered into the area. I volunteered to accompany it because I knew the terrain, but Captain Gossett said the other medic would go because he wanted me to go to Pleiku to pick up some needed supplies. This patrol had our XO and two other Special Forces sergeants in it. This patrol backtracked the route of my patrol, which had returned the day before. The enemy had booby-trapped the trail and two Montagnards were wounded. The patrol continued to search for signs of enemy infiltration to verify the radio intercepts from my patrol.

When the patrol left June 13, I was out of the camp. That night, however, I had the 2 a.m. shift for radio monitoring the patrol, which was in night positions when they were attacked. Our team XO called me and said in an obviously anxious voice, "We are receiving heavy small-arms fire." I heard in the background unbelievable small-arms fire. Then the XO said, "I have one American KIA." Shortly thereafter it was, "I have a second American KIA." Then the transmissions stopped. The olive-drab, khaki-clad NVA swept through our Montagnard force and they broke and ran. The XO had no choice but to attempt evasion back to our camp or he would have been killed also.

The morning of June 14, our Montagnards streamed into the camp. The XO made it back into our camp but was visibly in shock; I administered an IV and tranquilizer to calm him. He was airlifted out, but apparently came back two days later.

The Special Forces–led Mike Force with four American Special Forces men came by Chinook helicopters from Kontum and went to the site of the original ambush to recover our two KIA. The NVA knew our policy to recover our dead personnel, so they had moved the two dead sergeants' bodies to another nearby clearing to lure the Mike Force. The lure worked. Another ambush occurred, and two Americans were killed and the other two were missing in action. These Montagnards then staggered back into the camp for the next two days.

My own wound on June 17 during the mortar attack consisted of a six-inch shard of shrapnel embedded in my shoulder, extending another two inches outside. The wound missed my carotid artery by one inch!

The next day, a replacement Special Forces medic removed the shrapnel embedded in me. I had remained on duty and never left Dak To because there were so many wounded who needed attention. I probably treated sixty Montagnards and South Vietnamese Special Forces.

Either June 17 or 18, General Westmoreland came into our camp to assess the damage and confer with the 173rd Brigade, which had begun arriving on the 17th. He is the only four-star general whose hand I ever shook.

Eventually, a 173rd patrol recovered our two A-team members killed. They had them in a tent at the 173rd area, which had been established adjacent to our airstrip. I was called over to identify the bodies, but thankfully was spared the horror of seeing them, identifying them by their ID tags and a verbal description.

Several days after the attack on the 17th, I went with a patrol to the high ground on the ridgeline south of our camp. We traveled across the Dak Poko River through a banana grove and elephant grass where we discovered the enemy positions. They had prepared firing bases for the mortars by splitting bamboo shoots and flattening them on the ground to position their mortars. Their aiming stakes were still there. They had been setting them up the night before the attack when we had spotted them but thought they were local villagers.

In his book, *Green Berets at War,* Shelby Stanton described the events of June 14 this way:

> Later the same morning a company from the II CTZ (Corps Tactical Zone in Pleiku) Mike Force with four Special Forces personnel were inserted to recover the missing personnel. A reinforced North Vietnamese company had established a horseshoe-shaped ambush at the initial battlefield, realizing that a recovery attempt was probable. Their well-planned ambush disintegrated the Mike Force unit. When the bombing strike was delivered in response, the North Vietnamese rushed the defensive perimeter. This sudden assault allowed the NVA to escape the bombing and overrun the frail defensive line, leaving two more Special Forces troopers killed and the other two missing. The surviving native soldiers evaded NVA pursuers in the thick jungle and staggered into Dak To on 16 June 67. (Stanton: 166)

My dear Sergeant Jimmy Hill was spared a grisly sight by not having to personally view those bodies of his A-teammates recovered by the 173rd men. Here's the rest of that story. Once again, for the protected, they will never know what we face in our wars. The next paragraphs should be skipped by the weak of stomach.

> Charlie Company, 1/503d, received the mission of locating the missing Special Forces and CIDG from the 15–16 June incident. On 20 June Charlie, under Capt. Kirby Smith, found the missing men. It was a horrifying discovery. All of the men had been brutally tortured and their bodies mutilated.
> Captain Joseph X. Grosso, the battalion surgeon, had the unpleasant task of identifying the Americans' remains . . . .
> Captain Grosso arrived in South Vietnam and joined the 173d in April 1967. Since then he'd seen a lot of death. But nothing prepared him for the two Green Berets. Their bodies had been cleaved lengthwise, cut wide open from groin to head. Their insides were as clearly exposed as a cross-section drawing in an anatomy textbook. Grosso wondered just what kind of an enemy they were facing in the Central Highlands." (Murphy)

We who have been there know from past wars, and our brave men and women fighting the war on terrorism know again today, what kind of an enemy we always face. When our men come upon atrocities such as this, our own "rules of engagement" change in future actions with the enemy.

The events of June 17, 1967, resulted in monumental changes to my life. Ironically, on the same day that I was wounded, and ". . . at a time of great disenchantment with the Indochina War and rising frustration among his colleagues, Secretary of Defense Robert S. McNamara commissioned a major study of how and why the United States had become so deeply involved in Vietnam" (*The Pentagon Papers*, p. XVIII). The results of this exhaustive government study of the war would later become known as the infamous *Pentagon Papers* that would encompass forty-seven volumes of documents.

What if that study had been commissioned at the *beginning* of our involvement in Vietnam? What if we had called air strikes on June 16 because the enemy was setting up mortar firing positions? What if I had not volunteered for Vietnam? But as Betsie Ten Boom said to her sister, Corrie, in the concentration camp in Nazi Germany, "There are no 'ifs' in God's kingdom" (Ten Boom). It is God's business not ours, and God had other plans for that day and the days that followed.

CHAPTER 2

HOME FOR HEALING

Pleiku, Vietnam
June 18, 1967

The cone-shaped spray of shrapnel from an exploding mortar sprays out for yards, so if it hits five or ten feet away, a soldier may get hit in the stomach or even the head. I thought it incredible that I had no shrapnel wounds above mid-thigh except for a few very small wounds in my arm and hand. Although Sergeant Hill originally thought the round hit right between my legs, it most probably hit about eighteen to twenty inches to my left rear. I figured that must be why my left leg received the most damage and had to be amputated immediately.

Not long after my surgery, I began receiving visitors who told me that I wasn't the only soldier who had gone through hell at Dak To and lived. Sergeant Cramer, who had helped carry my litter into the medics' bunker, was now also a patient in the Pleiku hospital. Fortunately, however, his wounds were much less serious than mine. Cramer, a six-footer with sandy hair, approached my bed wearing the standard-issue faded-blue hospital pajamas.

"Captain," he said, "everyone on the ward has been amazed at the way you've taken this situation. Attitudes like yours put the 'special' in Special Forces." I was very proud to hear his words, even though I had not qualified in Special Forces at Fort Bragg and had only been assigned to this group in Vietnam.

Another visitor, Major George Nandor, my commanding officer, who had come into Dak To after the attack, told me that he would arrange for my medals to be forwarded. I remember telling him that it really didn't matter after what had happened to me. A soldier's badges of courage don't mean much when he's suffering. A small metal circle or bar seems little compensation for sacrifice and human suffering. However, with the passage of time, when the suffering had subsided and the full impact of Dak To settled in on me, I realized that it is their symbolism, not their monetary worth, that signifies the prices paid by so many. In later years, when well-meaning civilians asked about my medals, I usually jokingly, yet modestly, replied that they were given to me for things such as perfect attendance at morning reveille and well-shined shoes. However, in reality, I had become extraordinarily proud of those medals and what they represented.

Two orderlies wheeled a litter past my bed, and I looked at yet another familiar face. Sergeant Arturs Fisers had been only fifteen years old during World War II when he hitched a ride out of Russian-occupied Poland to reach the U.S. forces and join the American army. Sergeant Fisers rose up on his litter to wave to me as he passed. Working a mortar pit at Dak To on my instructions during the attack, he had taken mortar shrapnel in the back. I never saw Sergeant Fisers after that day, but I will never forget him. He was a great U.S. Army Special Forces soldier—a brave and courageous man who loved his country. I will care for him until the day I die, as I will Sergeants St. Lawrence, Cramer, and Hill, who put their lives in jeopardy for me. One of the many great things about American fighting men is that they truly care about one another and fight not to let one another down. The bond between us transcends many other bonds of life.

By Sunday, the morphine given to me for pain had induced a state of euphoria. It is evident from the positive tone of my letters home that the full impact of my wounds had not really hit me, even at this point. The second letter I dictated went to my father-in-law, Jack McAdams, a successful entrepreneur living in Dallas, Texas. An army corporal during World War II, Jack trained with a Texas unit, but when they went off to war, he remained behind because of problems with asthma. He lost many of his friends when his unit fought in the Battle of the Bulge. Jack once told me that when he received his discharge, he hung his uniform in the garage where he could see it every day when he got home from work to serve as a bleak reminder to him that civilian life could never be as bad as military service. So, it was with apprehension that I wrote him about my wounds. However, I wanted him to be the one to tell my wife, Jackie. I did not want her to be alone when she heard the news.

> Pleiku, Vietnam
> Sunday, June 18
>
> Dear Jack,
> What I'm going to say to you is going to be a real shocker, and I want to be sure that you explain it to Jackie. My camp fell under mortar fire on the seventeenth. I took mortar fragments in both legs. I suffered serious damage, and my left leg has been amputated below the knee. I want to be sure that you understand . . . that I'm getting excellent medical care.
> . . . I was evacuated to Pleiku Hospital immediately. I will probably stay here for two days and then go to the hospital at Qui Nhon. From Qui Nhon, I'll be going to some hospital in the States for fitting of a walking apparatus. It could be as long as eight or nine months before operations are completed.
> . . . I'll let you and Jackie know as soon as I can what my schedule is. You can't do anything at all about it. The sooner you accept the situation, the sooner everything will be all right. Tell Jackie I love her very much. . . .
> All my love, Allen

By Monday, I experienced excruciating pain, a sign that my body and mind were beginning to get a grip on reality. I began thinking about my wounds and wondering if I were really okay. I also began to wonder how my family would take the news—especially my wife.

Blind Date

After graduating from West Point on June 5, 1963, I departed with eager anticipation of achieving lofty goals in my career and in my life. By then, my parents had moved to Dallas. I had kept a rather thick little black book filled with contacts all over the country, which I had not opened for several months. When I looked for it, I discovered it was gone! We all have valleys in our lives, but this was one of my deepest. Fresh out of West Point with my future before me, I was new in Dallas and my acquaintances were few, so I did not have many opportunities to socialize outside my family. Now, to top it all off, my little black book was gone!

I began a summer job at a life insurance agency run by Tom McNiel, a 1945 graduate of West Point. Tom soon became like an older brother and wise counselor, who often offered sound advice and guidance—especially regarding my recent breakup from the girl I dated until just after graduation—that soon proved most helpful.

"Allen," he said, "there are more than a thousand women out there who you can meet, date, fall in love with, marry, and live with happily. The problem is exposure."

"Exposure?"

"Yes. You just need to network, work your contacts, get back into the dating game, and start meeting new girls."

After hearing Tom's words, I left the office full of renewed vigor and hope. I also said a silent prayer that I would meet the "right" woman in number one, two, or even three out of that thousand he spoke of, and that, hopefully, it wouldn't be woman number 999 or 1,000! After all, I had only five more weeks of leave before I had to report to Virginia and then go on to Germany for a one-month exercise with the Second Armored Division from Fort Hood, Texas.

I took Tom's advice and started "working my contacts." I remembered a West Point classmate, Lionel Ingram, who had mentioned that he had a cousin in Dallas. I called his cousin, Caroline Smith, and asked her to get me a blind date with one of her friends. We met at her house and proceeded to look through her high school annual, making a list of the women who seemed like the best possibilities. Together we came up with a list of ten women, and then Caroline ranked them from one to ten with number one being the best. (That was before Bo Derek's movie *10* ever hit the big screen.) Caroline showed the list to her mother and asked for further suggestions.

"What about Jackie McAdams?" Mrs. Smith asked.

"Oh, Jackie is 'dropped' to someone, so I didn't even consider her," Caroline answered.

Unaccustomed to civilian slang, I asked, "What does 'dropped' mean?"

"That," answered Caroline, "is the next step to becoming engaged."

"Well, if she isn't engaged, she's free to date as far as I'm concerned," I responded. "Work her into the list and rank her."

Caroline wrote Jackie McAdams' name at the top of the list as I peered over her shoulder to see her final ranking. "Great personality, good-looking, and fun to be with," Caroline said. "Definitely a number one."

Jackie was Miss Congeniality at the 1963 Miss Dallas Contest and both Valentine and Homecoming Dance princess at her high school. In addition, she was elected treasurer of the student body, "friendliest" personality of her class, and was chosen to be an officer of her high school drill team—all positive indicators of a well-liked person with an outgoing personality. Eager to meet this exceptional girl who stood out above all the others, I promptly asked Caroline to call her.

Two nights later, I called Jackie McAdams, assuming that Caroline had done her part and phoned her first. She had not. When Jackie answered the phone, she told me that she had never heard of me. Although disappointed and somewhat embarrassed, I asked her out anyway. She informed me that she never accepted dates with people she didn't know. What a blow to my ego!

More determined than ever, I asked, "Could I come over and get acquainted on Thursday night?"

After a moment's hesitation, I heard a very reluctant, "Okay."

I pressed on, "If we get along on Thursday, would it be likely that you would go out with me on Saturday?"

"I don't know you," Jackie said firmly. "I don't know if I'm going to like you Thursday night or not, so I'm not accepting a date with you for Saturday, period!" This proved to be only a minor setback. But, as a former college debater who hated to lose, I would not be deterred from my mission.

"Let's speak hypothetically, Jackie. If you like me on Thursday night when I come over, is it *likely* that you will accept a date with me for Saturday night?"

"Well, yes, it would be *likely*—hypothetically speaking, that is."

"I promise you'll like me on Thursday," I responded confidently. "Consider that we have a date for Saturday night." There, I did it! I won a date with Miss Congeniality. I hoped I'd sounded sincere, but pressed my luck even further and asked her to get a date for my classmate, Stephen Best, of Shreveport, Louisiana, for Saturday night. Steve was coming to visit for the weekend, and I couldn't leave him stranded. Besides, a double date usually eases the normal tensions present when two strangers go out.

"You'll like Steve, too," I said. "He was the gymnastics team captain at West Point, a cadet company commander, and a cheerleader." (My class called this group the "Rabble Rousers.")

Jackie paused for a few seconds and then responded, "Why can't I go out with him and get you another date?" Ouch! Blow number two! She must have contemplated a gymnastics star with bulging muscles and weighed the possibilities in her mind.

"Not funny," I replied.

On Thursday night, Jackie and I went dancing at Louann's, a local Dallas nightclub. On Saturday night, we double-dated with my friend Steve. Steve and I drank beer at each stop—a standard practice for me in those days. Unknown to me, however, Jackie soon became upset with our frivolity. A straight-laced Southern Baptist, she had grown up attending First Baptist Church in Dallas, then the largest Southern Baptist church in the world. I learned later that, because of my behavior that evening, she had decided not to see me again.

I didn't know her true feelings that evening. In fact, I thought we had gotten along fine. However, I suppose the alcohol, or perhaps my own heart, blurred my sense of reality. In either case, I was certain that I had fallen in love with Jackie after only two dates. I promptly informed Steve that I intended to marry her.

"Allen, you're out of your mind," Steve said. "You've only known her two days, and you've had only two dates with her. There is no way you could expect to marry her after such a short time." Jackie had overwhelmed me, and neither she nor Steve knew how determined I could be.

"Steve," I replied firmly, "I'm going to marry Jackie McAdams."

In spite of having had too much beer, I knew how I felt. I drifted into peaceful sleep Saturday night knowing that I had already made one of the most important decisions of my life. I certainly would save time, money, and heartache by being able to skip women numbers two through 1,000!

I called Jackie on Sunday only to have her tell me that it was *highly* unlikely that we would ever see each other again. Double ouch! Blow number three! Given my condition the previous night, I understood how she felt. Although disappointed, I refused to give up. This unexpected turn of events called for a new strategy. Instead of pleading with her to see me, I asked her to help me get dates with her classmates at SMU (Southern Methodist University) in Dallas. She agreed. Back to square one and Tom's concept of networking.

Shortly thereafter, Jackie underwent a tonsillectomy, so I lost time that I had been hoping I would be able to spend with her. However, during her convalescence, we spent two nights thumbing through her college yearbook looking at pictures of prospective dates for me. On the second evening, during a quiet discussion of one of her friends, Jackie suddenly closed the album and turned to me.

"Allen," she said, "I'm not sure I want to introduce you to any of my friends. I think we ought to give ourselves another chance." I was ecstatic! My strategy had worked. Jackie and I started seeing each other again.

On the sunny afternoon of August 1, we drove to White Rock Lake and parked at the highest scenic point overlooking the water. We had met on July 11, only three weeks before. I had loved Jackie since our second date. And once I make a decision, I don't like to waste any time. So, while we watched the sailboats skim across the lake below us, I asked Jackie to marry me, and she said yes.

Shortly after we became engaged, I had to report to Fort Belvoir, Virginia, for engineer officer basic training. One evening during one of my many long-distance phone calls to Jackie, we set our wedding date for December 28—that is, if we could overcome one major problem. I had been assigned to the 2nd Armored Division at Fort Hood, Texas, following my leave. In October, we were scheduled to participate in Operation Big Lift, an airlift to West Germany designed to test our ability to quickly transport an armored division from Texas to Europe during the Cold War. Because the exercises were scheduled to begin in October and last for several weeks, I did not know if I would be back in time for a late December wedding. The time had come to pull strings.

I called Colonel Henry Urrutia at the Pentagon. His sister had been a close friend of Mother's in Alexandria, Virginia, and he was a fellow West Point graduate. I would soon learn that West Point alumni would be *everywhere* as I progressed through my life.

"Colonel, would you please go to the operations room for 'Big Lift' and tell me if I'll be home in time to get married on December 28, even if the worst case happens and I'm on the clean-up detail after 'Big Lift' is over."

The colonel returned my call the next day, "You're safe, Allen. Set the date."

It is always nice to have friends in important places. I returned from Germany to Fort Hood about a month before our wedding.

One day as I entered one of our unit television rooms, I became curious as to why the news would be on so early in the afternoon. Other soldiers sat glued to the set, and as I listened to the newscaster, the impact of his words stung my heart and soul. It was November 22, 1963, and he was reporting that President John F. Kennedy had just been assassinated only 140 miles north of us in Dallas. As in all crises, we in the military are always cognizant of the added implications for us when there is turmoil such as this.

I went to Dallas to see Jackie the next day, and we were worshipping on November 24 at St. Luke's Episcopal Church when the priest came in and asked the congregation to pray because Jack Ruby had just shot Lee Harvey Oswald, the alleged assassin of the president. Another major historical event. It was with deep and heavy hearts that we spent the next few days watching the memorials and funerals. I learned later that just prior to his death, President Kennedy had decided to scale down the Vietnam buildup. Soon after his death, however, President Johnson reversed that decision and moved forward with the buildup—a decision that would cost him his bid for reelection. What if President Kennedy had survived? But again, there are no "ifs" in God's kingdom.

Since meeting Jackie, I had spent three of the five months I had known her at either Fort Belvoir or in Germany. We were married on December 28, 1963, after spending only two months together. Jackie saw me in my formal military uniform for the first time at our wedding at St. Luke's, where we had heard the news about Oswald. I know now, of course, that Jackie had no idea what being an army officer's wife would be like. We had not spent enough time together for that. Jackie's first exposure to the military was very glamorous and exciting. Reality, however, would soon take over. Life for her would change drastically.

Life as a Military Wife

As with most people, Jackie's heart, not her reason, had led her into marriage. She had no special preparation for life in the military, so adjustment problems became evident right from the beginning. My new bride found it difficult to adjust to military life in several areas: the low pay; demanding schedules that took an emotional toll on a spouse; frequent moves for military families who had no choice in where they were sent, which resulted in giving up friends, family, and familiar routines; tours of duty that required husbands and wives to be separated for long periods of time; and the knowledge that her husband was in a profession in which he might someday be killed.

Jackie first had to face economic changes. She had just left life in a college sorority where all the bills were paid to become the wife of a second lieutenant with an income that would barely make ends meet. When I met Jackie, my base pay was $222 per month. After we married, we received an extra $110 plus $47.88 a month for food, giving us a total of $379.88 per month on which to live.

In addition to economic adjustments, Jackie had to contend with emotional and social adjustments as well. I had a seven-to-six job as a second lieutenant at Fort Hood. Jackie soon began to realize that I wasn't an average husband who just happened to have a military career. From the very beginning, I worked toward my goal of becoming a general, so I constantly volunteered far and above the "call of duty." Also, as battalion athletics and recreation officer, I coached or played on several athletic teams that kept me away from home many evenings. When on maneuvers, I would also be gone for several nights at a time. As a new bride, Jackie only wanted to be with me so we could share our lives and get to know each other. After all, we had spent only two months together before we were married. Instead, however, she saw very little of me and spent much of her time alone. She found married life very lonely and discouraging. To help fill her hours, she enrolled at Mary Hardin Baylor College in nearby Belton to continue her interrupted studies in business.

When we talked about Jackie's concerns, she tried to explain how she felt. She had the same group of friends all through elementary, junior high, and senior high school. She had established roots and a support system of friends and family. She wanted to stay in one place, put roots down, and have the same pediatrician, the same church, and an attic full of memories. She enjoyed traveling on vacations, but didn't like relocating time and time again. She thought of military life as constantly being on the move, and she wasn't a good mover. She just didn't think military life could be very stable.

In all fairness, Jackie tried to deal with the realities of military life and tried to learn all she could from the veteran "experts." She often asked the older military wives about different aspects of the military that she didn't understand, such as separation tours. These tours of duty lasted an average of a year at a time away from wives and family. Men on these remote assignments were seldom allowed a visit home during that year. Some of the wives told Jackie they had experienced only one separation tour, while others confessed to as many as three. This disturbed Jackie greatly. That was not the kind of married life she had dreamed about, and she confided to me that the prospect of numerous one-year separations was unbearable to her.

In spite of the strain that military life placed on her, Jackie proved to be a very loving, caring, and devoted wife, and I am proud of the way she dealt with her own private adversity. I am very fortunate to have had such a woman for my spouse for so long. During the early years of our marriage, as she continually reminded me of the possibility of long separations, the probability of going to war, and other personal sacrifices, I began to have second thoughts about the career I had planned since I was eight years old. I also began to think that perhaps the personal sacrifices required by the military might not be worth the professional gains I would experience as a career officer. A soldier's wife must be totally understanding and supportive for him to remain in military service, much less succeed.

When I got married, my spiritual walk—especially in those early years—was misdirected. If I could have known and practiced one verse of Scripture, I would have been a much better husband early in our marriage. I Peter 3:7 teaches us that our duty as husbands is to "Give honor unto the wife . . . and as being heirs together of the grace of life, that your prayers be not hindered." The operative word here is *honor*. The way we treat our wives should pay honor to them. That must be our standard of performance in a marriage.

We all have our personal standards of performance—in academics, career, personal lives, and so on. I certainly had them at West Point and as a military officer. Honoring my wife so that my prayers would not remain unanswered was an unknown concept to me at this time in my life. Men honor neither God nor their wives when they love the "idols" in their lives more—idols such as money, fame, success, material possessions, pride of position, ambition, career, or personal interests. At the time, I had no idea that this concept of duty to my country and my men were idols. Jackie took a back seat to these priorities, as worthy as they were. As a basically nonpraying and spiritually ignorant young man, I did not have the tools that I needed to walk this tightrope of life, balancing all the facets of my life successfully.

Getting married had placed a new perspective on my life, and I found my priorities rapidly changing. I knew that as long as I was a part of the army, I must do the best job possible, but I had to face the reality that a long-term military career might not be the best thing for me and for my marriage. So, after a great deal of serious thought and discussion with my wife, I decided to resign from the army at the end of my four-year tour. I had already served half of my term, so I had only two years to go—or so I thought.

Qui Nhon, South Vietnam
June 20, 1967

Orderlies placed me in an ambulance to take me to a plane bound for Qui Nhon, South Vietnam. I twisted around on my litter to gaze hazily at the other occupants. Patients lay on tiered shelves four deep. I recognized two of the men as having been at Dak To, but we were all too drugged to wave, or even nod. A tall, slim blond Quartermaster Corps soldier lay across the aisle from me. During the attack, I had grabbed him and ordered him to load mortars. Now we merely stared at each other. Just above him lay the soldier whom Sergeant St. Lawrence ordered to stay and take care of me when I got hit. Frightened and confused, he had left me. Instead of finding protection, though, he too received serious wounds. Four of our nine wounded at Dak To had been touched by me in the attack.

When we arrived at the 85th Field Hospital at Qui Nhon, a gorgeous blond nurse approached the litters as they were unloaded from the ambulance. Playing the opportunist, I motioned for her to come closer.

"It's my twenty-fifth birthday," I whispered.

She bent over, kissed my cheek, and said, "Happy birthday, Captain."

That one act of kindness brought back feelings of warmth and caring so alien to the battlefield. One had to block out such feelings in order to survive with sanity. This small token of affection was my first step toward experiencing normal emotions again.

That evening we heard firing in the distance. Accustomed to harassment and interdiction intended to keep the enemy off guard, I wondered if the fire I now heard would result in the hospital taking a return hit. Panic and fear flooded my being. The drugs had started wearing off more and more, and I further realized that my wounds were real and permanent. My only thoughts were to survive this bloody war and get home safely with what I had left. Each time I heard distant guns like this, I thought to myself, *I've had it. It's all over for me. I've got to get out of here to safety.*

I called an orderly and demanded that he get me out of the hospital and explained, "What if this hospital is hit with mortar and I get hit again?" Understanding that my panic was real, the orderly patiently reassured me by telling me that, in spite of my fears, danger was not imminent. The hospital did not receive fire and I remained safe, but the sounds of the distant guns constantly reminded me of my own vulnerability and the battle at Dak To just three days earlier.

Because I got a Demerol shot every three hours, I had little control over my hands and had difficulty writing. I knew that I needed to write home regularly to maintain contact with my family so they would be assured that I was still all right. I still tried to keep the tone of my letters positive and upbeat, in spite of how I felt inside. I knew it was difficult enough for my family to deal with the uncertainty of my wounds and my future. I did not want them to worry about my mental and emotional state as well. I wrote home to Jackie, "I need you beside me more than I ever needed you before. . . . We still have a wonderful future together. . . . All in all, everything is quite okay. . . . I'll be home very soon."

How ironic that, while trying to stay focused, upbeat, and positive, my official military medical record reported, "While at the 85th Evacuation Hospital, (Captain Clark) had an episode of transient disorientation and anxiousness." What an understatement!

Clark Air Force Base, Philippines
June 21, 1967

I heard music playing as the plane crew lowered the ramp so that the litters of the wounded could be carried to waiting ambulances at Clark Air Force Base. A military band stood on the tarmac to welcome the wounded warriors to the Philippines. This was the first time I had been out of Vietnam in eleven months, and the music gave me a feeling of pride for the sacrifices our men had made there while fighting to free an oppressed people. In spite of it all, I was still gung ho army! That evening I wrote to Jackie, telling her how much more secure I felt about being at Clark Air Force Base and on American property once more.

"I've been moved to a six-bed room with a large window," I wrote. "I'm getting good care, and my spirits are high. I love you very much, and I want to see you so badly." My letters to Jackie had to remain upbeat. She must not lose faith and confidence. However, in a letter I wrote to my parents that same evening, I used a different tone.

"This experience has been horrible," I wrote, "and I can't let it happen again. I just want a quiet peaceful life with my wife and family." Little did I know that, as I wrote those two letters four days after the battle at Dak To, my family was hearing about my wounds for the very first time.

Allen Byron Clark Sr.

On June 21, 1967, I was at work in my office at Fort Bliss, El Paso, Texas, when my telephone rang. "Uncle, you have a telegram, and auntie isn't here." My niece Linda's words coming over the telephone startled me. Anyone who has been in the military knows that a telegram most often means bad news.

"How is it addressed?" I asked, " 'Mr.' or 'Colonel'?"

"Colonel."

"If your aunt comes in before I do, hide it. I'll be there as soon as I can." I quickly headed for home. I hadn't received a telegram in years, and I wasn't eager to read this one. I knew it had to be about Allen. I expected a death message, and all I could think of was that I had encouraged my only son to become a military officer.

The telegram advised me that Allen had been seriously wounded in a June 17 mortar attack, which resulted in the amputation of one leg. He would be returned to the United States via Japan. I cried. Although relieved that he was alive, I wondered if death would have been any worse than the pain he was having now and the pain he would endure in the future.

How could I tell his mother? I confided in a neighbor and his wife. When my wife drove into our driveway, my neighbors were waiting to help her unload groceries. She immediately sensed something was wrong by our demeanors. I slowly broke the news to her that Allen had been wounded and silently wished I could ease her pain, the pain we both felt. I called Colonel John Whitten, a military physician, who stopped by and gave her a sedative. The long night was just beginning. Other family members must be notified.

My daughter, Betty, and her husband, Alan Chalfont, had left their Tucson, Arizona, home that very morning on a camping vacation. Fortunately, I had their license number, so I called the Arizona highway patrol and explained the urgency of finding them. Within one hour, the highway patrol located them and had them call home.

The next day I tried to get more details about Allen's condition. Friends in the William Beaumont Army Medical Center in El Paso helped me track his progress. I soon learned that he would be returned to Brooke Army Medical Center in San Antonio.

Amalia Clark

I cried when Allen left Love Field in Dallas in August 1966, because I thought it would be the last time I would see him alive. As the plane taxied down the runway and the jet fumes billowed from its exhausts, I silently prayed, "God, don't let anything happen to my firstborn. He's so young."

I was upset all day on June 20. It was Allen's twenty-fifth birthday, and I prayed earnestly that he would come home safely very soon. The next day I played bridge and then shopped for groceries on the way home. As I drove into the driveway, I saw my neighbors standing by the garage. When they helped me unload my groceries, I thought it highly unusual. We were only casual acquaintances. My husband opened the door and just put his arms around me. I knew immediately that something terrible had happened, and I began crying.

After my husband told me that Allen had been wounded, I couldn't bring myself to read the telegram. I became hysterical. I wasn't really sure if Allen was dead or only wounded. I could only hold his photograph to my heart and say, "God, why Allen?"

Betty Clark Chalfont

My husband and I had rented a trailer and headed north to the White Mountains of Arizona for a camping vacation. We had just settled down to our first campout and were eating dinner when we saw a police car going from trailer to trailer. When the officer got to ours and learned who we were, he told us we were to call my parents in El Paso for an urgent message. I knew it had to be Allen Jr.

We found a pay phone down the road and called. Dad would only tell us that Allen had been wounded in the foot, but he thought we should come home right away. Dad seemed vague about both Allen's injury and where he would be taken.

"Is it serious enough to cut our vacation short, Dad?" We asked because it was our first day, and Dad seemed so unsure about everything.

Looking back, I believe Dad didn't tell us the seriousness of it because he didn't want Mom to overhear. The tone of his voice finally convinced us that we should get home to El Paso as soon as possible.

Alan and I packed early the next day and drove back to Tucson, and by evening we were on our way to El Paso. When we got home, everything was very hush-hush. Finally, Dad gave us the telegram to read: "One leg is gone . . . the other in bad shape . . . no danger of dying." I wanted to scream. I excused myself and went into the bathroom and sobbed quietly, but uncontrollably.

Alan knocked on the door and asked if I was okay. I let him in and he held me for a long time. I felt sick to my stomach. This couldn't really have happened to my big brother. It had to be a bad dream. In my eyes, Allen Jr. was as indestructible as our dad.

Jackie Clark

June 21, 1967, was a typically hot Texas day. That afternoon I took a cool swim in my parents' pool before changing to study for classes the next day. The doorbell rang just as I finished dressing. Looking back, I can't remember whether a postman or a special messenger was at the door. I only remember his words.

"Are you Mrs. Allen Clark?"

"Yes," I answered as fear struck my heart.

"Are you alone?"

I knew immediately that Allen had either been killed or wounded, and I became hysterical, screaming, "Is he alive? Is he alive?"

"Ma'am, I really don't know. You'll have to read the telegram. My instructions are not to give it to you if you're alone."

Mother heard my screams and ran to the door. When the messenger saw that I wasn't alone, he placed the telegram in my hand. The moment of truth had arrived, and I didn't want to face it. I forced myself to read the words blurred by the hot tears stinging my eyes.

> Mrs. Allen Clark, Jr.:
> The Secretary of the Army has asked me to express his deep regret that your husband, Captain Allen Clark, Jr., was placed on the seriously ill list in Vietnam on 17 June, 1967, as a result of metal fragment wounds resulting in surgical amputation of the left leg below the knee with open fracture. . . . In the judgment of the attending physician, his condition is of such severity that there is cause for concern but no imminent danger to life. Please be assured that the best medical facilities and doctors have been made available, and every measure is being taken to aid him. You will be informed of his progress when additional information is received. If there is a change in his condition, you will be advised immediately.
> Kenneth G. Wickham
> Major General U.S.A.
> The Adjutant General

I read the telegram over and over, blinking back the tears so I could reread the words "no imminent danger to life." In spite of my sorrow, I also felt irritated with Allen—irritated that he had chosen Vietnam over a safe assignment. Now I just wanted him to know as quickly as possible that I would stick by him through thick and thin. I composed my own telegram.

That evening my mother called a doctor to prescribe a sedative for me. Normally, a sedative would knock me right out, but that evening it seemed to have no effect whatsoever. Graduation from

SMU was only two weeks away, and I had to contend with finals while carrying this heavy burden. With the help of the tranquilizers, I made it to class the next two days. The importance of getting my degree was greater now than ever before because I might have to support both Allen and myself.

On Thursday, the day after I received news of Allen's injuries, I received another telegram at my parents' home (informing me that Allen had been evacuated to Clark Air Force Base, Philippines).

That same afternoon a major called from the Pentagon and asked me if I wanted to be kept informed about Allen's condition by telegram or daily telephone calls. I told him I preferred to receive phone calls. My first call came on Friday afternoon.

"What does 'seriously ill' mean?" I asked.

The caller matter-of-factly replied, "Oh, that means he might die, lady, but probably won't. Now, if you'll excuse me, it's about time for lunch, and I have to go now." He immediately hung up on me. How brutal and insensitive he sounded. Instead of relieving my fears, the phone call only intensified them.

While I was in safe surroundings at Clark Air Force Base on June 22 and my war was over, Lieutenant Colonel Partain's A Company was in heavy contact with the NVA on Hill 1338, the huge hill to the south of Dak To. That hill had always been a source of great mystery and wonder to us at Dak To. To my knowledge, none of our patrols climbed it during my Dak To tenure. Heavy casualties were taken by Partain's company in the vicinity of that hill. When a relief company of Partain's battalion reached the battle scene on the 23rd, this is how it was described:

> No one could comprehend the horrible scene. Dozens upon dozens of American bodies lay sprawled in death's grotesque grip. A heavy veil of black flies swarmed over the swollen corpses and the thick pools of blood and gore. The smell of death hung so heavily in the jungle that many of Charlie's paratroopers were unable to control their stomachs. They staggered behind trees to vomit.
>
> It was immediately apparent to Lieutenant Harrison

that many of Alpha's men had been executed; a large number of the bodies bore ghastly exit wounds in their faces. Other corpses had been mutilated, their features destroyed, ring fingers cut off, and ears removed. . . .

The final toll for Alpha Company was shocking. Out of 137 men in Alpha on 22 June 1967, 76 were killed. Another 23 were wounded. Of the dead, 43 suffered fatal, close-range head wounds. (Murphy)

I was now winging my way across the Pacific, sad enough not knowing of this massacre.

I left Clark Air Force Base, Philippines, on June 23 on a plane loaded with wounded soldiers bound for hospitals in the States. The large aircraft made a slow ascent and then a wide sweeping turn over the Pacific Ocean as it corrected its course eastward toward the United States. We stopped only once at Hickham Air Force Base, in Honolulu, Hawaii, for refueling and then continued on to Travis Air Force Base forty miles north of San Francisco.

Jackie Clark

For three days, I walked around anxious and sad, unable to deal with a situation over which I had no control. Around midnight on Friday, the telephone woke me from sleep. It was Allen. He called from Travis Air Force Base near San Francisco, where he had been taken from the Philippines. His familiar loving voice erased eleven months of separation and made him sound so close, so near. He sounded strong, but not exactly his old self. Looking back, I guess he sounded like anyone would sound while on large doses of painkilling drugs. In spite of the difference, he did sound lucid, which reassured me that he was okay. Allen told me he loved me and asked me not to worry.

"Will you meet me in San Antonio tomorrow?" he asked.

"I don't care where you go, I'll be there," I said.

There are only two amputee army medical centers in the United States—Walter Reed in Washington, D.C., and Brooke Army General in San Antonio, Texas. Walter Reed reportedly had an overcrowding problem at the time, so Allen was sent to Brooke.

After talking to Allen, I could not sleep for the rest of the night. I had missed him so much for so long. The excitement and anticipation of our reunion overwhelmed me. The few hours until morning seemed like an eternity.

The journey that had taken me from Dak To, to Pleiku, to the Philippines, and finally to San Francisco had taken only one week, but it felt as if it had taken a lifetime. When I finally heard Jackie's voice—warm, sweet, and full of love—stretching across the miles, I knew the journey ahead would be better because of the love and support my family would offer. Although I realized that eleven months of separation, frustration, and loneliness were about to come to an end, I also knew that the road ahead of me would not be easy. I understood that I faced many more months of agonizing pain and suffering as I took my first steps toward rehabilitation and recovery.

Brooke Army Medical Center
San Antonio, Texas
June 24, 1967

On June 24, I accompanied other wounded soldiers on the flight to Kelly Air Force Base in San Antonio. While waiting to be transferred to an ambulance that would take me to Fort Sam Houston, home of Brooke Army Medical Center, I lay on my litter and enjoyed the warm Texas sun streaming through a nearby window. The last eight days since the attack at Dak To seemed like a blur. But it certainly felt good to be on Texas soil again. It was almost too good to be true. As my litter was removed from the plane, a tall army colonel stepped forward from near the waiting ambulance and extended his hand to shake mine.

"Captain, the country appreciates what you did."

I had always meant my service to be for love of country, and that small comment meant more to me than anything else at the moment. I only wish other Vietnam veterans across the United States could have heard those words upon their return. Those words were all that any of us ever wanted to hear—that our sacrifices were recognized and appreciated by those for whom they were made.

If more veterans could have heard such words, perhaps some of the emotional wounds and scars from the war would have healed more easily and quickly.

The ambulance wound its way through the narrow San Antonio streets, the same familiar streets on which I had walked and played as a fifth- and sixth-grader. The excitement built within me. Each turn of the ambulance, each block we passed, took me that much closer to Jackie.

Jackie Clark

When I got the news about Allen, I was on the verge of completing my senior year at SMU, but after receiving that devastating telegram, I was much too upset to take my final examinations in business law and economics. (SMU later waived the requirement that the last thirty hours must be taken on campus and allowed me to complete my degree from SMU at St. Mary's University in San Antonio.) I had promised Allen that I would be there when he got to San Antonio, and I intended to keep my promise. Nothing could keep me away. He was much more important to me than final exams.

My parents decided that I was in no condition to make the three-hundred-mile trip from Dallas to San Antonio, so my mother and I booked an airline flight together. When we arrived in San Antonio, we rented a car and drove to a motel. I'm usually precise with facts, but to this day, I can't remember the name of that motel. I tried to rest for a while but could not, so Mother and I finally drove to the hospital at Fort Sam Houston. The world around us seemed at peace while my heart ached and my mind reeled in turmoil.

After taking what seemed like an eternity to find a parking space, we finally entered the Beach Pavilion, which served as the amputee ward. Parts of the building were being remodeled, and the sound of my high heels echoed in the empty corridors. One of the first people we met was Chaplain John Britcher. Allen's flight had just arrived at Kelly Air Force Base, and Chaplain Britcher took us into his office where we waited while Allen was transported across town by ambulance to the hospital. The chaplain suggested that I visit the amputee ward so I would know what to expect. He explained that Allen would probably smell bad from the stench of rotting skin. Even modern medical science could do nothing about this foul but familiar odor that permeates all amputee wards.

The sight of the amputee ward squeezed the breath right out of me. It was so large with so many, many beds containing dozens of men lying in agonizing traction with portions of their bodies missing. In one instant, I saw more pain and suffering than I had witnessed in my entire lifetime. Even the normal everyday sounds of radios and televisions shocked me. Normal sounds coming from such an abnormal place seemed terribly out of place. My life's experiences had not prepared me for this world.

Instinct told me that I must look at each man as an individual person and not focus on his handicap. These men were all united in a special fraternity. There were no differences among them here. All of them—black, brown, and white, rich and poor, Jews, Christians, and atheists—suffered equally. All of their families suffered as well. All of us were victims of this insane and bloody war.

Allen's ambulance finally arrived, and Chaplain Britcher took Mother and me to a window where we could watch medical personnel remove the patients. They secured each man on a gurney with army green straps fastened over white sheets. About seven men were unloaded that evening. I recognized Allen's handsome profile the instant they removed him from the ambulance. His evident helplessness and pain overwhelmed me, and my heart both ached for him and rejoiced that he had come home alive.

I waited impatiently for the medical team to bring Allen up to the amputee ward. I wore a silk turquoise dress that he had sent me from Vietnam. I originally intended to wear that dress for our reunion in San Francisco when his tour was up. I wanted to look my best when he saw me again for the first time in almost a year.

After orderlies placed Allen in his bed, Chaplain Britcher told me I could see him. Allen leaned up ever so slightly to hug and kiss me as the chaplain slowly drew the thin privacy curtain around the bed. Allen and I held each other for a very long time and cried. Our silent tears said it all. We were together again at last.

Although drugged and numb, I knew when Jackie arrived at my bedside. It had been ten and one-half months since we parted, and I thought she looked wonderful. I was home at last—home in the United States, home in Texas, home with my family, home in my wife's arms, and home in ward 43-A where I would live for the next fifteen months.

Jackie must have been overwhelmed by what she saw. She knew only about my leg wounds, and that was enough. But now she saw a soldier with one leg, one who could hardly move, lying in bed with an intravenous solution feeding into one arm and the other arm limp from paralysis. Apparently, when I fell forward from the force of the mortar explosion at Dak To, I landed on my right elbow, causing some nerve damage. The entire right side of that arm was paralyzed, and I had no feeling in the right two fingers of my right hand at all. It would take about eighteen months for the feeling to return entirely to my right hand and arm.

During that first evening at Brooke Army Medical Center, a medical team wheeled me into surgery for a dressing change. The dressings had to be changed every few days, and the dressing changes were so painful that I had to be anesthetized before doctors could strip the gauze off the raw flesh of my amputated leg. It would be more than a month before my dressings could be changed on the ward without the aid of anesthesia.

I woke up in the early morning hours of June 25 to what seemed like a surrealistic dream. I lay on a hospital litter in an intensely lit recovery room. The large round clock on the wall showed 2 a.m. My left leg was again tightly bandaged with a fresh dressing and hooked up for skin traction. Tape attached to the skin was tied to a rope at the end of my bed. Heavy weights on the rope held it taut as it stretched the healthy skin over my wounded leg. A large metal frame encircled my bed so I could use the grab bar to pull myself off the pillow.

Shortly after I awakened from the surgery, Dad came into the recovery room to see me. What a joy to see my father again! As he held my hand, I remembered one of my last memories of him just before going to Vietnam. We had a talk in the car just before I left for the war, and I knew he was worried that I might not come back. Our reunion would prove to be bittersweet.

Allen Clark Sr.

I arrived in San Antonio around midnight on June 24 with my wife, daughter, and son-in-law, but I went directly to the hospital alone. When I walked into the intensive care unit at Brooke Army Medical Center and looked at Allen, I saw a barely conscious soldier, but one who recognized me immediately. I could stay only a few minutes, although my son begged me not to leave. Seeing him alive helped me accept his injuries. As I left, I couldn't help but think of the long and arduous uphill climb he would have to make on his journey back to a healthy and normal life.

Amalia Clark

My daughter, Betty, and I suffered from upset stomachs during the entire six-hundred-mile drive from El Paso to San Antonio. Perhaps a combination of nerves and motion sickness caused it, but whatever the cause, neither of us was well enough to go to the intensive care ward when we arrived in San Antonio. I reluctantly sent my husband there alone.

I saw Allen for the first time the next day, June 25. Even though I had read the telegrams a number of times and knew what to expect, I had to restrain myself from crying out when I actually saw him lying there with only one leg. In a silent prayer I said, "I love him so much. I couldn't go on living if he hadn't returned alive. Thank you, God."

Betty Chalfont

When I wasn't crying during the trip to San Antonio, I was fighting to hold back the tears. I had to struggle to keep my composure for six hundred miles. I remember my husband taking my hand in his in an effort to console me. The next day, when the four of us went to the hospital together, a doctor on the elevator told us to smile and try not to cry or get emotional. I tried my best to smile, and that was the hardest thing I've ever had to do.

CHAPTER 3

PURSUING A LIFELONG DREAM

Brooke Army Medical Center
San Antonio, Texas
June 1967

The long, slow, painful process of recovery had begun, and I knew that I must face my life, one day at a time. The cast on my right leg seemed to grow heavier each day, and the toes on my right foot slowly turned black. Doctors frequently asked me to wiggle my toes, but that task grew more difficult instead of easier as time went on. The black color indicated poor circulation in my right leg and foot, and that diagnosis was confirmed when mold began forming on my toes. In addition, the pain in my right leg grew in intensity, and I couldn't move without experiencing extreme agony. Demerol shots every three hours were not sufficient to stop the excruciating pain, so I begged the nurses for pain shots more often than I was allowed to have them.

It wasn't long before my doctor admitted that if my right leg were to heal, it would never be healthy, would never function normally again, and I would have continual pain. All the doctors soon agreed that amputation was my best option for a healthy life. I told my doctor that I would rather have my right leg amputated than suffer as I was suffering. So, just ten days after the battle at Dak To, doctors ordered me off liquids at midnight, and nurses awakened me at six o'clock the following morning to give me a shot that would put me right back to sleep. I awakened in the recovery room several hours later. My right leg had been amputated three inches below the knee. The right leg now matched the left—two stumps tightly bound with bandages, gauze, and tape. I had been part of one statistic—one of 153,303 nonmortal woundings.

During those first few days after my second amputation, I slept most of the time. The pain never stopped, not even for a second. Both of my legs were suspended in traction. In addition to all of this, my hair began falling out of the back of my head from lying in bed twenty-four hours a day. Thankfully, it began growing back in by the time I could finally sit up a few weeks later. This period of my life was extremely difficult because I experienced constant pain, had to accept a second amputation, and constantly wrestled with dozens of questions going through my mind about my future. However, in spite of all the discomfort and pain, I felt a great sense of satisfaction knowing that Jackie, Mom, Dad, Betty, and Alan were nearby. Their presence comforted me at a time when I needed them most. Had it not been for my family's presence, life would not have been bearable.

Jackie Clark

I've been asked many times about the hardest part of coming to grips with Allen's wounds and his subsequent recovery period in the hospital. I think I was pretty much "up" for the whole thing. I felt it necessary to take each step as it came along.

When I saw Allen on his return from Vietnam, he had only one leg, and I kept hoping that the other one would make it. However, x-rays showed just how much damage the leg had sustained—muscles that would never heal, et cetera. In effect, doctors said that Allen would have to drag his right leg if it healed at all. They talked to me about preparing Allen for the prospect of a second amputation. In the end, Allen was in so much pain that he was almost glad to have the other leg amputated.

There were low times for me, of course. Once a woman came to the ward to show slides of how well double amputees could walk. I felt that wasn't good enough. In addition to his wounds from the loss of his legs, I had to look at a partially bald husband. I wondered what else could happen to him.

President Lyndon Johnson went on television every day, day after day and night after night, to say that we were winning the war. I looked at all the broken bodies in Allen's ward, their lives ruined forever, and thought, *We're winning the war? At what price victory?*

I guess I'm a lot like Scarlett O'Hara in *Gone With the Wind*. If things get painful, I just want to ignore them in hopes they will eventually get better or go away entirely. I always think I can face the problem "tomorrow." Allen's problems, our problems, didn't go away. The things that kept me going were my strong belief in God, the loving and positive support of my dear mother, family and friends, and telling myself constantly that I would not let all of this get us down.

Keeping Up with the War

During the weeks of recovery at Brooke Army Medical Center in San Antonio, most of the men on the ward kept up with the war and their units in Vietnam. We read every newspaper we could get our hands on and often clipped out articles about our units and the places we had just left. One such article, dated June 18, 1967, mentioned a communist mortar attack at Dak To that had wounded seven Green Berets. It felt strange reading a newspaper account of a battle I had survived just a few days earlier. A cold unfeeling newspaper account could never fully express the far-reaching effects, both physically and emotionally, that the battle had on these seven Green Berets and their families, not to mention the global effects felt by all those who served in Vietnam. Actually, as I later learned, the air force crew pilot and his passenger, who had spent the night of the attack in Dak To, lost their lives in the battle.

Another account dated June 24 told of B-52s striking at enemy troop concentrations after a company of U.S. paratroopers had been virtually wiped out. An Associated Press (AP) story regarding the same strike reported that "intelligence reports indicated that communists may have been planning an attack on a U.S. Special Forces camp and a small airstrip near Dak To." I guess they just couldn't leave us alone. Later AP stories reported that seventy-six members of the 173rd Airborne Brigade were killed, twenty-four wounded, and between four and five hundred communists killed. United Press International (UPI) described it as one of the worst defeats suffered by the American army in Vietnam.

Some of the heaviest activity in the war took place in the summer of 1967, and new patients poured into the hospital every day. Crowded wards necessitated that the beds be pushed closer together so more men could be squeezed in. Sometimes beds even spilled over into the long narrow corridors. Although excellent and competent, most of the doctors worked such long hours that they soon appeared like walking zombies. I was amazed that they could function at all, considering their tremendous workload. I don't know when they found the time to rest, much less see their families.

Dr. George Pomerantz
Brooke General Hospital 1966–1967

War is the best school for a surgeon. It is also an excellent school to learn about life.

Soon after the start of my orthopaedic residency training at BAMC in the fall of 1965, I found myself working on the amputee ward, which rapidly filled up with the unfortunate soldiers returning soon after severe extremity injuries sustained in the conflict in Vietnam. Allen Clark was a West Point graduate, assigned to Special Forces, who had lost both legs below the knees while serving in covert operations in Vietnam.

We were able to clear up his wounds and revise his amputations. Allen was able through many months of difficult rehabilitation to restore his ability to ambulate. He was fortunate to have great strength of character, determination, and support from a devoted family. He also had the determination to continue his very productive life over the years. I've enjoyed keeping in touch with him and never cease admiring him as an example of the kind of man who makes this nation a very special place on this earth.

One of the things that impressed me the most is how important it is for people to have depth of support to overcome such a loss.

Certainly the numbers and severity of the patients we served taxed the military community and medical facilities to the limit. We were blessed with an excellent, devoted staff of senior trained and experienced orthopaedic surgeons who taught us and guided us during all phases of care. It was also a wonderful thing when a Texas congressman, Henry B. Gonzales, came to visit our patients. When made aware of the lack of air-conditioning on these crowded wards—he returned to Washington and in a few days had arranged for General Electric Company to install window air-conditioning units in the old facility where we had our approximately six hundred patients.

All of us who have served this nation are aware of the destructive power of war. Allen Clark is an example of the strength of the human spirit to survive and succeed in life. It has been an honor to serve with him, to help in his care, and to enjoy his friendship over the years.

As patients filled the crowded hospital wards, visitors filled the corridors and surrounded the beds of their loved ones. Besides regular visits from family members, I was privileged to receive visits from old neighbors, longtime friends, and fellow officers. One of my old friends who stopped by to see me was Frank Santoro, my old debating partner from Gonzaga Jesuit High School in Washington, D.C. My parents, on the advice of a teacher who had told me it would benefit me academically, had enrolled me in Gonzaga for ninth grade when we lived in Alexandria, Virginia.

Gonzaga Jesuit High School

I confronted my first and only real obstacle to gaining admission to West Point at Gonzaga. My annual eye examination that year revealed that my vision didn't measure up to the standards of the academy. I had dreamed of attending the military academy for more than six years, and now that dream seemed unattainable. This was a blow that literally broke my heart. I became more distressed over that disappointment than any other I had as a teenager.

Looking for alternatives for colleges, I considered joining the Corps of Cadets at Texas A&M University in College Station, Texas, or perhaps studying engineering at Rice University in Houston. However, because of my lifelong dream to go to West Point, these considerations were never as attractive to me as attending the military academy, and I thought of them only as secondary alternatives. Looking back, I believe that God had a plan for my life and placed that desire to go into the military in my heart. When God has a plan, nothing stands in His way. He makes adjustments to fit His plan, not the world's plan, whatever that might be. The following year West Point lowered its vision standards and accepted applicants who had eyesight correctable to 20/20. Back on track, I saw my lifelong dream again turn into an attainable goal. I realized in later years that this was an early gift from God.

I relished competition, both athletic and scholastic. Gonzaga was known for its tough academic curriculum. Students were to expect three to four hours of homework every night. I relished an intellectual challenge inside or outside the classroom and, along with my partner and friend, Frank Santoro, participated on a winning school debate team for all the Washington area Catholic schools. I also reveled in athletic competition and started on a ninth grade homeroom touch football team of seven guys that included a future player at Navy and Maryland, Darryl Hill; a future New England Patriot center, Jon Morris; a player at Holy Cross, Henry Partridge; and myself—definitely of much lower athletic prowess than my teammates. Teachers at Gonzaga—many of whom were members of the Society of Jesus, the Jesuits—would serve as great sources of inspiration for me for years to come. What I learned from both mental and physical competition during high school would also serve me well in my military career and the rest of my future.

In spite of all the attractions and activities in Washington, my foremost thoughts were always of gaining admission to West Point. My father, ever the forward-thinker, had very wisely established and kept legal residence in Arkansas after his assignment there in 1946 to 1948. So, with Mother's Texas residency, my West Point nomination sources came to a total of six, including four senators. Admission to the military academy begins with congressional nomination. I could achieve my dream only with their help, and I didn't want these important men to forget about me. Gonzaga was located only four blocks from the capitol. Each month when grades came out, I walked those four blocks to visit my family's congressmen, Joe Kilgore of Texas and Brooks Hays of Arkansas, who was chairman of the House Foreign Relations Committee at the time. Joe Kilgore later became campaign chairman for Texas Senator Lloyd Bentsen's senatorial campaigns and a distinguished statesman residing in Austin after his retirement from Congress. A World War II veteran, he had always been a great inspiration to me.

Even though the strong and straight path for my walk as a follower of Christ was set at Grace Episcopal Church in Alexandria as a teenager, I had a lot of growing to do in my walk with Christ. Although I had become accustomed to taking the sacrament of communion as an acolyte and church member, like many other Christians, I did not have daily communion with my Lord. I did not build that personal relationship with my Savior that is so vital for every Christian until I was older. But isn't this the case with most of us?

While in the hospital, an outing with John Gepson, an old high school friend, provided another opportunity to reminisce. We had met at Exeter Academy in our teen years. John befriended me in the most magnificent way by inviting me to his home in Wellesley Farms, Massachusetts, after I had been at West Point for quite a while. John was a quiet, unassuming, balanced guy who became a dear and valued friend for many years.

Exeter Academy

Midway through my high school career, Dad informed the family that he would soon transfer to Europe. This presented yet another obstacle in my path to West Point. I knew that the strong academic preparation I needed to gain admission to the academy was available only in the United States, so I immediately began applying for admission to American prep schools. I wanted to complete high school at home in a school that would provide a better path to the military academy, so I applied to and was accepted at Groton, Phillips Andover, and Phillips Exeter, and finally chose Exeter Academy in Exeter, New Hampshire. My plans were back on track again. Even if Dad went to Europe (or possibly Fort Churchill in far northern Canada), I was at least established for my college preparation for West Point.

Exeter's principal, William G. Sattonstall, wrote my parents a letter that included very comprehensively the ideals and standards of Phillips Exeter Academy: absolute personal honesty, respect for other people, and, equally important, self-respect, eagerness to pursue the truth with diligence, and loyalty to the school. Founded in 1783, Exeter is an old, blue blood school with a long history of tradition. Although I attended Exeter on a scholarship, many of the former students or those there when I was a student were wealthy, paid their own way, and sported such names as Rockefeller, Salk, Trippe, Coors, Corcoran, Pershing, Hersey, Lincoln, Plimpton, Heinz, and Eisenhower. Even Iowa congressman Fred Grandy, the former actor best known for his role of Gopher in the *Love Boat* television series, also attended Exeter. It was what one would call an interesting student body all the way through its history. Of course, we never could match the alumni record of our archrival, Andover, which produced two presidents—George H. W. Bush and his son, George W. Bush. At the time I attended Exeter, approximately two-thirds of its graduates had gone on to attend Harvard, Yale, or Princeton.

The academic environment of Exeter was intensive. Students were required to study every evening and meet bed check every night. In addition to academics, Exeter students could participate in a wide range of extracurricular activities. I played both club (intramural) and touch football. I broke my ribs playing touch football before the beginning of our first season but always went to practices every day that fall anyway.

At Exeter, church attendance was mandatory, and each Sunday I attended the Episcopal church, which sat literally next door to my dormitory. My constant exposure to sermons and Sunday school throughout my teenage years helped keep me morally straight. I never wanted to let my God or my parents down. I know that in my teenage years I truly accepted Jesus Christ as my personal Savior, but I did not fully understand what that meant. I was certainly not filled with the messianic zeal of some young people to serve the Lord with all my heart. As a youth, I believed Jesus died on the cross for my sins and truly believed that I would have eternal life. However, mine was a very simplistic and rudimentary understanding of the spiritual "big picture." In my elementary, junior high, and high school Sunday school classes, my true knowledge of anything deeply spiritual was virtually nonexistent. As with all people, my life became a series of choices of actions that resulted in both good and bad consequences. It would take me approximately two more decades before I would even begin to understand the full ramifications of Christ's first coming. But during my teenage years, more worldly attractions held my attention.

Thankfully, I was never alone during my fifteen-month stay at Brooke Army Medical Center. I was greatly blessed by the personal visits from people who represented a virtual kaleidoscope of my life. In addition to my Gonzaga friend and debate team partner, Frank Santoro, and my Exeter friend, John Gepson, there were many others, including my elementary school principal, Elsie B. Jordt; my former neighbor and friend, Bruce Scoggins; another Gonzaga classmate, Frank Brophy, who went with me to physical therapy when I took my first awkward steps between the walking rails; and my West Point roommate and great friend, Peter "Bear" Kelly. During Pete's visits, we often reminisced about the days at the Point and our mutual love for our country.

A Dream Realized

On Christmas Eve 1958, as my family settled in for a relaxing holiday in Alexandria, Virginia, I received a telephone call from Congressman Hays of Arkansas. He had lost his bid for reelection that year and was currently serving the remaining portion of his term in office.

"Allen," he said, I have a principal nomination for you to West Point for next year. If you qualify, you're in."

"But, Congressman, you know I'm only a junior at Exeter and won't need the nomination for another year."

"I'm a lame duck Congressman, Allen," he responded. "I won't be around to nominate you next year. Why don't you go ahead and take the tests? If you pass them, simply decide whether or not to go without a high school diploma. If you don't pass the tests, you will have had the experience of taking them, and then you can try to get someone else to nominate you again next year."

His reasoning made sense, so I accepted with some hesitation. Filled with elation, I hung up the phone. A nomination to West Point as a junior in high school! Who would believe it? When I talked to the Exeter academic dean about the possible appointment, he told me he couldn't give me a high school diploma unless I completed my senior year. If the academy accepted me as a high school junior, I would have to enter as a high school dropout. I could receive my high school diploma upon graduation from West Point. After considering this option, I decided that if West Point didn't mind, why should I.

When time came to take the qualifying tests, I was lying in the Exeter school infirmary with the Asiatic flu. I could not let that interfere with the most important day of my life, so I dragged myself out of bed and went to Boston for the tests, including the required physical ability test. Three days later, I returned to Exeter only to check right back into the infirmary and fall into bed for another week.

The previous January, when Dad read the regulations for admittance to West Point, he had told me that it stated in order to be admitted to West Point, a candidate *should* be a high school graduate. As an attorney, he knew the difference between *should* and *must* and carefully explained the difference. On May 1, *the* letter arrived. I had done well enough on my tests to be accepted by the military academy without graduating from high school!

5 May 1959

Dear Mr. Clark,

You have been selected for admission and are authorized to report to the United States Military Academy, West Point, New York, on 7 July 1959 before 10:00 A.M., Daylight Savings Time. You will find helpful information in the enclosed instructions about transportation, baggage, funds, and other matters pertaining to admission.

I congratulate you on this opportunity for admission to the Military Academy, for it comes only to a select few of America's youth. It presents a challenge that will demand your best effort. I wish you a full measure of success and satisfaction, not only as a member of the Corps of Cadets, but later as a commissioned officer in the Armed Services of our country.

It is suggested that you give serious thought to your desire for a military career as, without proper motivation, you may find it difficult to conform to what may be a new way of life. If you decide to decline, I would appreciate your completing the enclosed form letter and mailing it at your earliest convenience in the envelope attached for that purpose. A definite decision is necessary, for should you decline, it is essential that another candidate be notified to report in your place.

Sincerely yours,

R.V. LEE
Major General, USA
The Adjutant General
Fully Qualified and Entitled to Admission.

As I read the letter, I knew that now there would be no way that anything would prevent me from attending West Point in the fall. Stunned by the incredible news, I read the letter over and over again, trying to grasp the reality of the situation—the reality that the dream I had dreamed for the past ten years was really coming true. My goal was within reach at last!

The summer after my high school junior year in 1959, I flew to Hawaii to join my parents for a few weeks. Oahu is steeped in history attendant to the Pearl Harbor attack of December 7, 1941, and I made it a point to work in a little military history by learning all I could about the timeframe and geography of that infamous day. However, this was a vacation, and I was also there to play. Summers in Hawaii were full of mainland girls, who are there to take courses in summer school, and they literally fill the beaches, clubs, and bars in the evenings. They were easy to meet, especially the Texans! Naturally, I checked out all the beaches, usually with some beautiful date I had just met. One or another of the various officers' clubs had a band every night, and the dates always seemed to be impressed by the military bases. I made the best of my last five weeks of youth, never really recognizing that the lazy and fun times on Oahu would be the last for a very long time. Once I became a cadet at West Point, life would never be the same.

West Point

As the weeks came to a close, I had to prepare for the approaching new phase of my life—both emotionally and physically. Plebes do not have off-campus leaves during their first year, so I left knowing that I would not see my mother and sister for eleven months. Dad assured me that he would have some opportunity to get to New York sometime during the year. Even though I knew I would face a very lonely year, boarding school as a junior had somewhat prepared me for separation from a family located 5,500 miles away. In addition, I wanted to be in top physical condition when military training began in July, so I started getting in shape and working off the Mai Tais to which I had become addicted. Each day I ran up and down the red clay hills behind our home at Tripler Hospital, the site of my dad's quarters. I turned seventeen on June 20, and on July 7, I entered the military academy for summer training as the youngest man in my class.

I spent the first night at the Hotel Thayer, at the south end of the campus. The following morning, as I walked across the 160-year-old campus steeped in tradition, I couldn't help but think about all those who had walked there before me, many of them national heroes. The academy counted among its honored graduates such historical figures as Ulysses S. Grant, Robert E. Lee, Stonewall Jackson, "Black Jack" Pershing, Douglas MacArthur, and Dwight Eisenhower. As a child and teenager, I had studied their biographies and their wars. They were my heroes, and I was proud and honored to be in their company. Yes, this was the day I had worked for, sacrificed for, and studied for when my friends were engaging in the more carefree activities so typical of teenage years. I realized that a new and exciting chapter in my life had just opened up before me.

In his opening speech to us on July 12, our superintendent, Lieutenant General Garrison Davidson, said, "You are not unique. Every one of the above named individuals pulled their chins just as far and raised their chests up just as high as you. They used the same kind of elbow grease shining their shoes and their brass, and they ran and drilled just as much. This is the system which produced these men, a system in which we believe" ("Lecture to the Class of 1963"). Those words were scant encouragement to me as I began the structured and disciplined weeks of dedication and training that lay before me.

An unbelievable whirlwind of activity filled the first day: equipment issue, pull-ups, push-ups, medical exams, and pictures to check our posture. Upperclassmen stood on every corner barking orders and instructions. They were known as the "Beasts," and the top-ranking cadet was known as "King of the Beasts." So it only naturally follows that our first eight weeks of cadet training were known as "Beast Barracks."

General Davidson had warned us, "In the next four years, we are going to control your diet, your sleep, your personal hygiene, and your exercise, so that you truly will be physically well qualified when you receive your diploma some four years hence" (Davidson). Everything he said was true in that regard. Confused by unfamiliar routines, rules, traditions, and places, 731 fresh-faced cadets tried their best to fit in and do everything the correct way. Double-time, double-time, double-time, set the pace for that first day and the days, weeks, and months to come.

As I finished each item on my orientation checklist, I was required to report to a cadet officer and say, "Sir, New Cadet Clark reports to the man in the red sash for further instructions."

In spite of the confused and hectic pace, however, by late afternoon, 731 plebes, dressed in gray trousers and dark blue woolen shirts with ties, marched in companies to be sworn in at Trophy Point overlooking the Hudson River. As I stood on the Plain and surveyed the beauty that surrounded me—the ivy-covered buildings, the majestic mountains meeting the Hudson River at Trophy Point, all dominated by the imposing granite Cadet Chapel—my very being swelled with tremendous pride and accomplishment. My dream had at last become a reality. At the graduation ceremony at West Point on June 1, 2002, President George W. Bush quoted Dwight Eisenhower: "Toward the end of his life, Dwight Eisenhower recalled the first day he stood on the Plain at West Point. 'The feeling came over me,' he said, 'that the expression "the United States of America" would now and henceforth mean something different than it had ever before. From here on, it would be the nation I would be serving, not myself.' "

True sentiments indeed, but Eisenhower's thoughts were much more high-minded than those on my mind at the time. I kept thinking how much gear I had to get put away in my room and the need to learn how to spit-shine my shoes and boots.

West Point proved to be a tough experience even for a gung-ho army "brat" with set goals and dreams. I lost ten pounds the first month because we plebes had to sit on the front three inches of our chairs in the mess hall, staring straight ahead, talking to no one, and taking small "polite" bites. I just could not eat enough for my teenage appetite. After three weeks, we were finally allowed to go to the "Boodlers," a cadet snack bar. I often loaded up with cookies and ice cream and returned to my room to eat them all at one sitting. I never knew how good simple junk food could taste. So much for the superintendent's controlling my diet.

I tried very hard to be a good cadet. I arose before reveille at 5:50 a.m. because I wanted everything shined and in good shape for inspection. I spit-shined my boots and shoes until my fingers ached.

I spent extra time on my equipment and learned everything a plebe needed to learn. During training, I ran, hiked, marched with my M-1 rifle, fired weapons, and trained with the bayonet. I fell into bed late, exhausted from both the physical and mental activity. All of us were in the same boat, and soon that special class attitude and *esprit de corps* began to develop among us. We were becoming lifelong West Point classmates. Little did I know how much these relationships would mean in later years and how much our lives would intertwine.

Cadets attended classes in the Honor Code, military traditions, and physical training each day during the summer. The Honor Code is simple: cadets do not lie, cheat, or steal, nor tolerate among them those who do. At West Point, we were taught that the Honor Code was especially important to soldiers because their word, translated as truth, could mean the difference between life and death in combat. General Davidson had said, "These then are the things that make up the West Pointer: a deep pride in our standards of honor and our code of living, the principles by which we pursue our profession" (Davidson).

Lieutenant Peter Dawkins, who had won the Heisman Trophy during the 1958 football season, spoke to one of our classes at Beast Barracks. Pete was what one would call a great big hulk of a role model. Elected as "Mr. Everything" in the class of 1959, Dawkins had also served as president of his class, captain of the army football team, and first captain of the cadet corps. Tall and rugged-looking, he stood ramrod stiff as he spoke to us about the Honor Code. This was nothing new to me. My parents raised me by these same principles. I felt fortunate to live again in a place that put the principles I had been taught as a child into daily practice.

On the fourth weekend at the academy, plebes were allowed a few hours out of the barracks to walk around the parade field known simply as the Plain. As part of the ongoing harassment, we had to wear woolen dress grays in the August heat while the upperclassmen strolled around in cool white cotton trousers. Besides making us physically uncomfortable (to help us learn to take orders and deal with pressure), the upperclassmen also played mind games with us.

During Beast Barracks, they constantly warned us about an upcoming climb up an artificial ski slope on which we would carry full packs. I worried about that climb for weeks, thinking it would be a terrible torture test. Actually, I was in such good shape when we finally climbed the slope that I climbed it with relative ease. That experience taught me that most things are never as tough as they first seem and that worrying about them only makes them seem even worse—a lesson I would need to remember in the years ahead.

On a stress scale of one to one hundred, I would rate Beast Barracks a 110! I got by on five hours of sleep a night during summer training. I soon began to feel tired all the time. To make matters worse, I missed my family. When I got lonely and homesick, I couldn't ask them to come all the way from Hawaii for a weekend visit. The loneliness, strenuous training, constant harassment and discipline by upperclassmen began to wear me down. This life didn't measure up to my long-held dream of tradition, ceremony, patriotism, and pride. I felt that I couldn't take it any longer, and I wanted out. I wanted to go home. Even Steve Best, my new best friend, could not talk me out of it. Steve was from Shreveport, Louisiana, and, in true Southern tradition, he just seemed to go with the flow in an easy fashion. He did not take the system as seriously as I did.

In August 1959, only one month after I entered the academy, I decided to resign and either finish high school or transfer to the University of Hawaii where I would be able to be with my family and relax on the beach. (*Relax* had long since become a word foreign to my vocabulary.) Disheartened and determined to get out of West Point, I went outside the chain of command, bypassed my squad and platoon leaders, and went directly to the new cadet company commander. Filled with trepidation, I reported to James N. "Nick" Rowe's room to ask permission to resign. He quickly got to the point.

"Clark," Rowe said, "my mother sent me an article about you from the McAllen, Texas, newspaper. She asked me to watch out for you here, and I don't think you should resign."

Uh-oh! Rowe was from McAllen, Texas, and, as fate would have it, our mothers were acquainted. Although stunned to hear this, I shared my feelings with him anyway. Later in life I realized this was one of God's magnificent blessings and provisions for me at a major turning point in my life! Even then, His hand was upon me, guiding me in the direction that He would have me go.

"I know that Beast Barracks is bad news," Rowe continued, "but it's really kind of a game. Why don't you try to hang on for just a little while longer? At least hang on for academics. When the academic year starts with football and all, it will be a lot more fun. Things will change around here then."

Rowe's voice had a ring of sincerity and understanding that I hadn't heard from anyone else since my arrival, compelling me to listen to what he had to say.

"You won't be a new cadet for the rest of your life," he said. "Besides, the end result is worth the price you have to pay to get there. You'll see."

I left Rowe's room knowing that he had spoken the truth. Every cadet probably wanted to resign at one time or another, especially during those first few weeks. I had forgotten for a while how hard I had worked just to get here. I had also forgotten that any dream worth having is worth working for, so I decided to take Rowe's advice and stick it out. I did not want to let my parents or myself down, and I certainly did not want to let go of my lifelong dream. I just kept telling myself, *I can do it. I can do it. I can . . .* Fortunately for me, I ended up in Nick's regular company for the entire academic year, with roommates John Dunn and Dick Walsh for the first semester.

Each year at West Point is the same. There are two months of military training in the summer followed by nine months of academics, and then a one-month vacation at the end of the school year in June. When the academic year began and we moved out of Beast Barracks, our lives did change dramatically as Rowe said they would. Every morning we fell into formation at six o'clock for head count and then had thirty minutes to clean our rooms for inspection. At 6:30 a.m., we marched to breakfast: two plebes sat at each table with eight upperclassmen, and we learned to do several things at once: eat in small bites, keep seconds available for upperclassmen, and answer their questions. The upperclassmen barked their food orders—"More eggs!" "More bacon!" "More toast!" The plebes, placed there to be at their beck and call, immediately responded, "Yes, sir!" and called for a waiter. This efficient system enabled 2,500 cadets to be fed quickly. It also taught us self-control and perhaps table manners in the process. (I know I didn't start putting my elbows on the table until I was an upperclassman!)

The common theme at West Point was daily pressure, both mental and physical. We were future officers and had to learn the discipline and principles necessary for good leaders. Classes at the Point were tough. Fortunately for me, however, my academic training at Gonzaga and Exeter had served me well. Cadets had to prepare lessons in each class every night in preparation for daily tests. We were then ranked by those test grades from number one on down to the last person and seated accordingly. As our grades changed, so did our seat assignments. We knew where we stood in each class at all times during all four years. Because of the daily quizzes, the pressure was overwhelming, and serious cadets couldn't slack off for any reason. Although extremely grueling, we knew the relentless academic grind helped build tenacity, steadfastness, and character.

Even though West Point was originally founded as an engineering academy in 1802, its primary mission today is to train tomorrow's regular army officers, and they are required to be in top physical form. If we were to set examples for the men who would someday be under our command, we had to learn to take care of our bodies. Every cadet has to participate in freshman or varsity athletics or intramurals. Physical ability is so important that a cadet cannot get through the academy without it. One cadet who ranked among the top five students in mathematics was so frail that he flunked out of the academy because of lack of physical strength.

On afternoons when I didn't have intramurals, I studied in my room or in the library. There were only a limited number of places a plebe could go during evening study hours. We had to sign out on a card in our rooms so someone would know where we were at all times. It was part of the Honor Code—a system that regulated even our social lives. Our code of conduct, honesty, integrity, and idealism, never changed. Lights were out at 10 p.m. The next morning, the rigorous routine started all over again. On weekends we attended classes on Saturday mornings and chapel on Sundays. Weekend free time lasted from noon Saturday until 6 p.m. on Sunday. If we had a weekend date or guest, we could sign up to miss meals. This practice, known as "dragging," was also part of the Honor Code.

I will never forget a scene from the movie *MacArthur* (portrayed by Gregory Peck), which depicted the general on a ship in the Pacific with President Franklin Roosevelt around 1943. Roosevelt asked the general to come back to the United States because things were changing. MacArthur had been in the Philippines since 1935. The general answered that the things he believed in never changed. I knew what he meant. These things make up the thread that runs through cultures, civilizations, and life itself. That thread is fragile and easily broken, but it is always there for a small part of humanity. It is unfortunate that only a few realize that these things are worth living for and, yes, worth dying for.

With only three exceptions, I was confined to West Point with my classmates for eleven months during my freshman year. We didn't even leave for Christmas, which was very tough. Experiencing Christmas 5,500 miles from family and friends proved to be one of the most difficult experiences in my young life. Most of my friends' families and girlfriends came to the campus to visit and exchange gifts. Because I was one of the few (and felt like the only one) who didn't have family or a girlfriend who visited on Christmas Day, I volunteered for duty officer. Needless to say, there wasn't much cheer for me that first Christmas away from home.

After Christmas, things perked up when I had *two* girlfriends who came to visit. The first one, a friend from Gonzaga, had such a good time she wanted to stay an extra day. It put me on the spot because the second girl was scheduled to arrive the next day. Things got pretty tight when I put girl number one on the bus and then walked across the street to meet girl number two in the lobby of the Hotel Thayer. She had been waiting for fifteen minutes, wondering where I was. The ski slope climb was nothing compared to the pressure of having two girlfriends within fifty yards of each other for fifteen minutes. Things hadn't been that lively since I enrolled!

Although most cadets had girlfriends, we weren't allowed to publicly display affection at West Point, a tough standard for red-blooded college men to follow. During the Christmas holidays, I received demerits when I was caught holding hands with girlfriend number one. I look back on that today and laugh, but it certainly wasn't funny at the time. I have to admit that I took cadet life much too seriously. Basically, however, demerits were never much of a problem. There was actually an eighteen-month period into my third year when my roommate, Bear Kelly, and I must have set a school record by not getting a single demerit. However, Bear finally broke the record one day in the mess hall when he was caught flipping food into the air with his belt.

When we started the second semester of our plebe year, William C. Westmoreland had been assigned as the new superintendent at West Point. He held a distinguished wartime military record and always enjoyed an incredible reputation with the Cadet Corps. Most of us who went to Vietnam later would serve in his command when he became the Commander, Military Advisory Command, Vietnam. My roommates were George DeGraff and Charlie Nahlik.

The plebes were allowed to leave the academy only twice our first year: once for the Army–Air Force football game in New York City (we tied 0–0), and another time for the Army–Navy game in Philadelphia (we lost 43–12). With two All-Americans in halfback Bob Anderson and the famous "Lonesome End," Bill Carpenter, one would think we could have done better. However, in the spring of 1960, I was given permission to make one extra trip to a church in New Jersey because I taught four- and five-year-old children at the post Sunday school.

I must admit that I carried out my work with children more from a sense of duty than from a real commitment of faith. I taught four- and five-year-olds because I figured they could not stretch me too far theologically. As a cadet, I had adopted a rather casual attitude toward formal religion. Although I had been an active churchgoer as a young person, I became less formally "religious." Frankly, I felt that the cadets who were members of the Officers' Christian Fellowship were too devout and prayed too much. I would learn in later years that those men really had something special, something that it would take me another fifteen years to discover.

One of the pictures that I have always tried to hide from my daughters is one of me in uniform in some German rathskeller in New York City on one of those Sunday school trips. Obviously holding up a beer stein in apparent emphasis to a significant line in a famous German drinking song, it appears that, at seventeen, I was not aware of the legal drinking age in the state of New York. Brigadier General Richard G. Stilwell, our Commandant of Cadets, wrote about the professional soldier: "He will sometimes talk from the pulpit, for he will always be part chaplain; but sometimes, also, he may be called upon to fight, perhaps to die, defending our country" (*The Army Information Digest*). He served as another of those sterling examples at West Point of everything toward which we strived. However, as a Sunday school teacher, my pulpit was very low, and the innocence of my youth was never more evident than that night in the New York nightclub so far away from the reality of where the rest of my life would take me in fulfilling the words of General Stilwell.

During the second semester of my freshman year, we began losing cadets who decided that military life was not suited to them. Some left to get married, and others simply sought a college home less physically and academically demanding. Many of the football players who quit transferred to other colleges where they started on first teams. Most were just flunking out. If a cadet failed only one course at West Point, he was out. Overall grade averages meant nothing. Only individual course grades mattered. Cadets who flunked out could "recycle," but they had to take the entire year over, including the courses they passed. The only advantage to that, however, was that during the second year repeating cadets did not have to endure Beast Barracks again. The chaff slowly separated from the wheat.

When our plebe year ended and the graduation parade dispersed, the upperclassmen finally recognized us as fellow cadets and allowed us to call them by their first names. We no longer felt like outsiders, but instead felt pride and relief that we were now finally a real part of the "Long Gray Line." As Nick Rowe had said, the end result was well worth the price we had all paid to get there. His earlier advice had served me well. I had worked hard and stuck it out, and now I would receive the payoff. (Nick graduated that year, became a Green Beret, and served in Vietnam. He was captured in 1963 and escaped after sixty-three months of captivity. The chronicle of his amazing survival is inspiringly recounted in *Five Years to Freedom* (Rowe). Our lives would cross again in later years.)

As promised, Dad came to the Mainland on a trip just after Christmas during my plebe year, and it was great to see him. But by the end of the year, I really missed my family. At that time, we all received a thirty-day leave, and I did not hesitate to use my cadet status to "hop" across the country to Hawaii on military airplanes. The leg from Maxwell Air Force Base in Montgomery, Alabama, to Phoenix, Arizona, proved uneventful until the termination of the flight when we met our pilot, none other than Major General and United States Senator Barry Goldwater of Arizona. I had no idea who he was then, though.

I savored those thirty days and filled them with time on Oahu's beaches, again meeting as many of the Texas girls who had come to study at the University of Hawaii as I could. While there, I found the exact location that the famous scene in *From Here to Eternity* was shot. In that scene, Burt Lancaster and Deborah Kerr lie intertwined on the beach with the surf lapping over them. In my youthful exuberance, I attempted to re-create that famous scene with my "date of the day," but my experience there lacked the impact of the same scene in the movie.

Three More Years

The second year at West Point is known as the "yearling" year. It began with summer training at Camp Buckner next to the main campus. Members of the Ranger School at Fort Benning, Georgia, conducted some of the training sessions. The Rangers are much like the Green Berets. *Impossible* is not a word in their vocabulary. The training we received under the Rangers was the toughest any of us had ever faced thus far. During hand-to-hand training, I sustained a hairline fracture in my wrist but continued anyway. Three years later, I would need surgery to correct damage from improper healing. I will never understand how it held up all that time under such rigorous training.

My yearling roommates were Pete "Bear" Kelly and Bob "Magoo" McGrath. Bear had entered West Point straight out of high school in North Arlington, New Jersey, where he had been a varsity letterman in at least three sports and all-state in basketball. I always seemed to land relaxed roommates. Bear was an easygoing guy, intelligent and warmhearted. I will always remember the intramural football game he quarterbacked when he passed the ball to the end zone even though there were three opponents trying to tackle him. Bob McGrath, a close friend with a big heart, hailed from Grosse Pointe, Michigan, one of the affluent suburbs of Detroit where so many of the auto industry executives lived. He was not sold on the options of our future careers in the army and resigned at the beginning of our third year.

January 1961 presented the Corps of Cadets with one of the more interesting experiences as a national service academy. Twenty-four-hundred strong, we were the lead parade element in the inaugural parade of President John F. Kennedy. We traveled by rail to Washington, D.C. from West Point and entered a wintry, cold city covered with several inches of snow. Because we were to step off at the front of the parade, we formed up early just to the east of the capitol building. In subfreezing weather, we marched in mass units up Pennsylvania Avenue, past my high school haunts from Gonzaga days, the FBI building, National Archives, the 12th Street bus terminal (which I passed through twice a day in high school), the Treasury building, and then took the left turn toward the White House. Popping our chests out a little more, we got ready for eyes left at the reviewing stand in front of the White House.

My view of President and Mrs. Kennedy was short indeed, but unforgettable. It surpassed my 1957 experience when I watched President Eisenhower's inaugural parade from the reviewing stands at Lafayette Park.

Just before we got to the White House, an eagle-eyed tactical officer, Major Ed Partain, who marched on the right flank of my unit, spotted a cadet chewing gum in my rank and commenced to have the cadets count off down the rank until he spotted the errant cadet and got his man. I'm sure a hole got worn into the pavement due to the punishment tours the cadet walked off back at the Point. He swallowed the gum before we ever reached 1600 Pennsylvania Avenue. Had we turned eyes right, I would have viewed 810 Vermont Avenue at the northeast corner of Lafayette Square, where I would later spend several years in public service at the Department of Veterans Affairs.

Once in a while, we find tiny jewels of wisdom that we all file away for future use. My yearling chemistry professor, King Coffman, uttered one of those memorable statements that I have never forgotten. One day in class, he said that there were three major criteria for success as an officer: "First, look the part by your posture, appearance, and grooming. Second, always be technically competent by knowing your job. And, third, maintain your integrity and personal honor." West Point provided a wealth of wonderful mentors and role models such as this to be our examples as we prepared for our military careers.

Perhaps one of the best leadership lessons I ever learned came during a counseling session with Captain Burke Lee during my second year. Captain Lee, class of 1950 (Corps of Engineers), served as the tactical officer in my company, M-1.

"Mr. Clark," he said, "if you were a commander of a unit with low morale, what would you do to correct it?"

In my youthful innocence (and indicative of what was still important to me at the time) I thought recreation would be important, so I responded, "I would make sure that the men had enough to do in their free time. I would set up pool and Ping-Pong tables, and so on."

"As important as that may be," Captain Lee replied, "the most important ingredient for high unit morale is to provide so much hard work for the troops that the work in itself lifts morale. Everyone wants to have a well-defined job, fulfill a mission, and achieve a goal."

I have since learned that the principles learned in that lesson carry over into life in everything we do. We all need to work hard at our responsibilities in order to feel good about who we are and what we do—mission, accomplishment, satisfaction. It began to set the stage for my life's work.

Upon returning to the Point for my third year, I again roomed with Pete Kelly and a new roommate, Dave Almy, a quiet and solidly mature guy who broke ranks with us and took his commission in the air force upon graduation. I was again assigned to Beast Barracks, only this time as an upperclassman in charge of eight plebes. I have to say I liked giving orders much better than taking them as a plebe. Perhaps the enjoyment I felt being in charge of underclassmen went hand-in-hand with the enjoyment I felt on the cadet debate team, where I learned to do combat of the mind as well as the mouth. Immersing myself into the research and techniques of debate proved to be the highlight of my third year.

At the end of the third year, in the summer of 1962, I spent my last summer in Hawaii. The 25th Infantry Division, "Tropic Lightning," conducted summer military training that year in the jungle environment of the Koolau Mountain range on Oahu Island. They simulated a prisoner of war camp, set up ambushes, taught us how to respond to ambushes, and sent us on a "slide for life," on a rope held by only a slingshot-shaped piece of guava wood across a mountain river gorge. Great fun! In later years, I remembered with fondness all the physical feats I had accomplished as a young man and never tried again. I am thankful that I was able to do so much as a cadet and an officer. Because of that I never wondered later what it would have been like to try something of great physical risk.

During summer training, I was assigned to the 65th Engineer Battalion at Schofield Barracks on central Oahu. This barracks was literally across the street from the quarters my parents had lived in the previous summer. The Japanese had attacked Schofield Barracks on December 7, 1941, and the buildings were still riddled with the bullet holes left from the attack. We could look west from the barracks over Kolekole Pass and imagine the Japanese warplanes swarming in like giant locusts on that memorable day—in President Roosevelt's words, the day that "would live in infamy." The images of planes with engines roaring and guns strafing in *From Here to Eternity* and *Tora! Tora! Tora!* suddenly came alive in my imagination.

While still in Hawaii, I had the privilege of going up in a small plane with my classmate Phil Mock and his father. We flew over the large volcanic crater on the big island as it spewed hot orange and yellow lava high into the air. That unforgettable vacation provided us with much needed enjoyment and rest—rest that would get me through year number four of the academy grind. I learned a hard lesson in military protocol from Phil's dad, Vernon P. Mock, who was then a brigadier general and assistant division commander of the 25th Infantry Division, when Phil and I were about to load up in a jeep. I always knew the senior person sat in the rear right seat in a car, so why not the same in a jeep? General Mock very politely let me know that he would sit in the front right "jump" seat in the jeep, and Phil and I would warm up the backseat.

I would attend my last Army–Navy game as a cadet in 1962, and this game proved to be one of my most memorable for two reasons. First, Navy introduced their new sophomore quarterback, Roger Staubach, who dominated the game by passing for two touchdowns and running for two more. Staubach later joined the NFL and became a star quarterback with the Dallas Cowboys under famed coach Tom Landry. I enjoyed watching him play that day and for many years after. In addition, President Kennedy attended the game that day, as is the custom with the commander in chief. And, as is the custom, he switched sides at halftime. As one of the group of seniors escorting him by providing an honor guard as he crossed over to the Navy side, my eyes had to remain focused straight ahead as he passed directly in front of me. As he walked past the cadet to my left, a man suddenly darted out of the crowd about five feet to my left and headed toward the president. His inebriated state allowed him to be collared and quickly turned away by the Secret Service.

President Kennedy, however, had more important things on his mind than an inebriated fan. The Cuban Missile Crisis occurred in the fall of 1962 over "a perilous thirteen days . . . that brought the world as close to nuclear war as it had ever come. The confrontation occurred after American spy planes detected the Soviet Union's construction of offensive launching pads on Castro's island" (Russell). In September and October, as army units were deployed to Florida, cadets had developed a personal interest in these current events and thus paid more attention in our tactics classes. Some instructors hinted that we might graduate early if we went to war, as had occurred in World War II for academy senior cadets. However, the situation was soon defused, and we returned to our normal routines and continued to enjoy our football and weekend activities.

I debated again my senior year and sometimes left for weekend tournaments as early in the week as Wednesday or Thursday. No question that my schedule had loosened up quite a bit since Beast Barracks days. Two Rhodes scholars, Captains Harvey Garn and Dale Vesser, served as excellent coaches. We traveled to approximately twenty different campuses during the two years I competed on the debate team and usually placed among the top teams at each tournament. I believe I derived more lasting benefit from that activity than from any other. In addition to learning self-discipline and logic, I enjoyed the fringe benefit of an endless line of girls to date. The girls we met on those trips thought cadet dates were a novelty. (Notice that I did not say an oddity!)

During my senior year, I roomed with James S. Dickey, a second generation West Pointer, who was as serious a cadet as I. He seemed to effortlessly succeed in academics, while I seemed to have to study so much more. We traveled together on a Debate Council and Forum field trip to Washington, D.C., in the spring of 1963 where we heard one of the great "grads" of our school speak in a room at the old executive office building of the White House. Retired four-star general Maxwell D. Taylor was a member of

President Kennedy's White House staff. One of the major lines of questioning concerned the role of the U.S. military in a small Southeast Asia country called Vietnam where the destinies of all of our classmates would eventually converge in one way or another.

At the end of my senior year, I received two awards that are still very special to me. First, the Consul General of Switzerland presented me with a wristwatch for being one of the best two debaters in the senior class. The credit for my debating success goes partly to my partner Frank Lennon from Providence, Rhode Island. He glided seamlessly through our debates due to sheer debating talent. Had he not left the team late in our senior year, I don't think I would have received this award at all. Next, my highest honor came when the chief of staff of the Argentine army, General Juan Carlos Ongania, presented to West Point, and thence to me, a special leather-bound book about a gaucho, Martin Fierro, to honor the top scholar in Spanish, which happened to be me that year. I am sure that my heritage and background of speaking Spanish since childhood can be credited in part for this second honor.

West Point instilled in me an extreme sense of love of country. I was proud to be a part of such an elite group and also proud that I had survived the rigorous and strenuous four years of intensive training. I still feel that pride. I never really *loved* being at the academy, but I did love what it represented. I loved the pomp and circumstance, the ivy-covered buildings, the traditions, and knowing that I shared the company of some of our greatest military leaders. As I would say in later speeches, "West Point is a great place to be from, but not at."

On May 12, 1962, General Douglas MacArthur gave his final speech to the cadet corps at West Point. He had been my childhood hero ever since I saw him in Tokyo, Japan, in 1949. His left hand thrust into his coat pocket, he stood before the cadets with no notes and spoke about the profession of arms. Those were some of the most inspirational moments of my life. General MacArthur eloquently expressed principles that would become my own personal soldier's code:

> A great moral code, a code of conduct and chivalry
> of those who guard this beloved land of culture and

ancient descent . . . The story of the American man-at-arms . . . One of the world's noblest figures . . .duty, honor, country. The code which these words perpetuate embraces the highest moral law and will stand the test of any ethics or philosophies ever promulgated for the uplift of mankind . . . The soldier, above all other men, is required to practice the greatest act of religious training—sacrifice . . . Through this welter of change and development, your mission remains fixed . . . It is to win our wars . . . You are the ones who are trained to fight . . . You are the leaven which binds together the entire fabric of our national system of defense . . . The Long Gray Line has never failed us . . . The shadows are lengthening for me, but in the evening of my memory I always come back to West Point . . . Always there echoes: duty, honor, country.

These words reflected my own standards, dreams, and ideals. I believed in them, and I tried hard to live up to them. These ideals may seem corny by so many standards evident in America today. They are, they were, and they will always be the standards for my life.

We heard another speaker several months later who was not quite so famous or illustrious as General MacArthur, but one who made a profound impression on me just the same. A West Point graduate and army captain, whose name I do not recall, lectured our class on military tactics and leadership. He had served in Vietnam as an adviser and had been wounded by the Viet Cong when they shot him through both legs. He spoke of their hit-and-run tactics and guerilla warfare and the atrocities they inflicted upon their victims. It was the first time I heard about Vietnam in detail, and the mental images he painted that day would remain ingrained in my mind for a very long time. I listened intently to his words, unaware of the major role Vietnam would later come to play in my life.

As I prepared to graduate, I began to consider entering the army and becoming a leader of troops. I was ready for that, but not especially philosophical about it. Actually, being a junior officer with our troops would lead to a later career when I would serve great men and women in our veteran ranks.

Obviously, not all West Point graduates go on to become well-known military heroes. Hundreds of men (and now women) in each class quietly and inconspicuously serve their country and then anonymously enter civilian life. They are all heroes in their own right. We all share a special camaraderie and feeling toward one another that cannot be experienced in a civilian college or university. I have discovered through the years that we all really do care about one another, in war and in peace. We have shared a common bond that cannot be broken and will continue throughout our lives. My associations there, in the present, and through the future are something no other association will ever emulate. After West Point, a West Pointer has usually been involved in every major turning point of my life.

When the Gulf War began in 1991, words spoken by Lieutenant Colonel Gregory Fontenot as he addressed his troops before the ground battle of Desert Storm were especially appropriate for the men and women cadets who were trained to lead and had led for 160 years when I graduated. "Like I told you before, this is not the 'Izod, Polo-Shirt, Weejuns Loafers Crowd.' Not a whole lot of kids here (have) dads (who) are anesthesiologists or Justices of the Supreme Court. We're the poor, white middle class and the poor black kids from the block and the Hispanics from the barrio. We're just as good as the . . . rest, because the honest thing is, that's who [sic] I want to go to war with, people like you. And you guys will do great" (*Washington Post*).

Today's governing elite don't usually send their offspring to war. In a January 23, 2006, article titled "Nation's Elite AWOL from Military," journalist Joe Galloway, the co-author of "We Were Soldiers Once . . . and Young," interviewed two authors, Kathy Roth-Douquet and Frank Schaeffer. They had written in 2006 "AWOL: The Unexcused Absence of America's Upper Classes from Military Service and How It Hurts Our Country." I think the most telling conclusion reached was that, "When those who benefit most from living in a country contribute the least to its defense and those who benefit least are asked to pay the ultimate price, something happens to the soul of that country." I feel this was certainly true for our Vietnam period in American history.

There are exceptions. In fact, Supreme Court Justice Antonin Scalia has a son, Matthew Scalia, who was in the class of 1995 at West Point and served in Iraq. President Reagan's administration's Attorney General Ed Meese has a son, Michael Meese, who graduated from West Point in 1981 and served in both Bosnia and Iraq. There have been a few distinguished citizens of our country whose offspring do choose the military, some for a career.

Reflections

The four-year military academy experience for me was an intensely elevating one relative to my sense of patriotism and the development of an ethical and moral code. However, my spiritual development as it relates to my religious development and biblical knowledge was still nonexistent. I chose not to participate in either Bible studies or the very active Officers' Christian Fellowship on campus. Instead, I spent my free time in my debate activities, which conveniently took me off campus to debate tournaments many weekends during my last two years. I do not recall needing to pray, because it was such an ordered and regimented environment with little to rock my boat, except for the occasional romantic entanglement. In some ways, the academy, the institution of the army, my country, and my flag became my "God." Instead of giving my allegiance, devotion, and dedication to God's world, I gave them to the elements of Caesar's world. I was definitely wrapped around my national colors and the history and culture that West Point personified. *Prideful* is the best word to describe me at this time in my life. I was proud to be a cadet, proud of my accomplishments, proud of my exalted status (in my own eyes), proud of being a member of the famed Corps of Cadets, and proud of being able to serve my country as an officer. I had become very comfortable in a life's path where I had a job in an honorable profession—the very thing that had always been my goal, my dream.

As I graduated, I really did not think much of spiritual things. Although my trust in God and knowledge of Christ's example had always been, and would always be, a moral and ethical governor in my engine of life, I had long since placed these things on the "back burner." I had set aside the Christ of my youth, ever prevalent in my acolytes, Episcopal services, Brotherhood of Saint Andrew, and youth group. Instead, I thought only of the trails of glory that I would blaze in the U.S. Army. In a way, I had a "country" covenant to fight and, if necessary, to die for. It was part and parcel of the payback for my free education, and I did not oppose it. Instead, I was proud and committed to this secular covenant. In my extremely earthly and very lowly existence as a child of God, I ended up fulfilling my "country" covenant by the spilling of my own blood and neglected the most important covenant in the life of man with the God who loved me so much that He came to earth as a man and spilled His blood for me.

I had grown up in the usual wide-eyed innocence of childhood amid a very wonderful family and parents that taught me the love of Christ, even though I did not take it all that seriously then. Just as I had read biographies of famous Americans and knew about them, I thought I knew all I needed to know *about* God, but I did not really *know* Him. I didn't have a personal relationship with Him. And there is a tremendous difference. After all, I had other priorities in my life and too many distractions to work on my relationship with the Lord—distractions such as studying, dating, having fun, and finding and marrying a beautiful Texas coed. I had been afforded an opportunity that most teenagers never even dream of—an outstanding education in the institution of my dreams, and I had valued that highly. In addition, I had a promising future and a loving wife. What more could one ask from life? Most would ask for good health and rank that as a high priority.

After returning from Vietnam, it would be many years before my health would be restored. However, had I returned home physically whole, I am not sure that I would have ever attained the spiritual growth that I have attained as a wounded veteran. I know now that nothing happens to God's children without His permission, and it is often through adversity, hardship, and challenges that many of us develop our faith and spiritual awareness. I began a journey in Dak To in 1967 that would continue for many decades of my life. That journey would become just the tip of the iceberg of the major challenges that I would face and opportunities I would have to share with others my experiences and what I learned from them. My military training had taught me much about the weapons of warfare. But my experiences in Vietnam on an earthly battlefield were simply a prelude for other battlefields of life where I would begin learning about and experiencing the ultimate chess game, that of the eternal struggle between good and evil in the realm of spiritual warfare. In some ways, my life and what God wanted me to do with it began in Dak To, Vietnam, on June 17, 1967.

CHAPTER 4

MY QUEST FOR INDEPENDENCE

Brooke Army Medical Center
Summer 1967

Seething beneath my seemingly smooth and uncomplicated path of physical healing that would eventually lead to walking out of the hospital lay a churning turmoil of my very soul and spirit. Sometime in June, after being on morphine every three hours since my injury, a most disturbing pattern began to appear. I began to have a great fear of how I was going to live my life, how I was going to walk, how I was going to support my family. Very depressed and anxious about my future, I felt diminished in importance and status and totally dependent on others.

I lived and relived the details of the attack, my wounding, and my seemingly endless surgeries. When my mind began to play games with reality, I needed to begin psychotherapy. I disliked having to see a psychiatrist because I believed it was a sign of weakness, though; it indicated that I was not strong enough to cope with the realities of life on my own. Originally, in my usual and positive gung-ho attitude, I believed that I would be able to meet and conquer this challenge the same way I had so many others. I believed that my legs would heal, I would be fitted with new legs, and I would walk out of the hospital the day I got my new legs and effortlessly begin a new life. But it would not be that simple.

At the end of June, I began to see a psychiatrist. Within a few weeks, it seemed that the psychological battle was over—at least temporarily. Two days after I had my second amputation, doctors wrote the following in my medical records: "29 June 67. Neuropsychiatry for onset of acute agitated behavior and hallucination." Two months later, the "external precipitating stress" factor reappeared as another neuropsychiatric consultation reported on August 31: "Paranoid state, acute, severe incomplete remission, manifested by delusional thinking, preoccupation with religion," and at that time there was felt to be "no appreciable degree of psychiatric impairment." Although continuing my physical healing, intellectually I had become an analytical observer and had begun to detest the hospital rules and questioned everything, especially the spiritual implications of it all. The notation about preoccupation with religion really interested me. Although I did not understand it at the time, this is when the spiritual war that would try to capture my very soul began.

As I have previously stated, although I had accepted Jesus Christ as my Savior during my teenage years, my true knowledge of anything deeply spiritual was virtually nonexistent. I believed in Christ intellectually—that He had lived and died for me. However, I had not reached that point where I took Him into my heart, developed a personal relationship with Him, and literally turned my life over to Him. And although I often prayed to God to heal my wounded body and soul, at this point in my life I did not fully understand what that meant either. My idea of prayer at the time was to make plans and ask God to bless them and to ask Him to meet my needs or give me what I wanted. Basically, I prayed from my own self-centeredness, not understanding that God was in control of my life, not me, and if my prayers were not answered, it was either because what I had prayed for was not in God's will for my life or it was not yet God's time to give me the answer I desired.

Gordon Lindsey, the founder of Christ for the Nations missionary organization in Dallas, writes, "Prayer must become as natural as breathing. Through prayer, spiritual forces that human efforts cannot overcome will be defeated. By continuous prayer, the enemy is kept at bay and a hedge of protection keeps evil from penetrating it" (*Prayer That Moves Mountains:* 40). Today, I know that when I pray, whatever happens will be God's will for my life, because, even though God does not always bless my plans, He does answer my prayers. And those answers, even if they are "no," are always for my good and within His will for me. I must constantly seek His will for my life, not my own.

Christian fiction writer, Jan Karon, says it best in her novels when she repeatedly refers to the "prayer that never fails": Thy will be done. When all else fails, this prayer, taken from the Lord's Prayer in Matthew 6, will never fail. When adversity strikes, when disaster befalls us, when tragedy occurs, and we just don't have the words to pray, this is the prayer that never fails. *Thy will be done.* Wondering about prayers and whether they will be answered or within the will of God should never be an inhibitor to prayer. God will *always* answer them—in His time and within His will.

As a young man and wounded soldier lying in a hospital with a double amputation, I certainly did not understand why this happened, much less how God could "fix it." It would not be until my fifth decade of life before I would really begin to understand the spiritual "big picture" and the ramifications of Christ's First Coming—and I am still learning. But at this time, I held a very simplistic and rudimentary understanding of God's ways. I only wish that I had known then that the earlier in life that we learn the basics of our faith walk, the easier life will be. However, in my innocence of the ways of God, I continuously held onto my faith and prayed constantly during my hospital stay.

Taking "Flight"

Independence Day has always been a festive day in my life. On July 4, 1967, the army provided a special fireworks display on the playing field at Fort Sam Houston. This time, however, it was not a celebration for me. The sounds of the exploding fireworks outside the hospital brought back the horrible memories of enemy fire. Those memories seemed to struggle with the drugs that would ordinarily put me to sleep within minutes. Although my drug-induced sleep eventually shut out the sounds of the fireworks, those same sounds gave many of the other men nightmares for the rest of the night, examples of post-traumatic stress disorder.

Each day we watched the endless procession of the wounded being brought into the hospital, read about the war in the newspapers, and watched daily reports on television. We tried to help and comfort one another and boost one another's spirits in any way possible. Amputees who had been there for a while and who were further along in their recovery process often ran errands for the rest of us. One soldier with two good legs and one arm often fed me and went for cigarettes for others.

One night, several days after my right leg had been amputated and probably due to the influence of the drugs, I found myself feeling better than usual and got the urge to get out of bed. I unhooked the traction ropes at 2 a.m. and eased myself into my neighbor's wheelchair. With great delight, I wheeled out to the nurses' station with a "Hey, look at me!" attitude. A surprised and stern-faced nurse promptly rushed me back to bed, tucked me in, and told me in no uncertain terms that the doctor would tell me if and when he wanted me out of bed, and that would probably not happen for several more weeks. In spite of the nurse's firm reprimand, I had enjoyed my few moments of freedom from the confinement of the bed and traction apparatus.

As the weeks passed and I began to feel better, the idleness of hospitalization began to take its toll on me. After being so disciplined and busy in a regimented life for so many years, I found myself with too much time on my hands and nothing to do. Jackie brought me a small portable TV set with an earplug so I could listen to television without disturbing the other men. More than half of the other patients had their own bedside televisions, which resulted in a very annoying noise when they were all tuned in to different stations at once with varying volume levels. In addition to watching TV, a couple nights a week we watched movies that Red Cross volunteers, or "Gray Ladies," brought to the ward. They often handed out gum and candy as well as magazines and books on loan from the local library.

Many times, celebrities and various local groups visited the ward to entertain and cheer up the wounded. Once, a choir group from Sul Ross State University came to the ward to sing for us. The women wore long white gowns, and the men wore tuxedos. When they asked if I had a favorite song I would like them to sing, I requested "Born Free." It seemed appropriate at the time. Other visitors included singer Anita Bryant and Christopher George, a TV actor who starred in *Rat Patrol* and *Mission Impossible.* A picture of Christopher and me somehow managed to end up in *Movie Screen* magazine shortly after that visit. However, in spite of the many celebrities who visited the wards, the person who cheered me the most was Frances "Mom" Mauldin. One of my favorite hospital employees, Mom Mauldin had lost a son in the navy during World War II. Always in a happy and cheerful mood, she brought a lot of sunshine into that depressing, pain-filled ward.

After eating only hospital food for weeks in the confines of the ward, I soon developed a thirst for a cold beer. When Jackie asked Dr. George Pomerantz for permission to bring beer to me, he granted it, saying that it might help me relax. Jackie periodically smuggled beer in a thermos past the hospital staff. Although seemingly insignificant, this was another small but important step on the journey back to the world I once knew.

In spite of the small things that helped boost my morale, it was difficult to keep my spirits up day in and day out in a place where all the men had lost an arm or a leg or both and where we all experienced great pain. One day, as a result of feeling really depressed, my feelings bubbled to the surface in the form of a few insensitive, negative comments. The double amputee in the bed next to mine was a black draftee from New Orleans. We usually talked all day and had come to know each other very well. He soon grew tired of my negative, pessimistic diatribe.

"Captain," he said, "knock it off. You're an officer, and you're supposed to set an example for enlisted men like me."

He was right. His comments reminded me of my years of training, and I knew that I should be the leader and set the example for all the men—difficult as that may be under the current circumstances.

From then on, I tried to keep a positive mental attitude. Some days it was very difficult to keep that stiff upper lip, especially on days like the day one of the double amputees died on the operating table during surgery. That was bad for us all because we each knew, but for the grace of God, that it could have been any one of us.

On July 3, 6, and 12, I had dressing changes, again each time under anesthesia in the operating room. The dressing change procedure became less and less painful as time wore on. After the July 12 procedure, my doctor decided to begin changing the dressings in the ward. I was one of the four double amputees who occupied a row of beds on one side of the ward. As a favor for all of us, I asked the doctor if our dressings could be changed before the single amputees across from us so we wouldn't have to watch them and feel terrible anticipation gnawing in the pits of our stomachs as we each waited our turn. After thinking about it and realizing that we had twice the discomfort and pain to endure, he agreed. That, too, proved to be a small, but very important triumph.

After a couple of months in traction, I had to face skin grafting for my legs. In preparation, the doctors showed me photographs of the bottoms of my stumps. I had not seen them before and was not prepared for what I saw. The pictures revealed bone and raw tissue still exposed after so many weeks. I couldn't believe that they really looked that bad, so I asked Jackie to bring in a mirror so I could see for myself. The gruesome reflection in the mirror only confirmed what I saw in the photographs. My legs still looked awful. I knew in spite of how my own legs looked, there were worse cases than mine on the ward. One soldier came in after losing two legs, an arm, and his eyesight. A shell had exploded directly below him. In addition to losing three limbs and his sight, he also had a large hole in the bottom portion of his body. His recovery, if one can call it that, would take the rest of his life. I could not imagine how anyone can recover from something like that, and I realized that I was very fortunate in comparison. Those cases will haunt me my entire life.

Physically, I got increasingly better each day. The bandages and gauze were taken off for good, and medical personnel placed a wire basket-type apparatus over my stumps for protection. A lamp placed at the end of my bed helped dry out the raw flesh and speed up the healing process. It also served to prepare my legs for skin grafts taken from my stomach and placed over the bottoms of my stumps. After grafting surgery, I had to wear my pajamas slung low around my hips until the four-inch square of skin near my navel healed enough to no longer be sensitive to the touch.

Still on Demerol every three hours, I certainly experienced the euphoria of not having a care in the world until the drugs wore off. I suppose the effects of drugs are similar to those of alcohol, giving one a sense of magnanimity and bravado that is never or seldom evident when sober, or perhaps it is simply kept under control. This became evident to me when I later looked back at the words of a letter that I wrote to President Lyndon Johnson on July 19 while still under the influence of pain killing drugs.

> As a representative of all American fighting men, I am writing this letter to you from my bed at Brooke Army General Hospital in San Antonio, Texas. I am a commissioned officer who was wounded in an enemy mortar attack in Vietnam on June 17, 1967, and as a result, both of my legs have been amputated.
>
> There are many other men in this ward with me who have served and fought in Vietnam and have also given their flesh and blood for our great United States of America.
>
> Our morale is high because we are all in the same situation. We aid, comfort, and assist each other. We have suffered for our country, but the greater majority of us are not bitter that we have lost limbs and have incurred other wounds due to the armed conflict in Vietnam.
>
> Some are war heroes and have received their wounds by brave fighting. Others are just ordinary servicemen who went to Vietnam to do a job. We are a cross section of American youth of this generation who are fighting in Vietnam to preserve freedom, not only for our United States, but also for Vietnam and the entire free world.
>
> We are distressed, naturally, that we are disabled in varying degrees, but we all feel deeply in our hearts and

souls that we have suffered for a good cause—for a very real, worthy and just cause. We are proud to call ourselves United States fighting men.

We are very thankful for the legislation that has been passed on our behalf that will enable us, despite our handicaps, to leave Brooke Army General Hospital and other hospitals all over the country and once again live normal, productive, and healthy lives.

It is my understanding that you sometimes come through San Antonio, Texas, on visits to your home near Johnson City. If it is possible, Mr. President, for you to visit us in the future, we would all consider it a rare privilege for you to stop by for just a few minutes to talk with us.

If it is not possible, Mr. President, I will understand. I am well aware that you are granted few periods for private time within the framework of your responsibilities as our Commander in Chief. At any rate, Mr. President, I, myself, wish to compliment you for the outstanding manner in which I think you are making the decisions in regard to the conflict in Vietnam.

I know that, in spite of the drugs, I did mean what I wrote at the time. I would not have written it had I not actually believed in what I wrote. Jackie dutifully typed the letter and never discussed its contents. Thirty years later, with the hindsight of maturity and all the revelations of the debacle that this particular war represented, I am amazed at the naïveté and innocence of that young soldier that I once was. If my father or any other family members recognized any of this in me, thankfully they did not say anything. I suppose they knew that wisdom most often comes with the maturity of age, and I was not yet quite there.

A New Taste of Freedom

Jackie rented an efficiency apartment near the hospital, and we were anxious to be alone together without the constant presence of other patients and hospital staff members. Because of the painkilling drugs I had to take, I had difficulty getting a temporary pass to leave the hospital, even for a few hours. Though still in pain, but motivated to acquire a pass, I began to wean myself from morphine to Demerol and then from Demerol to Darvon. Once I finally received a pass, I had to overcome one more obstacle—the three-inch ledge at the apartment threshold that presented a problem for my wheelchair. My good friend, former Green Beret sergeant and single amputee, John Graw, voluntarily fashioned a ramp for our apartment entrance, and I finally used my permission pass to go home for a few hours.

On August 1, 1967, exactly four years since I had proposed to Jackie, one year since I had left for Vietnam, and six weeks since I had sustained my wounds, I left my hospital bed for three precious hours to go to the apartment for a private visit with my wife. Graw lifted me from my chair, placed me on the sofa, closed the wheelchair, chatted for about thirty seconds, and left Jackie and me alone for three hours of blessed privacy. It was a wonderful way to spend the anniversary of our engagement. (Graw told us later that he spent those same three hours trying to get the blasted wheelchair to open because it had jammed shut. He didn't get it open until just before he returned to the apartment to take me back to the hospital.)

My first taste of freedom lifted my spirits tremendously. Jackie and I often bought records by Frank Sinatra, Roger Miller, and other 60s recording artists and listened to them in the apartment. By the third month of my hospitalization, I received permission to take rides regularly through San Antonio with Jackie in our 1963 Corvair.

One day as she pulled away from the curb at the hospital, I found myself grabbing for something to hold on to and exclaimed, "Jackie, you're going too fast!"

"But, I'm only going thirty-five miles per hour," she responded.

Because of the narrow roads filled with potholes in Vietnam, we seldom drove faster than twenty to twenty-five miles per hour. So after nearly a year in Vietnam, I had become accustomed to that slow pace and felt like I was hurtling through space at Jackie's meager speed of thirty-five. I knew then that it would be necessary for me to make many adjustments in order to settle back into life at home. At least, I wanted to keep my movements at much lower speeds for a while.

By September, I was finally able to wheel around the wards to visit friends. During one of those excursions, I learned of a Green Beret sergeant in ward 43-D who reported to Dak To shortly after I left. We visited for a while, and I told him that I had served as captain at Dak To and received my wounds there.

"Oh, yeah," he said, "everyone at Dak To is shown the spot where you were hit. There is still a stain from where the blood soaked into the concrete."

His insensitive words brought back vivid memories of that day, and it was more than I could stand. Without saying much more, I turned and wheeled my chair away as quickly as I could. I never visited him again. The memories of that day and that battle were still much too raw and elicited emotions I did not want to feel and images I did not want to remember.

My Own Red Badge of Courage

In August, Colonel George Omer Jr., chief of orthopedics at Brooke Army, conducted an awards ceremony in the Red Cross lounge. Colonel Omer walked over to my wheelchair and pinned the Bronze Star, Purple Heart, and Air Medal on my new set of khakis that Jackie had bought me for the occasion. I received the Air Medal for a certain number of hours in flights over enemy territory. In his remarks regarding this medal, Colonel Omer said, "During the period 7 September 1966 to 17 June 1967 he actively participated in more than twenty-five aerial missions over hostile territory in support of counterinsurgency operations." The helicopter pilots and crews deserved their Air Medals much more than I. The Bronze Star Medal for Achievement was somewhat a good conduct medal for officers, but I still wear it proudly. The citation (standard for all of us) read: "Materially contributed to the efforts of the United States mission to the Republic of Vietnam to assist that country in ridding itself of the communist threat to its freedom." We all cried. The Purple Heart, my own "Red Badge of Courage," spoke for itself.

Although it was a touching and traditional ceremony, such ceremonies had become rather perfunctory. Because most of the

Vietnam War "heroes" were hospitalized wounded soldiers, private medal ceremonies for family members only were conducted there on a regular basis. The frequency of the ceremonies diluted their glamour, and we all began to take them as a matter of routine. For Jackie, however, the ceremony brought all of her harbored emotions and feelings about the war to the surface. She loved me dearly, but she hated what Vietnam had done to me and to us. She felt that no medals could ever compensate for the loss of my legs. The war had robbed us of so much, including what should have been the most carefree and happy years of our marriage.

We often heard that there were many divorces among the severely wounded men. Jackie and I had been married only three and one-half years, but that short time was considered to be a long marriage by those on the ward who had experienced divorce after less time together. Although the divorce rate on the ward was very high, the suffering that Jackie and I shared seemed to bring us closer together. We had all been warned of this possibility. Perhaps it was because of those warnings and the effects that military life seemed to have on Jackie that I had made a promise to her earlier that would hopefully ensure a long and happy life together.

In the fall of 1967, Jackie and I were able to travel for the first time to El Paso to see my family.

A Promise Kept

Until 1963, Vietnam had been labeled a *police action,* a term that has now become familiar military jargon. After the assassination of South Vietnamese President Diem in 1963, the *action* began to intensify, and everyone around the world knew that our government was simply using this term as a euphemism for *war.* I stood by and watched as more and more of my friends and classmates left for Vietnam. By the spring of 1966, a close friend and classmate, Burt McCord, had already died there. Burt and his wife, Eddie, had lived only two doors from us at Fort Hood, and we had babysat his son, Mike.

As a first lieutenant, I had been assigned as the Engineer Battalion operations officer (S-3), normally a major's slot, when the heavy Vietnam troop levies began in 1965. It was my duty to oversee the annual completion of the individual physical fitness tests. To my chagrin and disappointment, I discovered that many of the older officers and senior noncommissioned officers were accustomed to taking what is called "pencil tests," tests taken in their offices without going out on the course. I refused to allow this and got the battalion commander to order that everyone under forty years of age take a real test. As the first person in the battalion to perform the test on the scheduled day, I watched some soldiers with modest paunches struggle through the exercises. My West Point leadership training meant that I led my men. That meant that I physically trained with them daily, although there were many other officers who conveniently had "prior commitments" during the scheduled runs and exercise periods. In spite of my unpopularity for this decision, I know that I did the right thing, and I believe the rank and file troops appreciated all their leaders being required to fulfill the same standards that they had to fulfill.

In the summer of 1965, I had several alternatives to consider. First, I could take advantage of an offer to become aide to Division Commanding General John E. Kelly and spend at least some of the remainder of my four years in a continuing safe assignment. On the other hand, I could go to Korea as aide to Brigadier General Robert Safford, assistant commander of the 2nd Armored Division at Fort Hood and avoid Vietnam. Most soldiers during the '60s would have paid handsomely for such a choice. So, after serving two years as a combat engineer officer at Fort Hood in the 17th Armored Engineer Battalion of the 2nd Armored Division, I decided to accept General Kelly's offer and became his junior aide.

Serving as an aide to General Kelly proved to be a wonderful professional experience for me. A 1936 West Point graduate, General Kelly had been awarded the nation's second highest award for valor in World War II, the Distinguished Service Cross, when he commanded a battalion in Europe. I looked to him as a role model. Under his guiding hand, I sharpened my organizational skills and observed an inspiring leader and family man. On the other hand, however, this unfortunately soon became a stressful situation for Jackie as well. As my wife, instead of just being on time for functions,

Jackie was expected to be there an hour before the function started to socialize with other officers' wives. I couldn't really be her date at these affairs because I had to take care of the general and other dignitaries. Even when she was with me and surrounded by a crowd of people, Jackie felt on the outside and alone.

In addition, I must admit that, after observing General Kelly, I experienced some disconcerting thoughts about the decision I was making to resign from the army for family reasons. General Kelly and his wife, Jane, had seven children, three of whom eventually graduated from West Point. During my years as an army "brat" and then as an officer, I noted many successful and happy military families. They, like General Kelly, had successfully integrated military and family life, and I knew that it could be done. Sadly, I also knew that kind of life was not to be for me.

Therefore, to ease the strain my career placed on our marriage, I transferred from the Corps of Engineers to military intelligence in 1965 with plans to become a counter-intelligence officer. I did this for two reasons: First, I originally intended to ensure another stateside assignment before my four years were up so I would not have to go to Vietnam. Second, I wanted to be an intelligence officer like my father, whom I greatly admired. I hoped that Jackie's mind would be eased in knowing that, as an intelligence officer, I would not be sent into active combat, even if I had to go to Vietnam.

In spite of all my rationalizing, however, I was still a trained regular army officer, and those West Point traditions—mental tapes if you will—of duty, honor, and country were hard to erase. Eventually, it didn't take much thought or soul searching to know what I must do; I stayed at Fort Hood and eventually *volunteered* for Vietnam without telling Jackie. If I had not gone, the guilt of not going would have eaten at me for the rest of my life. My Vietnam assignment cut short my cushy job as a general's aide. Army life would never be that good again. In April 1966, I went to Fort Holabird, Maryland, for intelligence branch training.

Making such an important, life-changing decision without consulting my wife was admittedly a huge error in judgment on my part and one that would haunt our relationship for decades.

Twenty-two years old, brunette, and beautiful, Jackie would plan to graduate from Southern Methodist University in Dallas during my absence. I don't think she ever had a serious worry in her life, and, with all good intentions, I wanted it to stay that way. I wanted her always to feel as cherished and protected as she had felt while living with her parents. I delayed telling her of my decision because I wanted to protect her from the inevitable anguish it would bring. To tell her good-bye now and leave for a war she did not understand was the hardest thing I had ever had to do. I could never have anticipated how much harder my life would become in future years.

In my opinion later in life, there is no way that any spouse could ever totally understand a patriot soldier's commitment to serve his or her country by volunteering to be placed in harm's way. No one ever anticipated the conflict engendered by my volunteering, but in retrospect, it was inevitable. Even after two and one-half years of marriage to an army officer, Jackie did not understand the military nor my motivation for military service. However, I believed that, as an intelligent and capable woman and given time and experience, she would eventually understand. I was wrong. I could not fathom in my wildest imagination that she would later be forced to face the consequences of my dedication to service in such an intense fashion.

To this day, it is still difficult to put my reasons for volunteering into words, because those reasons are more easily felt than expressed. I felt a strong inner desire and sense of duty to do my part in fighting the communist menace—a menace I had learned about firsthand as a child and one that I had grown to hate. I simply followed the pattern of so many other West Point graduates who had gone to Vietnam before me and who, like myself, had been trained for four years to serve and defend the cause of freedom. Unlike some of them, I had been prepared for military service since early childhood. A war raged, and I volunteered. It was just as simple as that. It was something I had to do. Perhaps that is why I signed and sent in the volunteer papers without telling Jackie until after the fact, when I could no longer keep what I had done from her.

Although Jackie had begged me many times not to volunteer for Vietnam, and although she said she understood my reasons, she eventually confessed that what I had done created raw emotional wounds that would take twenty-eight years to heal. It wasn't a matter of abandoning her, and she knew that. She had no doubts about my love and devotion for her. She has said that she understood that my not telling her was simply a protective measure on my part to postpone her mental anguish for as long as possible. Yet, in spite of her apparent understanding heart, I could see the pain on her face and wished the year in Vietnam was behind me, not before me. However, I did keep my promise to Jackie and submitted my resignation to the army before I left for Vietnam. I planned to do my part as an intelligence officer, and then return home and settle down to civilian life with my wife and the family we planned to have together. Life was supposed to be just that simple.

Vietnam Hits Home

In May 1966, just two and one-half months before leaving for Vietnam, I read a newspaper account of an attack at Gio Linh, an outpost at the DMZ (demilitarized zone between North Vietnam and South Vietnam). My good friend and M-1 classmate, Michael Kilroy, served as an adviser to a South Vietnamese battalion there. I didn't give it much thought because in those days we read reports of skirmishes and battles in Vietnam every day. A week later I learned that Mike had died in the attack. Mike's captain wrote his parents that he was killed by mortar fire during an attack by the North Vietnamese. He had chosen to remain standing beside the Vietnamese battalion commander whom he was advising rather than take cover in a concrete bunker. He chose to do what he thought he had to do. It was a tragedy for such a good life to be snuffed out in such a manner.

Mike was one of the most popular cadets in Company M-1 at West Point. We had double dated together. He was a very strong Catholic with a big heart, and I thought of him as one of my best friends. His death brought the war home to me in a vivid, special, close, and personal way, causing my desire to serve in Vietnam to intensify. Although that desire grew, I began to experience more fear than I had ever felt before. What if that same thing happened to me?

Over Memorial Day weekend, Jackie and I drove to Packanack Lake in New Jersey for Mike's funeral and then on to the burial at West Point. Mike's funeral and the reality of war seemed eons away from our innocent, tranquil lives as cadets. Our lives would never be the same again. I wrote to Jackie's parents that nothing had touched us as much in all my life.

"Mike is home," Pete Kelly, my roommate of two years at West Point, said as Jackie and I stood beside him at Lieutenant Michael W. Kilroy's grave in the cemetery at West Point.

The cemetery faces out over the Hudson River and up the Hudson Valley flanked by the green mountains of the Highlands. Mike's grieving mother clutched the American flag that had draped her son's casket all the way from Vietnam. Volleys were fired and *Taps* played the last time for another fallen American soldier. This had been one of my dearest friends for four years. We had laughed, drunk, studied, and dated together. Mike was a sterling Christian, dear friend, and fine soldier.

Jackie and I witnessed an outpouring of love at this funeral that we may never see again, and I pray we never have to see again, but probably will because Mike was certainly not the last soldier ever to fall. We saw truly remarkable expressions of admiration and respect from Mike's town, family, friends, and classmates. Two of my West Point roommates and several former M-1 Company men, including Magoo, flew in from Chicago and Detroit for the funeral. People packed Mike's home church to capacity for the memorial service. The Catholic chapel at West Point sent twenty cadet choir members to sing the litany, and six cadets served as pallbearers. At the termination of the service, 140 cars in the funeral procession began winding the fifty miles through the mountains to West Point. About two hundred Bluebells, Girl Scouts, and Boy Scouts lined the block leading from the church in silent tribute to their hero. Mike had been a very religious person whom all respected and loved, and he belonged to all of them. The Town Council voted to name a park after him and ordered the flags at Packanack Lake, Mike's hometown, flown at half-mast for a mourning period of thirty days. The entire Memorial Day weekend was packed with emotion, and Jackie and I shared something that we will never forget.

Jackie Clark

It was my first time to see the academy, and I was glad to have an opportunity to see the school that had meant so much to Allen. Trophy Point, where the mountains and the Hudson River meet, is incredibly beautiful. However, knowing that Allen would be going to Vietnam placed a dark cloud over the beauty I saw there and filled my heart with fear for his safety.

The loss of such a good-looking, well-liked West Point friend moved me deeply. The reality of war truly struck home as the twenty-one-gun salute fired. The sound of the guns made me realize the finality of it all. My mind searched for meaning in the insanity of this war. Tears streamed uncontrollably down my face, as I feared the same thing might happen to Allen. I wrote my parents: "I know that I have a much more healthy attitude and appreciate more what our boys are trying to do over there." Although this was very simplistic, it was heartfelt then, but my emotions changed with time.

The weekend after Mike's funeral, Jackie and I again drove to West Point for June Week (graduation). I stood proudly as a graduate at the end of the Long Gray Line on the Plain, surveying my familiar surroundings—the chapel, the barracks, and all the monuments to our academy and to our military heritage. With the loss of my friend still fresh in my heart, I think I realized for the first time the true impact of West Point and its purpose. Many of those who graduated from the academy would not come home alive. War signified not only duty, honor, and country, but also pain, grief, and loss. It had been a very sobering week.

Preparing for War

Prior to leaving for Vietnam, I spent six weeks at Fort Holabird, Maryland, where I received basic training in military intelligence, including five days of intensive training on how to interrogate prisoners. Some of the people we interrogated were professional actors. As the entire class looked on, we performed interrogations that lasted for what seemed like an eternity. By watching our classmates take their turns, we learned from one another's mistakes. Members of our class grew very close to one another, and we developed a special camaraderie in knowing that we were all on our way to a place from which some of us might not return.

Being at Fort Holabird again and being so near to Washington and New England, where I had lived and gone to school as a young man, provided a homecoming of sorts for me. I pointed out all the old familiar sights to Jackie as we toured New England and the Washington area extensively. We toured the Old North Church in Boston where Paul Revere saw his signal light, Independence Hall in Philadelphia, and the capitol, White House, and Lincoln Memorial in Washington. We partied late in both Washington and Baltimore, a habit that caused me to struggle to classes on the "mornings after." We knew these would be our last few days together before I left for Vietnam, so we tried to make the best of them, spending all our free time making memories. My main goal, however, was to get through my classes, get to Vietnam, serve my year there, and get the war experience over and done with, so I could put it behind me and come home to resume my life with my family.

CHAPTER 5

THE BEGINNING OF MY OWN PERSONAL WAR

Brooke Army Medical Center
Summer 1967

My slow but certain recovery proceeded day by day, as did the daily routine on the ward. Nurses flipped the lights on promptly at 6 a.m. and brought in food trays by 7 a.m. Jackie massaged my back twice a day during those first few weeks. Orderlies helped me shave, brush my teeth, and bathe. Next to my family's visits, one of the brightest spots during this time was when Irma Presswood, a wonderfully cheerful black orderly, came in to help me each day. Her beaming personality and bright smile lit up my mornings. We soon became very good friends.

I soon became an avid clock-watcher as I waited for Jackie, who faithfully came to the hospital every day at 2 p.m. for two hours and then again at 6 p.m. for two hours. Once, when the pain dragged me down and she had not arrived, I asked a single amputee in the next bed if he would hold my hand. Without a second's hesitation, this understanding black enlisted man rolled his wheelchair next to my bed and held my hand until Jackie arrived. His sympathetic touch not only helped take my mind off the pain, but also helped me realize that I was not alone. In addition, this act of kindness helped me see that neither race nor rank nor status of officers and enlisted men existed on the ward as it did on military bases and battlefields.

Here we were all as one. We were united as wounded warriors with no differences among us.

My family soon had to leave to return to their homes and jobs in El Paso and Dallas. Their talk of flying into Dallas brought back memories of that hot August day in 1966 when we all sat in the restaurant at Dallas Love Field, waiting for the departure flight that would take me to the other side of the world, to a war in which I had volunteered to fight—a war being waged to free yet another oppressed nation.

Dallas, Texas
August 1966

As I lay in the hospital and reflected on the intervening months since the summer of 1966, I felt as if an eternity had passed rather than one short year. I could not believe that so much had happened. The summer of 1966, the last sweet innocent time of my youth, had been a period of renewal for me, a recharging of my batteries of commitment to what our country stands for, to the cause of freedom, and to the joining of other American service people who had served before me when called upon to do so. I was to go into that thin line of soldiers and become "as one with the band at Thermopylae, with the Knights Templar in the Holy Land, with the men of Concord and Lexington, the Alamo, Bastogne, and Iwo Jima" (Stilwell). I left the East Coast that summer as ready for Vietnam as I would ever be.

When intelligence training ended, we returned to Texas for a few more vacation days, so I could visit with my family in Temple. While there, Dad and I went for a long drive. Sometime during our drive, Dad pulled over and parked the car. He told me how much he loved me and how concerned he was for my welfare.

"I'm very worried, Allen," he said. "If you get hurt or killed, I will feel responsible because I raised you in a military family."

"It won't be your fault, Dad," I said reassuringly, "I'm on my own now, and I made the decision to go, not you."

Tears streamed down his cheeks as he spoke, and I could see the pain in his eyes. I knew he carried a very heavy burden for me, his only son and the last male in four generations of Clarks.

After our visit in Temple, Jackie and I traveled to Dallas so we could visit with her parents before I left for Vietnam on August 1. Mr. and Mrs. McAdams invited many of our friends for a going away party beside the swimming pool at their home. Some of our friends couldn't understand why I volunteered when so many men were trying to avoid Vietnam in various ways that included fleeing across our borders into Canada and Mexico. I remember telling them that although no one really wants to go to war, I was very proud to have an opportunity to serve.

The Turning Point

August 1, 1966, had been a typical Texas summer day—clear, warm, and not a cloud in the endless blue sky. I sat at the breakfast table with Jackie, my parents, and Jackie's parents. Although we were bathed by the morning sunlight that streamed through the restaurant windows at Dallas Love Field, our hearts remained somber. We stared at our plates with no appetite for the pancakes before us. Today would be a difficult day for all of us, and one none of us would ever forget. Like so many other young men who had gone to war before me, I desperately wanted time to stop so I could stay with my family and my wife of two and one-half years. However, time would naturally not stop. The clock ticked on, and I knew I must leave. I had to get on that plane in order to make connections to Travis Air Force Base in California, a connection that would take me across the Pacific to that small, embattled country of South Vietnam. I had a personal as well as a military mission to perform—to do my part in the war, however small that part might be. It would become the end of a path that had begun in elementary school. The career I had been associated with since birth because of my dad was now my own career, my own life. I could easily accept the need for military sacrifices.

After breakfast, my family slowly walked the short distance to my assigned gate at the airport terminal. My feet felt heavy, making each step an arduous undertaking. All our hearts and minds were full of words we could not voice, words we wanted so much to say to one another, words that welled up within us and made our hearts ache. When we arrived at the gate, we stood in somber silence and stared out the window into space. A male voice crackled over the public address system with a special news bulletin, which I heard in the back of my consciousness, but filed away for future reference. For me, there were more pressing matters at hand. The inevitable, the moment we had all dreaded, had arrived when yet another unfeeling, crackling voice on the airport PA system finally called my flight number. I quickly pulled Jackie around a corner in the terminal for privacy, held her close, and gave her a long, lingering kiss, a kiss that would have to last for an entire year. We clung to each other trying desperately to burn this moment deep into our memories.

I turned to say good-bye to my family and quickly shook hands with my father and Jack. I gave big hugs to Mom and my mother-in-law, Adell, picked up my bags, and quickly headed for the waiting plane. Unwilling to let go of Jackie, I still held her hand. Letting go would be so final. I knew there could be no turning back, and lingering over good-byes would only make leaving that much harder. Knowing that it was finally time to let go, I bucked up, trying to hide the black emptiness in my heart. If sadness in life creates a hole in one's heart, a small one began to develop that day. I climbed the steps to the plane and turned for one last wave, and then slowly inched down the narrow aisle to my seat. As I looked out of the window, I managed to catch one last glimpse of Jackie before embarking on a long journey that would change my life forever.

Jackie Clark

We all watched Allen go up the steps and into the waiting plane. Allen was handsome, strong, and muscular and had always been in excellent shape. As he turned for the last wave, I wondered if I would ever see him again. And, if I did, what kind of condition would he be in?

When the airplane door closed behind Allen, I fell apart. I believe everyone in the family cried, but I was too shaken to notice things going on around me. I was glad that Allen couldn't see that I had lost my composure. My mother and Allen's mother each suggested that it might help if they took me shopping. "After all,"

Mother said, "shopping is an escape, and it usually makes most women feel better."

Shopping didn't help. At the very first store, I broke down and couldn't stop crying. Allen had been gone less than an hour, and I really suffered the grief of separation as well as the fear for my husband's future. I had to go home and sort out my thoughts alone. I had neither children nor a desire for any other occupation other than that of being Allen's wife and helpmate. The center of my life was gone, and I was miserable.

I looked around the plane, and I saw dozens of strangers, some of whom perhaps would accompany me to Vietnam. As I sat in my seat contemplating the enormity of what I was doing and the year that lay ahead, the words of that earlier news bulletin coming over the terminal loudspeaker began to trickle into my consciousness. Two hundred miles away in Austin, a sniper sat perched atop the University of Texas Tower shooting people with a high-powered rifle as they strolled across campus. Charles Whitman had already killed fourteen people and wounded thirty, and the siege continued. This date would go down in history and be forever remembered in Texas and the nation, but not for the same reasons my family and I would remember it. As my plane taxied down the runway, my mind couldn't shake the irony of the events taking place in Austin at the same time a vicious war raged halfway around the world. Although cold-blooded and violent, Whitman's shooting spree seemed small in comparison to the Vietnam war zone that I would face in forty-eight hours.

The roar of the plane's engines grew increasingly louder as it picked up speed, lifted off, and soared into the cloudless sky. Faces of my loved ones flooded my mind. I again saw my parents standing in the airport—Mother fighting to hold back the tears and Dad, always the exemplary military officer, standing tall, straight, and proud. His example and influence were key factors for my being where I was on that day. I knew I would miss the warmth, love, and tenderness of Jackie. It crossed my mind that my sister, Betty, newly married to air force officer Alan Chalfont, might soon face her own separation of war.

My civilian flight from Dallas took me to San Francisco, California, where I boarded a bus bound for Travis Air Force Base. I settled into my seat feeling enveloped in a shroud of loneliness and homesickness while at the same time anticipating what lay ahead. Even though I had already accomplished a great deal in my life, that part of my life for which I had prepared for so many years was now just beginning. I surveyed the faces of the men sitting all around me and wondered if they felt the same mixture of feelings—excitement, anticipation, loneliness, and fear. I wondered if I would change, and I wondered if I would ever go back home.

My heart and soul filled with confusing and contradictory feelings. I missed my wife and family already. I knew it would be a year before I saw them again, and despair swept through me at the thought. At the same time, I desperately wanted to serve my country. After all, that's what I had dreamed about since early childhood, and that's what I'd worked so hard for. I wanted to serve in a way that would make my family proud and in a way that would honor my country and West Point and all they both stood for. Duty, honor, country—the three things all cadets held sacred—could best be served by answering the "call." In the mid-60s, the call rang out from a small and seemingly insignificant country called Vietnam— the place where my destiny would come to be fulfilled.

At Travis Air Force Base, I boarded a military transport that would take me on a long and lonely flight across the Pacific Ocean to this strange little war-torn country. War. That was really the whole purpose of my profession, the profession of arms that pro-vides a defense against the enemy. And although I had trained for it so vigorously during the past three years, I didn't think I would be a part of it so soon. I was not a young man who wanted to kill any-one; I just wanted to do my duty to fight the forces against freedom. Here I was, ready to do just that. I found myself a long way from Mom's West Point bridge partners and the scenes I remembered when, as a child in the hospital, I had looked through the latticework at wounded soldiers. Would I become one of them?

Saigon: Pearl of the Orient

Soldiers green from hometowns and military bases stateside crowded the small windows to stare at the approaching countryside around Saigon, as it seemed to rise up to meet our plane. Curious and anxious, we all wanted to see what the infamous Vietnam looked like. From the air, Saigon looked like any other large city in just about any Asian country. However, as the plane's tires squealed and bounced on the tarmac at touchdown at Tan Son Nhut Air Force Base and we began taxiing down the runway, we saw a different sight. Bunkers and sandbagged machine-gun pits dotted the air base while armed security guards stood at strategically placed intervals. Jet fighters lined the edge of the runway awaiting the next assignment. No matter which way we turned, we saw evidence of war. When the jet engines droned to a stop, so did the soft music playing on my earphones. *End of the line, soldier,* I thought. *Your war is just beginning.* Ski slope climbs, debate tournaments, daily quizzes and grades, and even airborne and jungle warfare training on a Hawaiian island now seemed like nothing more than child's play. This was the real game of life—a soldier dropped into the middle of a war-ravaged country.

Army personnel directed us to waiting buses that would soon head for Camp Alpha, a tent city designed to hold incoming soldiers as they awaited orders and transportation to various assignments in Vietnam. As we arrived at the holding camp and our bus pulled up to unload, I saw soldiers boarding an outward bound bus and recognized a West Point classmate among them. Lou Sill had served with the 101st Airborne Division in Vietnam for the past year and had fought in the battle of the Toumorong near Dak To. In later years, I would read in General S. L. A. Marshall's book, *Battles in the Monsoons,* that Lou contracted jungle rot on his hands during the 1966 battles in the Central Highlands. Although his hands were eventually both totally bandaged, he refused to leave his command (Marshall, p. 383). I tried to push past the other men crowding the narrow aisle of the bus, but Lou's bus drove off before I could manage to get off mine. He probably went to the air base and boarded the same plane on which I had just arrived. He was going home, and I was just arriving. In spite of my sense of duty, which had caused me to volunteer, I envied him.

Destination: Nha Trang

I spent two days in Camp Alpha before boarding a C-130 for Nha Trang, a seaside town situated halfway up the Vietnamese coast. It was known locally as the Riviera of South Vietnam because large villas and nice restaurants lined its beaches. Our detachment building contiguous to the First Field Force Vietnam (1FFV) was blocks from the beach. Nha Trang was filled with military people and relatively safe and removed from the war. I was assigned a room with a bed in a house with the luxuries of a bathroom, refrigerator, and hot water (sometimes). I ate hot food three times a day in the military mess hall and drove my own jeep—not the typical assignment normally associated with Vietnam. I was housed with the counter-intelligence corps section of my unit.

Although by now a junior captain in the 55th Military Intelligence Detachment, I soon found another interrogator was not needed at Nha Trang. So, as luck would have it, I became a technical intelligence officer instead. My "intelligence" assignments were to make certain that all the vehicles in the compound ran properly and to examine the different weapons picked up in action to determine if any new weapons were coming into the country. The Soviets and Red Chinese supplied most of the weapons used by the NVA. In turn, they supplied arms to the VC (Viet Cong, a contraction of Viet Nam Cong San, meaning "Vietnamese communist"). The VC were South Vietnamese communists who lived and worked in South Vietnam and received military backing from the North Vietnamese Army. During my short stay there, I came across only rudimentary weapons to include AK-47s captured in battles. Nothing spectacular.

My typical eight-to-five job began in my downtown office building, which included two cells for interrogating prisoners, cells that I never got to use. I first examined weapons—many of them homemade—and then forwarded them to Saigon for inspection. After that, I went to the motor pool to check on the vehicles, visited with the men (many of whom had been in the field and told interesting stories), and returned to the air conditioned van that served as our main headquarters near the beach.

By late afternoon, I had accomplished all I could in one day, so I took off in my jeep to tour some of Nha Trang's beautiful sites, one of which was a dominating large white Buddha that sat on a hilltop overlooking the city. While touring, I usually headed for the beach where I jogged through the sand and swam in the rolling surf of the South China Sea. For all I know, I may have even swum beside Viet Cong soldiers as they were known to use Nha Trang for rest and relaxation. It wasn't a bad life for someone assigned to a combat area. In fact, I never even carried a weapon while at Nha Trang.

Most people would have been grateful for such a cushy assignment that seemed more like a vacation than work. Nevertheless, I decided that I didn't want to spend my time this way while in the midst of a raging war. My West Point classmates were serving, and even dying, in combat. My conscience wouldn't allow me to leave the war after a year in a cozy, comfortable place just to go home and tell my friends that I had done my duty. We had all trained for war, and I couldn't let myself, much less my classmates, down. It was that emotion and vanity of pride that had always perched itself on my shoulders where it clung tenaciously. It seemed I could never do enough. A quiet, inner voice always seemed to say, "Do more."

Transfer to the Green Berets

On a plane trip to Saigon, I had met Lieutenant Colonel Eleazar Parmly (West Point, 1946), who had served as a tactical officer at West Point and now commanded a Green Beret unit at Pleiku. As we visited, I told him that I wasn't satisfied with my work and asked him about the possibility of transferring to Special Forces (Green Berets), a fabled unit for which I had always felt a special fascination.

Colonel Parmly told me that he needed an intelligence officer in his B-team detachment in Ban Me Thuot, Darlac Province, Central Highlands. That was all I needed to hear. I started the paperwork right away, and amazingly, my transfer sped through channels in only two weeks, helped along by the fact that my intelligence unit's executive officer, Major Drake Wilson, had been my engineering professor at West Point. I moved to the headquarters of Fifth Special Forces. Fifth Special Forces Headquarters was spread out over a large expanse of land on the far side of Nha Trang from the beach. It was in low buildings all enclosed by heavy barbed wire because it faced open terrain on the edge of the city.

After a few days there, I was frustrated that I had not received orders to Colonel Parmly's C-team in the Central Highlands. I began asking questions about what was happening and the answer I received was not what I had expected to hear. I had been reassigned.

"Captain," a senior sergeant said, "your records are kept under lock and key in a safe. We don't want the Vietnamese who work at headquarters to know anything about you. For the record, you don't exist." My new unit was B-57.

I didn't exist? That was a shock. What if something happened to me? How would anyone know who I was? The mystery surrounding our unit and its mission increased as did my questions, but I could never successfully get any satisfactory answers. Finally, during a visit to Ho Ngoc Tau, a camp outside Saigon, I pinned down a major and asked him why our mission was such a big secret.

"Espionage in Cambodia," he replied.

It seemed our initial and simplistically stated mission would be to observe troop movements down the Ho Chi Minh Trail through Cambodia. The NVA often infiltrated South Vietnam via the Ho Chi Minh Trail to select their targets. Sometimes they raided the crops of surrounding villages, and sometimes they attacked the Special Forces camps or regular U.S. units and scurried back to their Cambodian base camps protected by a supposedly "neutral" country.

What a revolting development that was! Allen Clark, army brat, hero worshiper, and fan of "The Ballad of the Green Berets," was about to get in up to his neck. Espionage. I had visions of James Bond. Well, I had asked for a job with more excitement and, thus (by my own definition) meaningful fulfillment, and now I had just such an opportunity. I was to be the "first" military intelligence branch officer assigned to a unit that would end up being one of the most controversial of the Vietnam War.

Special Forces History

It was my honor to be joining a unit I had always considered as something really special in the annals of their short military history. I would never be qualified as a Special Forces officer as defined by the "Q" (Qualification) course at Fort Bragg, but assigned to the unit in Vietnam, because I was airborne-qualified, I was authorized to wear the beret as my headgear.

By 1952, our army was committed to unconventional warfare outside the normal conventional army methods. As a consequence on June 20, 1952, the first Special Forces unit was formed at Fort Bragg as the 10th Special Forces Group, which deployed to Germany the next year. They began training for insertions deep into enemy territory for purposes of disruption of the enemy behind their lines in the countries behind the Iron Curtain.

President John F. Kennedy, still stung by the Cuban Bay of Pigs debacle, was seeking a way to counter the communist encroachments all over the world by a method other than regular army units. His visit in late 1961 to Fort Bragg and the Special Warfare Center convinced him of the need for Special Forces, and that was what it took to solidify their value and official support. The beret was now authorized.

Colonel George C. Morton (USA, Ret.) in his foreword to Stanton's *Green Berets at War* said that President Kennedy described the beret "as a symbol of excellence, a mask of distinction, and a badge of courage" (Stanton).

Special Forces personnel began to be assigned in Vietnam by 1957 to train Vietnamese army personnel. U.S. Special Forces would be engaged in "three tasks (special unit, clandestine, and paramilitary projects) . . . throughout the Vietnam War" (Stanton). Special Forces A-teams eventually became the principal means by which any kind of government presence to fight the Viet Cong and eventually the North Vietnamese Army (NVA) was able to operate in the Central Highlands along the Cambodian and Laotian borders, and the isolated provinces away from populated cities. Much of their success depended upon developing loyalties among the Montagnard Tribes of the Central Highlands.

In his book, *Green Berets at War*, Shelby Stanton described the principal mission of the Special Forces in Vietnam as that of hiring and training Montagnards and other indigenous people in the Civilian Irregular Defense Group (CIDG). He goes on to say that the primary objective of the CIDG program "was blocking VC encroachment into Vietnam's back country by developing the loyalties and fighting abilities of various native contingencies. The Montagnards were fundamentally village-level aborigines scattered in more than a hundred different tribes that relied on hunting or slash-and-burn farming. Their most significant common traits were a deep hostility toward the Vietnamese and a strong desire to be left alone. Under French rule, the Montagnards had lived in a large territory under a French commissioner, similar to an Indian reservation in the United States. This territory included Kontum, Pleiku, and Darlac Provinces" (page 57).

Throughout history, the Montagnards have been used as pawns in war. The Japanese used them when they invaded Vietnam during World War II. Although defended by the French during both the Korean and Vietnam wars, the Montagnards easily and often changed loyalties in order to survive. According to the Associated Press, Green Berets, posing as butterfly collectors and geologists, built camps on the central Vietnamese plateau and defended the camps with the Montagnards as early as 1961 and 1962.

By late August 1966, with less than four weeks in-country, I was assigned to a positive intelligence-collecting unit of Special Forces way outside the mainstream of Special Forces, which was way outside the mainstream of the regular army.

CHAPTER 6

COVERT
OPERATIONS
IN B-57

My assignment to B-57 began when I reported to a Green Beret villa, the "liaison office" in Saigon near General William Westmoreland's headquarters. I didn't know who my commanding officer would be, but I did have an idea about our mission: send agents across the Cambodian border to see what the Viet Cong and NVA were up to. As yet, we had no real plans for investigating that "privileged sanctuary." Nevertheless, when volunteers were requested throughout Vietnam, many Green Berets came forward. The more the risk, the more they seemed to like it. That is the way it always has been and always will be with the Green Berets. They were and are a breed unto themselves. For the next several months, I was to live only in rented "safe houses" in Saigon.

My world at that time consisted of six Green Berets, one other intelligence officer, and myself. One of the Green Berets, Major Curtis D. Terry—short, stocky, and built like a boxer—had been camp commander at Ban Don in the Central Highlands in September 1964 when the Montagnards staged one of their frequent revolts against the government for the purpose of establishing their own country. The Montagnards finally earned representation under the Vietnamese constitution drafted in April 1967. A legend in his own time, Major Terry had been instrumental in quelling the 1964 revolt when on September 20 he persuaded his Montagnards to return to Ban Don.

Major Terry instructed me to stuff my military uniforms in duffel bags, put on civilian clothes, and forget that I was even in the army. I wore no uniform, no nametag, no dog tags, and nothing else that could identify me with the U.S. military. He went on to say that before I began my mission, I must first learn the city of Saigon. Because we weren't directly associated with the Special Forces chain of command, though, we couldn't use military vehicles. He recommended that I take one of the two taxicabs we had already hired and ride from one end of the city to the other until I could find my way around in the dark.

"I want you to know your way around Saigon so well," Terry said, "that if you're ever out on an operation or mission at night, or if you ever get robbed or beaten up, you'll be able to find your way back to a main street to get help or get back to us. Knowing the city that well could save your life."

I commandeered one of the cabs and spent twelve hours per day for two days riding around Saigon until I knew it like my own hometown. I directed the driver to turn right, turn left, go straight, back up, and so forth, never stopping except when he returned me to my villa for lunch. The Vietnamese driver never said a word, but near the end of the second day I could tell he was getting pretty angry. Although I didn't know his language, with few exceptions, body language is basically the same throughout the world. When we turned onto a street for the third or fourth time, he shot me a look that clearly communicated his feelings. I'm sure his opinion of American soldiers changed drastically after that—or perhaps it was merely confirmed.

In spite of my frustrated driver, I had a wonderful tour of Saigon. Dirty and teeming with people, Saigon's crowded streets overflowed with motorcycles, bicycles, taxis, and rickshaw drivers pulling their cabs. As we drove slowly through the mishmash of vehicles, I watched recent history come alive before my eyes. We drove past the sandbagged entrance of the Brinks Hotel, which had been bombed in 1965 and now served as an officers' billet; the rebuilt My Canh floating restaurant, also bombed by terrorists; as well as the magnificent presidential palace. Not only did I learn the city, but I learned much about the history of the war as well.

Within a few days, an intelligence officer who had worked with cross-border teams in Korea took over as commander of our unit. Major Pat Murray brought a warrant officer with him and named me liaison officer responsible for making contact with other intelligence units. Together, the three of us formed the nucleus of the new intelligence unit. During our time in Saigon, we had to have dealings with the Vietnamese when we needed to rent a building for our unit headquarters or rent a "safe house" in which to keep our agents for a few weeks. More times than not, the owners were high-ranking Vietnamese officers. I did not understand the significance of this until years later when I understood the graft and corruption that had become an integral part of that country.

I began to learn the craft of "intelligence" under the tutelage of Major Murray and other career military intelligence branch officers. Our first mission began in October 1966 when I developed the operations order when we sent three Cambodian nationals and two Green Beret sergeants to an outpost near Tinh Bien, South Vietnam, in the Delta area SW of Chau Doc. They set up about two hundred yards from the Cambodian border next to a Buddhist pagoda. The security force for our team consisted of about fifty Cambodians who were armed to the teeth, and each time I went in to check on operations, one of the guards shadowed me so I wouldn't be kidnapped while I was on the ground. This was B-57's first outpost and Captain Steve Alpern, who became one of my best wartime friends, soon went there to oversee the team.

Captain Alpern
Story of Tinh Bien

When I first arrived by helicopter to Tinh Bien, I was greeted by the two NCOs on site. This was Stephanski and Hudkins. Hudkins was a commo specialist but really somebody you would want on your side. He could do just about everything, and he was good with an M-16 as well. We needed good commo back in Saigon as we were using one-time pads and Morse code and Hudkins was an expert. Also, he was the one with a few years' experience in Vietnam. Stephanski, on the other hand, was the intel specialist.

We lived outside of the district town of Tinh Bien (about one-half mile away) in a small Cambodian village. Hudkins and Stephanski had built a small wooden shelter. We had a couple of bunk beds and a table along with a kerosene refrigerator that allowed us to cook meals and keep some cold Viet beer. Our cover was that we were rice researchers, so we wore black pajamas and civilian clothes.

As three Americans in this isolated spot, we were very concerned with security. So we hired, and paid for, a security force of about fifty Cambodian men from the village. We outfitted them with Swedish K rifles and had them build a few bunkers around our little wooden house so we could at least find some protection should we be targeted by any Viet Cong or North Vietnamese who crossed the border into Vietnam.

The main purpose of this operation, as well as other early B-57 operations, was to locate any downed American pilots who were being processed through Cambodia back either into Laos or North Vietnam. The whole idea was to be able to penetrate across the border and have the presence of real people on *our* payroll to locate any possible movement of a captured U.S. pilot.

So we had a very unique scheme to provide a cover for a Cambodian agent, trained by our team, to cross the border without actually being suspected of its being an intelligence operation. A plan was written to have several of the Cambodian villagers act as cross border smugglers. What could be smuggled and sold across the border? The bright idea was to smuggle whiskey. So we proceeded to stock our location with about fifty cases of Seagram's Seven from Saigon, cheap stuff, but good for smuggling purposes. We trained several Cambodians on what to do (via our Cambodian interpreter, Danh), and sent them off across the border in a cart of some sort each with a case or two of whiskey. One of them had a small radio, which they could use to contact us should an opportunity exist where they actually had observation of any U.S. prisoner. Otherwise, they really were eyes and ears to come back in a few days and be debriefed on what they had seen and heard.

Everything seemed to be running smoothly. The Cambodian guards would provide us some protection, especially at night, as we posted them around our shelter. One incident did occur when one of the guards shot himself in the neck. Hudkins was also a very good medic; when they brought in this guard, I really wasn't sure what Hudkins could do for him. Part of his neck was missing from the gunshot wound. Fortunately, we were about three miles from an SF camp above a mountain peak that overlooked Tinh Bien, so we contacted them for some advice on this wounded guard. It was two in the morning and we couldn't move around at night. With some good advice from the SF camp, Medic Hudkins was able to patch up the guard, and so, he survived, albeit with a scar in his neck area from the stitching performed by Hudkins.

Intermittently Hudkins, Stephanski, or I would take a trip on the road from Tinh Bien to Chau Doc, the provincial town. This was more for R and R than anything else. But this could have been one of our most dangerous experiences. We would rent a taxi from Tinh Bien, and then have the taxi drive as fast as it would go on the road to Chau Doc. It became about a forty-five-minute drive over totally unprotected roads. We dressed in our civilian clothes and had only a small .38 pistol for protection. Needless to say, this wouldn't be much help if someone were to have a roadblock or intercept the taxi. Such foolish things we did when we were young. Without doubt, living in this little village was not the most enjoyable experience. Just going to the bathroom at night, we would have to cross a two-hundred-meter rice paddy to a "john" located in a monk's pagoda. Squatting in the middle of the night is quite an experience. Who knows who might come in? This is the only time I can remember having a loaded M-16 pointing out the door of the facility.

Things seemed to be going fine, but then came an intelligence report from our headquarters about the possibility of a compromise on our little operation, which indicated that a North Vietnamese unit was targeting us for destruction. We were very concerned about this intelligence report because we had very modest means to protect ourselves. We were out of range of any artillery from an American unit or mortar support from the Tinh Bien Special Forces camp. We were three Americans with M-16s and a starlight scope acquired by Hudkins. The fifty guards were bodies, but we were really not confident of their abilities to repel any type of real North Vietnamese attack against us.

So the decision was made by Saigon that we should evacuate and close down the operation. Our problem was what to do with the guards, weapons, and so forth. The guards did not want to give up their weapons, and we were not in a position to argue. We had one day to get ready to totally abandon the operation and leave. So we decided to just let them keep the weapons; we made a final payment to our guards and then offered them our abode and everything in it. We wanted out without incident.

The next morning we paid the guards, and shortly thereafter the big air force Chinooks arrived to pull us out. It was a successful pullout and the operation was closed in February 1967.

(In early 1967 Alpern was medevac'd due to an illness from Loc Ninh Special Forces camp one week before it was overrun by the enemy.)

In November 1966 while riding a bus from Tan Son Nhut Air Base to downtown Saigon, I sat with Bob Foley, a classmate. Standing six feet seven inches, Bob had served as captain of the academy basketball team, 1962 to 1963. The secrecy of my mission was such that I couldn't tell him what I was doing, and his modesty was such that he didn't even mention that he had just been nominated for the Medal of Honor—the only member of our graduating class to receive it. I would learn about Bob's medal much later. During the course of their service there, most all recently graduated West Pointers would eventually cross paths with classmates serving in Vietnam.

"Robert Foley was a basketball star in high school. At six foot seven, he had received fifteen college scholarship offers by the end of his senior year. He was still considering his options when the hockey coach from West Point happened to pass through

Massachusetts on a weekend Foley scored forty-four points in a game. He told the West Point basketball coach about Foley. The coach invited him for a visit and asked him to play army basketball. Foley knew that going to West Point would eliminate the possibility of his playing professional basketball, but he was impressed with the history and sense of purpose he saw at the academy and decided to enroll" (Collier and Calzo).

Excerpts from his citation indicate that "on November 5, 1966 near Quan Dau Tieng, South Vietnam, Capt. Foley's company was ordered to extricate another surrounded company of the battalion. Moving through the dense jungle to aid the besieged unit, Company A encountered a strong enemy force occupying well concealed, defensive positions, and the company's leading element quickly sustained several casualties. Capt. Foley immediately ran forward to the scene of the most intense action to direct the company's efforts. Deploying one platoon on the flank, he led the other two platoons in an attack on the enemy in the face of intense fire. During this action both radio operators accompanying him were wounded. At grave risk to himself, he defied the enemy's murderous fire, and helped the wounded operators to a position where they could receive medical care. As he moved forward again, one of his machine gunners went down. Seizing the weapon, he charged forward firing the machine gun, shouting orders and rallying his men, thus maintaining the momentum of the attack. Under increasingly heavy enemy fire he ordered his assistant to take cover, and alone, Capt. Foley continued to advance firing the machine gun until the wounded had been evacuated and the attack in this area could be resumed. When movement on the other flank was halted by the enemy's fanatical defense, Capt. Foley moved to personally direct this critical phase of the battle. Leading the renewed effort, he was blown off his feet and wounded by an enemy grenade. Despite his painful wounds he refused medical aid and persevered in the forefront of the attack on the enemy redoubt. He led the assault on several enemy gun emplacements and, single-handedly, destroyed 3 such positions. He was under intense enemy fire during the fierce battle which lasted for several hours."

His own men recommended him for the Medal of Honor, and President Lyndon Johnson presented it to him on May 1, 1968. This is a classic example of a star athlete from Newton, Massachusetts, accepting a challenge for military service as an officer and eventually performing magnificently in heavy combat.

Our intelligence group next established an outpost at Duc Co, a border surveillance post west of Pleiku. For forty-eight days in the summer of 1965, Duc Co had been under a siege in which the Special Forces A-team there had suffered heavy casualties. For our mission in the fall of 1966, we first outfitted a Montagnard agent with a basket in which we had placed a camera. We then sent him off to take pictures of enemy positions. When the agent returned with the film at three one morning, we thought it so important that we took it immediately to an air force photographic lab in Saigon for development. The first few pictures developed revealed 105mm howitzers.

"The NVA are really moving in the big stuff," I said, feeling that we had made an important discovery.

The seventh picture revealed a shirtless Caucasian soldier standing beside one of the cannons. At first we thought he might be Russian, but it didn't take long for the mystery to unravel. Our "reliable" agent had brought back pictures of a U.S. Army artillery battalion set up to fire at the enemy. To make matters worse, the army post he had photographed was located just down the road from Duc Co. Obviously, we had mislabeled this "reliable" agent and, needless to say, didn't use him again.

On the first of November, our unit commander told me about Inchin Hai Lam (probably an assumed name), a very thin five-foot-five-inch Cambodian national. Lam, a supposed member of the Khmer Serei (free Khmers), who were fiercely anti-communist and anti–Prince Sihanouk of Cambodia, was in a group that we named the Dirty Dozen after the World War II movie by the same name. These men were twelve of the top Khmers that we recruited to use as agents. The command authority of the Khmer Serei had pulled them out of several Special Forces camps to perform our missions for B 57. Our commander first suggested that we use Lam because he could speak seven languages—Cambodian, Vietnamese, French, Russian, a smattering of two Chinese dialects, and English. We felt he was one of the smartest Cambodian nationals around and thought it prudent to take advantage of his knowledge and use him in some way, even if only as an interpreter.

Apparently the Khmer Serei leadership used Special Forces to train their troops. A platoon of Khmer Serei in one of our camps would disappear and another platoon of these Cambodians would take their place for the training cycle to start anew. Our camps must have been unwitting training sites for these Khmer Serei, who perhaps went back into Cambodia possibly to fight for an overthrow of Sihanouk's regime.

American intelligence units bid on potential agents, and once a unit acquired an agent, no other unit was allowed to use him. We quickly placed a bid for Lam and acquired him as our agent. Lam had only recently entered South Vietnam and had gone immediately to the American embassy to sign up to assist the Americans. It was only because of a bureaucratic foul-up that the embassy sent him back to a Saigon Cambodian Buddhist temple, where he remained until Sergeant Stephanski, a member of our detachment, discovered him while scouting around the temple. According to an officer in B 57, Operational Intelligence (OI) to use In Chin became a tug-of-war due to his supposed value.

According to Lam, his mother served as the head housekeeper on the Royal Palace grounds of Prince Sihanouk in Phnom Penh, Cambodia. Growing up there, he had become the best friend of Prince Sihanouk's son. As a curious child, he remembered standing close enough to Sihanouk's desk to see different kinds of papers, but he claimed that he couldn't recall what they were about. Lam never mentioned his father, so I assumed that his father had either abandoned him and his mother or had been killed. A story made the rounds in our detachment that he was the illegitimate son of Sihanouk himself. Lam was such a good student that the communists under Prince Sihanouk sent him to Peking, China, and then to Moscow for two years of study at Patrice Lumumba University, a training center for revolutionaries around the world. He told me that he had once been a Cambodian army lieutenant, but had defected to South Vietnam after becoming disenchanted with the events in his native country.

I first met Lam at a "safe house "where I hid a tape recorder behind the curtains to record our conversation. His English, although slightly broken, was very good. Following that first interview, I met with Lam approximately fifteen more times during November 1966. I had to learn everything he knew, so it was important to find out whether he could be trusted. At each meeting, Lam and I spent three or four hours in either his home, a one-room apartment just outside the wall around the Cambodian Buddhist temple, or in a rented hotel room. When we met in his home, his wife, a very small good-looking woman with fragile features, usually lingered nearby. When I met Lam in a rented hotel room, I played a radio loudly to drown out listening devices, which could have been placed there by eavesdroppers or hotel guests. I paid the bill at the end of the day, and the next time we met in a different room perhaps at another hotel.

After spending a month with Lam, my superiors removed me from the case and thanked me for my work. Other interrogators would take over and delve more deeply into Lam's background for strategic intelligence on particulars we had already discovered, such as his involvement with Patrice Lumumba University. My future commanding officer, Major George Nandor, would serve as the new contact for Lam. When I left Lam for the last time, I felt that I would never hear of or from him again, but that was not to be the case. He remained on the payroll of Detachment B 57, and others in my unit frequently used him as an interpreter.

I suppose in peacetime I would have liked Lam; however, the possibility always loomed over us that he could be a setup, a plant, to gather information from us to feed back to the communists. One never knows in intelligence work who the enemy really is. We could never trust a foreign agent completely. As seemed to happen so much in my life, Inchin would indirectly enter my life again in the future.

Mission Cambodia

In December 1966, Major Pat Murray called me to his office where he pointed to a spot on a map on the wall.

"This is the tri-border area, Allen. Cambodia, South Vietnam, and Laos meet here. We have information that the communists are using this sanctuary area as a staging ground for attacks into South Vietnam, and General Westmoreland wants to know for certain. Would you like to try your hand at getting him the needed information?"

"It's a great assignment," I replied promptly.

"Okay. I want you to train and put a team in there to find whatever intelligence is available."

I named the mission "Operation Cherry," a name that would be splashed all over the pages of the *New York Times* years later.

Because I felt the need for physically stronger agents, it never occurred to me to use Lam for this mission. Because of his small build, I didn't think he would have the necessary staying power to make it through the jungle, not to mention the fact that we still didn't know whether he was a plant. We picked three of the original Dirty Dozen Khmers to infiltrate the area. For three months, I lived with them and trained them. Rumor had it that one of them was the son of Son Ngoc Than, the Khmer Serei leader. Rumors run rampant in intelligence work.

The Khmers slept across the hall from me in a rented Saigon villa. I had one bedroom; they had the other two. Even though they spoke very little English, we did manage to hold a few casual conversations, usually about Cambodia. I learned that they were violently opposed to Sihanouk, whom they felt to be an oppressive dictator. One of my most memorable times with the Khmers occurred on Christmas Day 1966. While listening to the radio at the villa, I heard that Bob Hope had brought his USO show to Tan Son Nhut Air Base just two miles away. Although sorely tempted to desert my post, leave my agents alone, and go watch the show, I remained on duty and shared a rice and fish Christmas dinner with the Khmers. All through the following years, whenever I watched a television broadcast of Bob Hope entertaining the troops on Christmas Day, I remembered that Christmas of 1966.

During training sessions, several other members of B-57 and especially my good friend, Mike Eiland, taught the Khmers weaponry, patrol techniques, compass work, and radio communications. We jogged along the streets of Saigon early each morning to keep them in shape for the long jungle trek ahead of them. Under Mike Eiland's leadership we also took field-training trips to Ban Don in the Central Highlands as well as to two islands off the coast of Nha Trang. It would be on one of those two islands that future Senator Bob Kerrey would lose his leg in battle, resulting in his receiving a Medal of Honor as a U.S. Navy Seal.

I experienced one of the greatest thrills of my life on one of the training missions at Ban Don. Just after dusk, we bedded down on the ground for the night when, suddenly out of the darkness, a huge Asian elephant came crashing toward our camp. Everyone jumped up as quickly as possible and scattered, trying desperately to get out of the path of the massive beast. As it turned out, a Montagnard rider atop the giant elephant spotted us just in the nick of time and quickly turned the animal away. Needless to say that, after that rousing interruption of our modest campsite, none of us fell asleep easily that night. Mike Eiland was a very calm, cool, and collected officer in all my endeavors with him. To his surprise, in the late nineties his picture was on the front cover of *Spies and Commandos* by Kenneth Conboy and Dale Andrade.

In early January 1967, I went to Kontum to scope out the area for my first infiltration mission. The Central Highlands altitude temperatures were much colder than in Saigon. The nights were so uncomfortable because of the climate change that I wrote to Jackie and asked her to send me some long underwear. While at Detachment B 24, the Army Special Forces camp at Kontum, I stayed in the same room with classmate John Goorley. We spent some free time visiting with a missionary group from the Midwest that was translating the Bible into native dialects. John and I also visited a hospital just outside town that was operated by an American female physician, Dr. Pat Smith. Dr. Smith did a marvelous job with modest resources caring for some very sick Montagnards who walked many miles to receive her care. I later read that she had been captured by the communists but was released unharmed after five months of captivity.

When I went back to Saigon, we made final preparations for the trip north. Obviously, one of our most important responsibilities was to "sanitize" our agents to make them appear to be NVA soldiers, so I went to a CIA supply building to obtain captured NVA uniforms, ID cards, and weapons for our men to wear and carry. Major Murray and I received our final briefing in the CIA headquarters building in downtown Saigon. We would be ready for our mission as soon as we completed training sessions.

As our first assignment, we had to make arrangements to drop our three agents by helicopter into a landing zone next to Cambodia. Our plans were to go to Kontum to find a drop zone using a two-seater observation plane piloted by an air force officer. These guys flew missions every day and knew their areas so well that they could spot a log lying across a creek that had not been there the day before. However, after I marked a clearing on my map that my pilot told me we could use for a landing zone, another pilot informed me that I had picked a landing zone in Cambodia. If we used that zone and got shot down, it could cause an international incident, not to mention the extra risk we would be taking with our lives. After that close call, I decided to drop the team in a landing zone that was far enough east to be assured to be in South Vietnam so the agents could walk into Cambodia and then back out again when they completed their mission. I finally settled on a landing zone and took my team to a small hotel in Kontum.

As we made preparations to begin our mission, the weather could not have been worse. Rain poured from dark clouds that hung low in the sky. On the morning the helicopters were due, I went outside every five minutes to check the sky toward Nha Trang. The helicopters were late, and I feared they wouldn't be able to make it in the bad weather. Finally, I spotted the first chopper coming in low beneath the looming clouds, its spinning rotor blades sending rain swirling around the aircraft. Then, through the mist, I saw the second, third, fourth, and fifth choppers slowly rising above the horizon. Operation Cherry was a "go." To show just what a small world this is, the flotilla commander that day turned out to be Captain Eldon L. Smith, my former engineer company commander at Fort Hood in 1964.

We flew the team through pea soup weather to the designated drop area, which appeared from the air to be a clear landing zone. As we drew closer, we could see that twelve- to fifteen-foot bamboo shoots rose from the ground like giant porcupine needles. The place had been a quick landing zone for our 101st Airborne Division paratroopers the year before, and the enemy had set up the bamboo shoots as a deterrent. Naturally, my men didn't want to jump for fear of becoming impaled on one of the spikes. I couldn't much blame them, but this mission was too important to abort at this point.

"Go," I shouted as I pushed them out of the helicopter.

Fortunately, they all landed safely, but as the helicopter curved back over the jungle, I remember thinking that if there were any enemy soldiers below us, not only would our agents not make it, but it would also take only one well-aimed bullet to our rotary blade stem to put us out of commission forever.

Two days later, we received a radio signal that our agents were ready to be pulled out. Once again we climbed into heavily armed choppers and headed the flotilla toward their signal. Anxious and nervous, we flew toward the designated pickup area. Tops of trees and small villages darted beneath us as I contemplated the many questions flooding my mind. Did the mission succeed? Did the enemy follow our agents out? Could we get them out safely and successfully? Then we finally spotted the bright orange panel marker spread out to mark the pickup location. We all let out a collective sigh of relief, and the tension flowed from our bodies as we flew out with everyone on board, safe and unharmed.

I threw a lot of questions at the team during the debriefing session. We didn't want to miss any detail of this key mission. The agents reported that, on the second night while they were sleeping, a communist patrol came within ten feet of their campsite. Frozen in terrified silence as the patrol walked quietly by, the Khmers remained undetected. Although it appeared they had not even reached Cambodia, they stayed only one more day. And although the patrol they encountered indicated communist activity, they did not come across any military installations of any kind. They had nothing further to report except to say that two of the three men would not go back again. It was simply too dangerous. This tri-border area was heavily covered by triple canopy jungle, and young men who were not trained soldiers could not succeed in this area. I learned this again at Dak To in late spring 1967.

"You can't pay us enough to go back," one of them said—at least that was the American translation of their remarks.

I had to start all over again. I gave another agent a two-week crash course and sent him off with the one remaining man from the original team who was willing to return. The second mission would be sent into "Landing Zone Viper." This time we flew the men in after dark to a different drop area about three hundred yards from the exact tri-border point.

When we flew back to Kontum after dark to await radio contact, we found that people were celebrating Tet, the Vietnamese New Year. Vietnamese soldiers stationed at outposts and camps shot their weapons off, lighting up the sky with flashes of tracer bullets. As we landed, after flying under an arc of brilliant but deadly fire, I breathed a sigh of relief to have both feet back on solid ground. To toast our deliverance from the evening's revelry, the chief helicopter pilot and I went across the river in Kontum to have a few beers in the military clubhouse of the super secret Studies and Observation Group (SOG). Led by Green Berets, these special units infiltrated into Laos to harass the North Vietnamese Army by not only performing prisoner snatches, but also by sabotaging their movements down the Ho Chi Minh Trail through Laos. We considered these guys the toughest of the toughest of soldiers.

This camp across the river from Kontum was the headquarters of a "Special Forces–commanded Golf-5 Commando Security Company, a reaction force for the Leghorn radio relay site" (Stanton).

While we were in the clubhouse, a fight erupted in town between Chinese Nung mercenaries from the SOG camp and Vietnamese soldiers. It seems the Nungs had killed a soldier, and as a security precaution, the Vietnamese army blocked the river bridge that we needed to use for our return. With beers in hand, we drove to the bridge where five Vietnamese soldiers promptly brought their rifles to their shoulders and aimed them directly at us. (Drinking while driving laws are suspended in a war zone.) My friend, the chopper pilot, quickly stepped out of the jeep and offered his beer to one of the soldiers, who unhesitatingly took a big swig. The other four dropped their rifles and followed suit, each taking a swallow in turn. They all grinned giant grins, stepped aside, and allowed us to pass. I have to admit that as I watched this tense scene from the jeep, I imagined one of our obituaries reading: "Killed by friendly fire while drinking!"

Our men supposedly made it into Cambodia successfully and came out unharmed, but again with nothing to report. However, in hindsight, they very well could have stayed near the place we dropped them off the entire time. The thick jungle made it impossible for them to see anything at all. Trying to find military installations there was like trying to find a specific tree in a vast forest. There had to be a better way.

I completed my involvement with Operation Cherry in February 1967. The fact that it had not gone well greatly discouraged me. I would learn years later, however, that the original plan for missions into the tri-border area had been a good one because later teams discovered the area honeycombed with enemy installations, including underground hospitals and supply depots. The enemy soldiers were masters at camouflage and had successfully used the jungle to hide their installations. Because of the inroads made by those first intelligence missions, Americans moved a base right up next to the border at Ben Het from 1967 to 1970 when heavy fighting ensued. That base was probably no more than a few miles from our original Viper landing zone. We had been right on target after all. Of course, I didn't know the impact our missions would have later on the war when my commanding officer, Major Pat Murray, asked me to lunch at the air force officers' club at Tan Son Nhut.

Over beef tips and noodles, he asked, "Allen, how would you like to go to Dak To and set up a field operations team?"

Straight talk. Military talk. I knew it well. I had been in and out of Dak To several times and knew the intensity of the fighting in that extremely sensitive area. I wondered, *Why me?*

The hesitation in my voice was obvious, "Major, I'm a professional soldier, a regular army officer. If that's where you need me to go, I'll go. But, I'm *not* volunteering."

Already a double volunteer, I was not anxious to volunteer a third time. We all know what happens after three strikeouts. He told me that I was needed there and that I was to report to Dak To within twenty-four hours. I was to go back into uniform as an infantry officer under an assumed name and use a fake ID.

I had only twenty-four hours to prepare for a new assignment and find an assumed name—a requirement of my secret intelligence unit at that isolated site. With so little time to prepare, I decided to stop by a local nametag shop to see if I could locate any unclaimed nametags. I did. An American soldier had not picked up the nametags he ordered, so I paid for them and assumed his name. From that point on, I became Allen Copley. As I put on Copley's tags in preparation for my new assignment, I had to wonder if he had failed to pick them up because he was killed in action. And, given the intensity of the war situation at Dak To, would that be my fate as well?

I finally began to understand about this country much more than my training had ever prepared me before I was deployed to Southeast Asia. I went to Dak To much more informed because of my exposure to my Operation Cherry interpreter in Saigon. From him, I had learned that the majority of the Vietnamese people were basically apolitical and just wanted to be left alone. Their allegiance changed from day to day in the rural areas, based on which side could ensure their safety. The Catholics, who had left the north in 1954, had moved south so they could worship in freedom. The main populace did not have any great grounding in democracy. Basically, our cause was initially well conceived, but as we eventually discovered, we had taken on an impossible effort under which the rules of engagement for strategic political purposes did not favor a real victory on the battlefield along traditional American military standards—a situation our government seems to experience again and again.

CHAPTER 7

UP COUNTRY
TO DAK TO

Nothing except thick, dense jungle stretches east from the tri-border area to Dak To located in the central plains on the Dak Poko River. This dense jungle surrounding Dak To provided a haven for enemy camps and installations. Operating out of a square fortlike structure, the Special Forces unit at Dak To was responsible for coordinating constant patrols throughout this massive intertwining of trees, foliage, and undergrowth to make certain the enemy did not infiltrate the area and overrun the camp again as it had done in 1965.

In August 1963, Dak To was built as an isolated Special Forces camp near the tri-border point. Its purpose was to act as a fortified position and a base to send patrols of Montagnard commanded by Vietnamese Special Forces troops (Luc Long Dac Biet or LLDB) and advised by U.S. Special Forces to monitor the enemy movements through the heavily jungled areas of the border. The Special Forces camp at Dak To consisted of approximately twenty-five Americans. Although I reported directly to Major George Nandor, my new Detachment B-57 commanding officer in Saigon, Captain Larry Gossett, commanded the camp at Dak To. Heavy-set and partially bald, Captain Gossett was a big-hearted man who soon became my good friend. Others included the Quartermaster Corps personnel and two Green Beret medics from Walter Reed Army Institute of

Research (WRAIR) in Washington, D.C., who were conducting medical research on malaria strains and various tropical diseases. In addition to the Americans, about a dozen Vietnamese Special Forces personnel were present along with 350 Montagnard soldiers and their wives and children. The combat force numbered approximately four hundred.

Americans may find it highly unusual for women and children to be present in a combat zone, but this practice was commonplace in Vietnam for several reasons. First, by 1967 small villages surrounded practically every Special Forces outpost. Tribes moved their villages close to the camps for protection from NVA and VC invaders who raided their crops and sometimes killed villagers in the process as they perpetuated their campaign of terror and control. Second, it was a common practice in the South Vietnamese Army for soldiers and Montagnards to bring their families into camp with them. Under attack, the women passed the ammunition to firing soldiers. As we know from many publicized reports, their children played a role as well. Families lived in underground huts surrounded by firing pits and gun positions. All one could see above ground were the sandbag-covered thatched bamboo roofs of the huts as well as circles of sandbags, which rimmed the firing pits dug in preparation for combat. During my first fourteen weeks there, we stayed on constant alert, although we did not come under attack once. However, all the other nine Green Beret camps in our team were constantly attacked by enemy mortar fire.

Two walls surrounded our camp. Claymore mines, which shot pellets toward the enemy if tripped, and punji stakes (sharpened bamboo sticks) interspersed among barbed wire outlined the outer perimeter. The mess hall, team house, living quarters, and bunkers lined the inner perimeter, which also included ammunition bunkers, one 4.2-inch and two 81mm mortar positions. I slept on a cot and shared a space with two other men in a building just outside the inner perimeter. Two large tents just outside the inner wall housed ten Quartermaster Corpsmen and two signals intercept men.

The American Quartermaster troops were responsible for guarding and servicing our Dak To supply point, which included an ammunition site, food supply building, and an airstrip containing supplies of oil, gas, and lubricants for refueling aircraft. Technically, the South Vietnamese Special Forces team commanded the Montagnards, and the Americans served only as advisers. Our men went on patrols with them and paid them through the Vietnamese. The difference between us appeared only in the rhetoric used to describe our mission.

Soon after arriving at Dak To, I witnessed firsthand the strange weather phenomenon known as the monsoon season in Vietnam. Every afternoon for several weeks, incredible torrents of rain poured from the sky in sheets for thirty to sixty minutes at a time. Rivers of rainwater swept through valleys and camps. Newcomers at first feared flooding, but soon became used to the regularity of this strange phenomenon. Just as suddenly as it began, the rain stopped, leaving a strange, eerie silence and sticky mud everywhere. The sun came out again and shone blindingly bright, causing steam to rise from the wet mud and foliage, creating an oppressive, humid atmosphere. It is no wonder that so many soldiers like my friend Lou Sill suffered from various tropical skin diseases. Our bodies weren't used to such rapid changes in climate and temperature.

The camp at Dak To was fairly comfortable as long as we weren't under attack! We ate hot food in a mess hall where several Vietnamese cooked for us. Our mess boy, a waiter about fifteen years old, turned out to be the brother of a Viet Cong soldier the Americans had captured in the jungle. The Americans brought the soldier back to Dak To and then sent him on to a prisoner stockade in Kontum. The mess boy chose to remain loyal to the government, and although his brother had elected to join the Viet Cong, he had not. We were never quite certain if that was true. Brother fought against brother in this war, just as in the American Civil War. But, then again, our "brother" could have just as easily been planted as a spy.

As a cover for our intelligence mission, I became part of a medical/civic action patrol (MEDCAP) team made up of two Green Beret medic sergeants and myself. Ostensibly, we treated ill villagers in isolated areas, but while carrying out this "cover," we kept our eyes open for signs of the enemy as my Montagnard agent walked through the village making contacts. Each morning after breakfast, I got in my jeep, followed by two trucks full of Montagnard soldiers, and headed for a jungle village. The Montagnards acted as a security patrol that swept through the village checking all the huts before setting up a defense line on the perimeter. The fact that we came in peace to help sick villagers would not have deterred the communists from killing any of us.

Once the Montagnards secured the village, the MEDCAP team entered with an interpreter who introduced us to the village chief. Most days we traveled up to seven miles, visiting each village along the way. We never stayed overnight. Lines began forming as soon as the word spread that "doctors" were in the village. The medics were soon busy pulling teeth, bandaging sores, treating for head lice and earaches, and caring for people so ill they had to be carried to us on blankets. The medical problems were just as numerous and varied as any treated in a medical clinic in the States—perhaps more so. We tried to visit each village within a two-week period, and then began all over again the third week. It was on one such foot patrol that I received my introduction to leeches. After walking through the damp jungle, I found a leech attached to the calf of my leg. One of my men promptly lit a cigarette and burned it off. That experience served as only one of numerous menaces and consequences of living in the jungle.

At Dak Roleang, a village near the end of the jungle road, we met a French Roman Catholic priest who had ministered to the villagers in that area for more than twenty years. I had been raised an Episcopalian, but, again, never really made a total commitment to my faith. After Jackie and I were married, we practically ignored the church altogether for the first two and one-half years of our marriage. To see such dedication to other people, the church, and God was incredible to me. That priest and his commitment to his faith inspired me, and I would remember him for a long time to come.

Just past Dak Plon stood an old French fort, abandoned since 1954. Beyond the fort, I had discovered the drop area where I left my Cambodian agents during Operation Viper. To me, the abandoned fort represented the very end of civilization—an eternity away from family, home, and reality. We never traveled by vehicle to this camp, but I flew over it often. Just east of it was later built the Ben Het A camp, terrain described as "rugged, and covered by triple canopy jungle, bamboo, and brushwood" (Stanton: 284).

The medical side of our mission paid off twice when we evacuated ill villagers to better medical facilities. These people were so ill that they surely would have died without our assistance. One published estimate reported that Green Beret medics in Vietnam treated approximately forty thousand civilians a month in the many dispensaries opened and operated just to treat local villagers. Working in Dak To made me feel I was doing more for the war effort than I could have done in a comfortable hotel room in Saigon or the villa back in Nha Trang. There were some positive aspects to this extremely controversial war after all. The Green Berets accomplished their mission of pacification and of winning the hearts and minds of the villagers very well.

On several of our MEDCAP patrols, we had a real physician with us. I became a close friend to a Special Forces and Ranger-qualified Captain Andrew J. Cottingham, M.D. He visited Dak To as a member of the Walter Reed Army Institute of Research. There were two combat medics at Dak To with whom he worked in the Special Forces Field Epidemiologic Survey Team (Airborne). A real mouthful. They were involved throughout Vietnam with the myriad tropical diseases prevalent in that country that were not present in the United States.

The camp at Dak To sustained a major epidemic of bubonic plague in early 1967 because some of the Montagnard troops and their families ate rats as a part of their diet, but it became more complicated. We had to quarantine the camp by hanging skull and crossbones signs to indicate that the camp was off-limits to everyone except the Americans. We had all received gamma globulin shots and were spared from the plague. The wails and cries of the families standing vigil over the corpses pierced our nights for several days. Captain Cottingham was intimately involved with containing the plague in our camp.

Captain Andrew J. Cottingham, M.D.
Plague Outbreak at Dak To Special Forces Camp, 1967
Plague was used as a biological weapon in the Middle Ages when armies catapulted dead plague victims into cities under siege in order to spread the disease. Japan used plague as a biological weapon against the Chinese during World War II by dropping plague-infected fleas over populated areas and causing outbreaks.

Plague presents itself in three forms. Bubonic, the most common form, occurs when an infected flea bites a person or material contaminated with the bacteria enters through a cut or break in the skin. Bubos, or large tender swollen lymph glands, develop. The pneumonic form is spread from person to person by an aerosol of bacteria as a result of coughing or spitting. Septicemic plague occurs when the bacteria multiply in the blood. It can be a complication of pneumonic or bubonic plague. It is a severe overwhelming infection.

Plague first appeared in the RVN in 1906. It was imported by rats, transported in bundles, from Canton and Hong Kong to the port of Saigon. Plague spread outward from the Saigon-Cholon area, appearing in the lower Mekong River Delta at Soc Trang in 1907. In 1908, it was imported from the south, by junk, to the port of Phu Hai, and then to Phan Thiet and through most of Binh Thuan Province. From 1911 on, the disease moved northward, appearing in Phan Rang (Ninh Thuan Province), Phu Yen, Quang Nam, and Quang Binh. Plague has appeared sporadically in these and other areas, with some sharp outbreaks, since that time.

An outbreak of plague at the Dak To Special Forces camp during the period February 21 to April 2, 1967, resulted in twenty cases. Diagnosis was confirmed bacteriologically and serologically. All but one were bubonic. There were four deaths. Cases ranged in severity from acute infections with death, to mild infections in which the only manifestation of illness was with low-grade fever.

In addition to the Montagnards infected, the disease was found in the daughter of the (LLDB), Vietnamese Special Forces commander at Dak To. She had a very large bubo on her neck. A photograph was taken of her and the bubo. Eventually, she was healed. Additionally, my immediate commander, Lieutenant

Dak To 1966–67

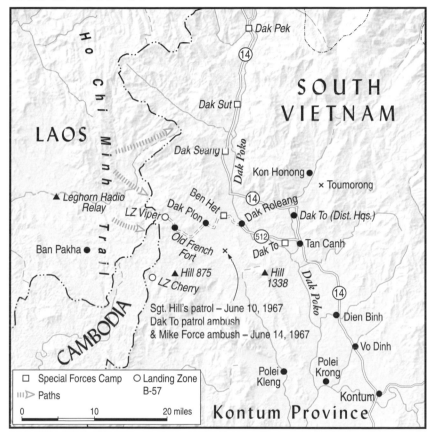

Dak Pek □

(14)

Dak Sut □

SOUTH
VIETNAM

LAOS

Dak Seang □

Dak Poko

Kon Honong ●

× Toumorong

▲ Leghorn Radio
Relay

Ben Het

(14)

Dak Roleang

Dak Plon ●

LZ Viper ○

Dak To (Dist. Hqs.) ●

Ban Pakha ●

Old French
Fort

×

(512)

Dak To □

Tan Canh ●

▲ Hill 875

○ LZ Cherry

▲ Hill
1338

Dak Poko

(14)

● Dien Binh

CAMBODIA

Sgt. Hill's patrol – June 10, 1967
Dak To patrol ambush
& Mike Force ambush – June 14, 1967

● Vo Dinh

Polei ●
Kleng

Polei
Krong

□ Special Forces Camp   ○ Landing Zone
B-57

IIII▷ Paths

Kontum ●

0   10   20 miles

Kontum Province

Southeast Asia 1967

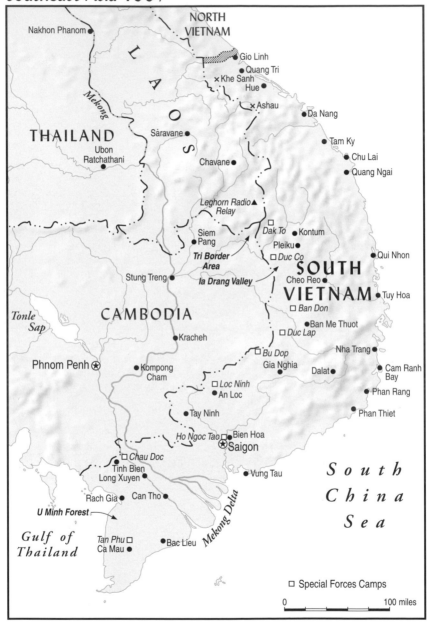

NORTH VIETNAM

Nakhon Phanom

L A O S

Mekong

THAILAND

Ubon Ratchathani

Sàravane

Chavane

Gio Linh
Quang Tri
× Khe Sanh
Hue
× Ashau
Da Nang
Tam Ky
Chu Lai
Quang Ngai

Leghorn Radio ▲
Relay

Siem Pang

□ Dak To   Kontum
Pleiku
□ Duc Co

Tri Border Area

Ia Drang Valley

Stung Treng

Cheo Reo

SOUTH VIETNAM

Tuy Hoa

□ *Ban Don*

Qui Nhon

CAMBODIA

Tonle Sap

Kracheh

Ban Me Thuot
□ *Duc Lap*

Nha Trang

Phnom Penh ⊛

Kompong Cham

□ *Bu Dop*
Gia Nghia
Dalat

Cam Ranh Bay

□ *Loc Ninh*
• An Loc

Phan Rang

Tay Ninh

Phan Thiet

Ho Ngoc Tao □ Bien Hoa
⊛ Saigon

□ *Chau Doc*
Tinh Bien
Long Xuyen

Vung Tau

S o u t h
C h i n a
S e a

Rach Gia   Can Tho

U Minh Forest

Gulf of Thailand

Tan Phu □
Ca Mau   • Bac Lieu

Mekong Delta

□ Special Forces Camps

0   100 miles

Here I am as a second-year cadet at West Point, age eighteen, 1960.

In January 1967, I trained with Mike Eiland and three Operation Cherry Khmer Serei Cambodian agents near Ban Don Special Forces Camp in the Central Highlands. I am holding a Chinese AK-47 rifle, which the agents would carry on their intelligence-gathering mission into Cambodia. I was five feet nine inches tall prior to my amputations.

In January 1967, we spent three days near Ban Don Special Forces Camp with our Cambodian agents. "What am I doing here?" I wondered at the time.

On the Ban Don area training mission for Operation Cherry my Vietnamese interpreter takes a break with me. The night before we almost got trampled by an elephant.

My Montagnard security squad leader spoke several dialects of Montagnard tribal languages, especially Rhade and Sedang, which were the predominant languages of our Civilian Irregular Defense Group soldiers at Dak To. When we entered villages to perform our cover mission of medical/civic action efforts, he would circulate through the villages to locate villagers who would go into Cambodia to gather intelligence on the enemy base camp positions.

In May 1967, we had a steak and beer party for our Montagnard security force at Dak To. When we visited villages, they fanned out to the outskirts to protect us. The squad leader is in the white T-shirt on the other side of the hood of my jeep, which was "procured" for me through "midnight requisitioning" at a U.S. Navy installation in Saigon.

I obtained building materials for a school on the opposite side of the runway from the Dak To camp and obtained a teacher for the children of the camp soldiers. Thirty-six children attended (only one a girl), and this was the first formal education any had ever received. May 1967.

Montagnard children at the village of Dak Plon near Dak To. March 1967. We took them toys and soap on our visits to their villages. My Montagnard squad leader would talk to men in villages to recruit as agents.

Captain Andy Cottingham, M.D. accompanied Allen Clark on medical/civic action patrols when he visited Dak To. Here he is shown in the center of the photo treating villagers. *Courtesy of Colonel (USA-Ret.) Andrew J. Cottingham, M.D.*

Living quarters of Montagnard soldiers on west side of Dak To camp.
This side experienced several cases of bubonic plague because
rats came over the roofs and their fleas bit the family members on
the upper levels of the multilevel underground bunkers. Fighting
foxholes are in front of bunkers. The enemy mortars fired into our
camp were set up on the ridgeline in the middle of the picture.
Courtesy of Colonel (USA-Ret.) Andrew J. Cottingham, M.D.

When I was wounded on June 17, 1967, I was taken on a stretcher
to the bunker of Special Forces medic Sergeant Jimmy Hill. His
bunker is immediately to the left of the one-story sandbagged
building in the front of the picture. My shrapnel wounding
occurred just on the other side of the one-story building as I
attempted to spot the enemy gun flashes. *Courtesy of Colonel
(USA-Ret.) Andrew J. Cottingham, M.D.*

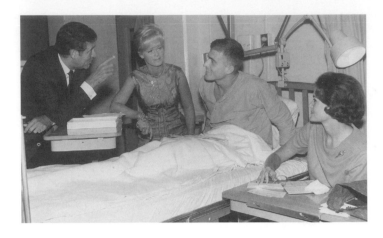

Various United Service Organization (USO) groups visited our amputee ward at Brooke General Hospital in San Antonio. Jackie was with me during a visit with producer Martin Rackin, and actress Carol Andreson of the movie, *Rough Night in Jericho,* on August 7, 1967. Dean Martin and George Peppard also appeared in the film. When outsiders visited me, I always covered up my stumps. *U.S. Army photograph*

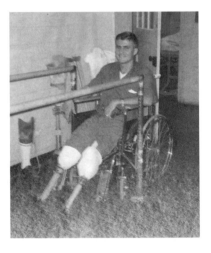

In October 1967, Jackie and I were able to take my first trip from San Antonio to El Paso to visit my parents, Byron and Amy Clark, and my sister, Betty, and her husband, Lieutenant (USAF) Alan C. Chalfont. I guessed my height was about four feet six inches.

October 5, 1967, was the landmark day when I was first fitted with new training legs to try out on the parallel bars. They were very crude and uncomfortable as they were made of plaster.

A rather belated Silver Star, the army's third highest decoration
for heroism, was awarded on September 17, 1970, to me for my
actions at Dak To on June 17, 1967. This was two full years after
my return to civilian life. I was five feet eight inches tall on my
first artificial legs. Brigadier General Harold Parfitt, the Southwest
U.S. Division Engineer, U.S. Corps of Engineers, Dallas, Texas,
presented me with the decoration. *U.S. Army photograph*

My sister's family joined mine for a 1975 Dallas Christmas portrait.
Pictured are Jackie, me, Elizabeth, Christi, Chad Chalfont, Amy,
Byron, Charlene, Betty, Chuck, and Alan Chalfont. Chad and Chuck
became officers after graduating from West Point. Charlene married
a West Pointer. Cheryl, born later to Betty and Alan, married a naval
academy graduate.

It was my distinct privilege and pleasure to serve as special assistant for administration from 1979–1981 to Texas governor William P. Clements Jr., who was a great leader of Texas during his two four-year terms. I had his complete backing in my efforts on behalf of disabled citizens of Texas. To demonstrate "growing in all my jobs," I became five feet eleven inches tall when I went on his political staff. *Courtesy of Bill Malone Photography, Austin, Texas*

When I was a cadet, General William C. Westmoreland had been the superintendent of West Point and he was the American commander in Vietnam from 1964–1968. We were pictured together at a veterans' gathering in Washington, D.C. in May 1989. When I went to Washington in 1989, I was fitted with new legs that elevated me to six feet one inch tall.

President and Mrs. George H. W. Bush hosted a reception at the White House on December 6, 1989, when I was an assistant secretary at the Department of Veterans Affairs. My daughter Elizabeth, a White House intern, also attended. They were always very gracious at their social events. It was one of those times when I endured one of my frequent stump irritations requiring use of my wheelchair. *Official White House photograph*

The Department of Veterans Affairs annually co-sponsors with the Disabled American Veterans a winter sports clinic in Colorado for disabled veterans. At Grand Junction, February 16, 1990, it was a big thrill to learn to ski on my artificial legs.

Bob Hope was the guest of honor at a fund-raiser on May 1, 1990, in Washington, D.C. to raise funds for the Korean War Memorial. My father served in the Korean War. I remember telling him I missed his 1966 USO show at Tan Son Nhut Air Base in Saigon because I was at a safe house with my Operation Cherry agents.

At the Republican National Convention in Philadelphia in August 2000, Texas Governor Rick Perry visited with the Texas delegates. I had been elected from my congressional district as a delegate.

Senator Bob Dole, one of the best-known and respected WWII veterans, visited the Dallas VA Medical Center in November 2001 when I was the public affairs officer. Before I began working at this medical center in 1995, I reached my original goal set in 1967 of six feet two inches tall.

Ross Perot gave me my first job after I completed graduate school at SMU in 1970. I was unable to keep up the fast pace of his busy company, EDS, and had to have a slower job. He has done many untold deeds for America's military men and women and our veterans. He has always been most kind to me. We were pictured together on October 30, 2004, at a dinner recognizing supporters of Dallas disabled citizens.

Texas Senator Kay Bailey Hutchison has been an incredible advocate for our nation's military and veterans. We are pictured on February 1, 2006, when Linda and I attended the National Prayer Breakfast in Washington, D.C.

Best Wishes, *Allen,*
Kay Bailey Hutchison

My retirement party in August 2005 was held at the American Legion Post in Duncanville, Texas. My older daughter, Elizabeth, was a guest also.

My younger daughter, Christi, and her husband, Matthew Bieberich, at Linda's and my wedding on September 11, 2004, in Dallas.

My height rose to ten feet tall when the former Linda Frost of Dallas married me on September 11, 2004, at the home of former Texas secretary of state David Dean and his wife, Jean. Our children Vincent, Elizabeth, and Christi celebrated with us.

Special Forces medic Jimmy Hill finally receives his long-overdue Purple Heart at a ceremony April 15, 2005, at Dallas VA Medical Center where Allen Clark was public affairs officer. The medal is being pinned on by Medal of Honor recipient Colonel (USA-Ret.) James Stone with Medal of Honor recipient Lieutenant (USN-Ret.) Michael Thornton and Major (USA-Ret.) George Petrie, Special Forces participant in the 1970 Son Tay Raid.

At the conclusion of Jimmy Hill's Purple Heart award ceremony, my wife, Linda, introduced my "Band of Brothers": Jimmy Hill; Abe Stice, who had been in the First Cavalry Division in Vietnam and my best friend at Brooke General Hospital; and Andy Cottingham, my best wartime friend. I am in a wheelchair because I had fallen the month before and broken my femur bone.

At the Purple Heart ceremony, my younger daughter, Christi Bieberich, is shown hugging the medic who saved my life on June 17, 1967, at Dak To Special Forces camp with his battlefield medical treatment. Jimmy told me later that as she hugged him, Christi said, "Thank you for bringing my daddy home."

Colonel Llewellyn Legters, who had flown up to help with the epidemiology studies of the outbreak, developed plague while in the camp. He began to run a fever and complained of malaise and pharingitis. Plague was cultured from his throat. While at Dak To, he was started on an antibiotic regimen and finally evacuated to Saigon.

Selectively higher attack rates among dependents of CIDG soldiers, compared with those among the soldiers themselves, suggest that plague transmission occurred primarily in dependent housing. This proved to be due to the fact that the housing was either in a two-level arrangement or in deep underground bunkers. The relative darkness within the bunkers during daylight hours, where dependent wives and children unquestionably spent more time than the soldiers, was perhaps a significant factor in accounting for the higher plague attack rates observed among dependents. Fleas convey plague to man at night. The flea found in the Dak To study was known to prefer dark areas. The predominant rat captured in the camp was a roof rat, preferring upper levels. This also helps to explain why the individuals in the upper levels of the houses were more affected. Plague occurred only among CIDG soldiers and their dependents housed along the east and west sides ("walls") of the camp, and virtually simultaneously on both sides. Along the east and west walls, lallang grass, scrub brush, and short grasses extended up to the outermost defensive barbed-wire perimeter, while to the north was an asphalt aircraft runway and parking apron; and to the south, the Dak Poko River, with sparse grasses and scrub brush between the camp and the river. A burn-off in the lallang and brush on the east and west sides during the weeks just preceding the outbreak suggested that plague-infected rodents might have been driven into the camp. Plague cases at Dak To were the first ever in Kontum Province to be bacteriologically confirmed, though suspect cases were seen for the first time in Kontum City in October 1966. At the time of the Dak To outbreak, major plague outbreaks were in progress in Nha Trang, from which supplies frequently were delivered by air. It is possible that the source of infection (i.e., infected rats and/or fleas) was introduced via food shipments aboard cargo aircraft.

The Walter Reed unit medics at Dak To acquired small wire cages to catch the rats for examination. An interesting phenomenon discovered in the camp was that the majority of the Montagnard mercenaries were of the Rhade tribe, who had multiple wives. The Rhade soldiers always lived on the lower level of their living quarters with one of their wives so the rest of the family got infected from the fleas of the rats on the upper levels.

Eventually, the problem was solved at Dak To with antibiotics, warnings not to eat the rats, removal of the rats from the roofs and living quarters, and lastly, explaining to the Montagnards that they should not use body parts of the rats in the amulets they wore around their necks.

Next, in spite of the humanitarian efforts connected with our mission, the isolation of the camp location, and the tension caused by my secret and sensitive intelligence assignment soon began to take a double-sided toll. I suffered both physically and emotionally. The extreme isolation of the camp made it seem that all contact with the outside world was lost. We had no radio or newspapers, and our magazines were at least two weeks old. I often found myself extremely depressed. Because no one could know of my true assignment there, I could not talk freely with anyone in camp except for Captain Gossett. This only compounded my depression. In addition, I began to suffer from severe headaches. I wrote home that I no longer felt like my old carefree self. Although I did not regret my decision to transfer to Special Forces, I could feel myself slowly changing inside, and the change felt permanent.

Back to Saigon

Once in a while, I could take a plane 280 miles south to Saigon to buy items for the villagers, obtain new radio code books, or replenish the cash supply with which I paid my agents. These trips offered welcome relief from the boredom and tension of camp. While in Saigon, I had lived in a six-story building near the Cholon (Chinese) section of the city, and I looked forward to returning to these comfortable surroundings where I had my own room with indoor plumbing and could visit the club and mess hall located on the top floor of the building.

Just before one of my trips to Saigon, word reached Dak To that a guard had caught a man lurking outside the headquarters building. Under intense interrogation, the man finally confessed that he was scouting the building in order to bomb it. This revelation resulted in tightened security in the area, and, beginning in the spring of 1967, none of us at the field stations were allowed to return to our headquarters building for brief trips. Consequently, we had to set up new headquarters in a nearby Vietnamese hotel, causing us to sorely miss our old comfortable quarters.

Staying in the Vietnamese hotel posed a major problem, though, that had nothing to do with comfort. One of the primary reasons any of us looked forward to trips to Saigon was that we could visit with Americans. Ironically, however, under the new conditions, our commanding officer sent messengers to bring us money and pick up our reports. We were given strict orders to talk to no one. We couldn't even visit with our friends. These conditions robbed us of our sense of camaraderie and opportunities to sit down with fellow soldiers to drink beer and simply talk to one another. On one visit to Saigon, I found the companionship that I longed for so desperately. I ran into my former West Point debate coach, Major Dale Vesser, at the Rex Hotel, which was run by the U.S. Army. We were able to share a steak dinner and talk for one precious evening. Most of the time, I ate alone. The loneliness I had felt at Dak To only intensified in Saigon. On another evening there, I shared a meal with Dr. Andy Cottingham and told him my real name a few days before my wounding.

He was a physician, accustomed to keeping information private, so I felt I could share my real name with him. As it transpired, he forgot my real name but heard about my later wounding. I have discovered his involvement in another disease case that relates to malaria.

Andy Cottingham was a unique medical doctor to be assigned to Special Forces. He was starting fullback on the Duke University football team in fall of 1958. He became qualified in Special Forces by taking the officer's course at Fort Bragg and would attain thirty-seven paratrooper jumps in his career.

In his story below of the malaria among our troops, it is important to point out that he made a combat airborne jump with the Mike

Force unit that was the subject of his malaria research and was with the unit when they were in action against NVA troops. He collected blood samples from the dead enemy troops to assist in his research that ended up having very positive results for malaria treatments for our troops and our Montagnards.

Captain Andrew J. Cottingham, M.D.
On Malaria in Vietnam

Throughout the history of warfare, in virtually every major conflict, more soldiers have fallen from the battlefield as a result of disease than from battle-related injuries. History is replete with examples of how non–combat-related disease has affected the effectiveness of armies and the outcome of a battle, a war, and perhaps even the outcome of a nation. During the Civil War, more men were killed than in all previous American conflicts combined. The casualties of Antietam were twice the casualties suffered at D–Day during World War II (WWII); yet, twice as many men died of disease during the Civil War from malaria, dysentery, smallpox, and other rampant diseases than died of wounds sustained from enemy fire. Napoleon's magnificent army was ravaged and almost completely destroyed by louse-borne typhus during his Russian campaign and retreat from Moscow. The entire WWII Asian-Pacific campaign was constantly threatened by malaria and other exotic tropical diseases. During the battles for the Solomon Islands, malaria casualties overwhelmingly outnumbered enemy casualties by at least eight to one.

Hippocrates taught "If one wants to become a surgeon, one should follow the army." As in ancient times, this has proven to be true throughout more-recent history as well. Many of the best medical techniques and practices were developed during times of military combat. During these stressful periods by virtue of necessity an increased impetus has been given to developing the necessities to successfully complete the war.

Gerhard Johannes Paul Domagk, a German biochemist, discovered a class of drugs that could be transformed into sulfanilamide. When transformed, this agent proved to have antibacterial properties highly effective against many bacterial diseases. He published his findings in 1939. American chemists transformed the drug, and this agent was used extensively during World War II by American soldiers who sprinkled the powder on open wounds to prevent infection. Every soldier's first aid pouch contained not only bandages, but also a package of sulfa powder. Sulfa in the form of tablets which prevented dysentery was a major contributing factor relating to the effectiveness of North African British operations in the battle of El Alamein against Rommel's German divisions.

A Scottish bacteriologist, Sir Alexander Fleming, discovered penicillin in 1906. As knowledge of its antibacterial properties emerged, Pfizer began working on a method of mass production. By 1942, this highly safe and effective antibacterial agent began to flow into U.S. military medical facilities. Penicillin saved countless lives during World War II and the subsequent Korean War.

Mothers are eternally worried about their sons marching off to the risky business of war, but hardly any realize that the major enemy is not the opposing army, but rather a multitude of microscopic microbial agents known by funny Latin and Greek names.

In Vietnam, the situation in 1966 was no different. The United States was involved in a communist-inspired guerilla war taking place in a remote, hostile jungle environment. It was in 1964 that the first knowledge of Plasmodium falciparum parasites (one of the three forms of malaria parasites) resistant to chloroquine began to occur in U.S. combat troops serving in that distant land. The prevalence of chloroquine insensitive to this type of parasite in any given geographic area of RVN had not been determined, and such information was vital to the understanding of the malaria situation and for planning future treatment and control or eradication. The information would be useful to military commanders in the planning and conduct of tactical operations.

By 1966, there was growing evidence that heavy regular North Vietnamese Army (NVA) troops were infiltrating down the Ho Chi Minh. Medical intelligence estimates derived from captured documents and prisoner interrogations indicated that NVA units operating in the Central Highlands of South Vietnam were sustaining high rates of noneffectiveness from malaria. Nevaquine (choloraquine), paludrine, and atabrine (quinacrine) were the principal antimalarial drugs administered to NVA troops. In addition according to some documents, NVA troops were treated once a month with 2100 mg of nevaquine, paludrine or atabrine, administered over a five-day period. The type of drug used by a particular troop unit was apparently dependent upon availability. It was also becoming increasingly evident that infected enemy personnel represented the principal reservoir of malaria infection for U.S. units engaged in combat operations. Malaria transmission among U.S. personnel had been observed repeatedly to be apparently related to contact with enemy forces or to areas recently occupied by the enemy. In 1965 and 1966, scientists at WRAIR hoped to improve on the defenses of malaria then available by providing to the U.S. soldiers an effective regimen. At the time U.S. soldiers were given chloroquine to take once weekly. Laboratory evidence suggested that by the addition of dapsone daily, an effective prophylactic scheme would be attained. Before instigating this regime into the diet of all U.S. forces in Southeast Asia, field tests needed to be conducted. Recommendations were made for administration of test drugs to indigenous units (CIDG, Mike Force, Strike Force). It was apparent that a number of field studies need to be conducted— but by whom? Remember this was a war zone—a dangerous zone. Typically, doctors are used in the relatively more safe rear zones of evacuation or at least in somewhat more secured headquarters company locations.

My research team was formed in late 1965 and 1966. It was composed of physicians and other medical personnel, highly skilled in their individual medical fields, but also Green Berets (Special Forces–qualified) trained in guerrilla warfare. All were volunteers from various Special Forces groups. Although the entire theater of operation technically was behind enemy lines in the true sense of guerrilla warfare, this medical intelligence needed to be obtained from deep within the hazardous enemy territory, perhaps directly from the enemy.

Operation Paul Revere IV, a U.S. military operation conducted in the Central Highlands of II Corps Tactical Zone (CTZ) in

November and December of 1966, provided an opportunity and a focal point to begin the investigation of certain of those problems.

To summarize, I was the medical officer in charge of the malaria project in II Corps, Central Highlands RVN during late 1965 and 1966. Working with the Mike Force, I took blood smears from the 1st Company Mike Force prior to deployment on Operation Paul Revere IV, and I administered various regimens of drugs to platoons within the company while on operations. We came in contact with the NVA. I took blood samples off dead NVA soldiers. Some strains of malaria were acquired when our troops made contact with the enemy being brought into RVN from outside that country. This was the information we were looking for—the NVA were bringing new strains down the Ho Chi Minh Trail, and some of these strains were not treatable with our standard medications. To my knowledge, no new cases of malaria were observed in our forces who did use this new combination of chloroquine and dapsone, which we had discovered from our study. I took it for the rest of my stay in RVN. The question as to exactly where these new strains were acquired by the NVA was somewhat speculative. Laos, Thailand, North Vietnam, or China—these were the suspects. Some evidence suggested that it came down from the Yunnan Province of China.

Obviously many of our troops were spared malaria infection from the research of Dr. Cottingham.

My experiences at our Saigon hotels were most often lonely or even surreal. One time, from the tenth floor of the Rex, I looked across the Saigon River and saw helicopter gun ships using tracer bullets to repel a Viet Cong attack on an outpost. The irony of it wasn't lost on me. There I was, comfortable and relaxed with a beer in my hand, while only two miles away people were dying in a raging war. It seemed as if the whole world had turned upside down and nothing made sense—as if we had all somehow passed through Alice's looking glass.

Rest and Relaxation

In her own way, Jackie had as much frustration and loneliness to deal with as I did. She had returned to SMU in Dallas to complete another year toward her degree. Fellow students often talked to her about Vietnam. She knew that some West Point friends had served not one, but two years there. The realization that I might have to stay an extra year in service upset Jackie terribly. A positive was she lived with her generous parents.

The fact that rules for military service seemed to change constantly during the 60s also contributed to Jackie's confusion and frustration. First, if a man got married, he did not have to serve in the armed forces. The rule changed so that if he had one child, he did not have to serve. That changed, too; if he had two children, he was exempt. With such confusion, it was no wonder that Jackie's thoughts in her letters reflected her frustration and loneliness. Many of her friends got married and had children very quickly to avoid the draft and the war. It all seemed so easy for them and so unfair to her. She was married, but her husband was gone. Neither of us could avoid the war. It had already invaded our lives.

We both survived in our separate worlds the best way we knew how. Yet, we both knew our relationship was going downhill. We felt that if we could only see each other and spend some time together, we might be able to resolve some of our problems. As one possible solution, Jackie and I planned an R and R trip to Hawaii in February 1967, but she became ill and had to cancel. We planned another trip for May, but that time I had to cancel because my radio operator at Dak To returned to the States on an emergency leave because his mother died. That, of course, took precedence over my request for R and R with my wife.

Jackie and I both felt very lonely and helpless. We could not talk to each other; so the next best thing was to write letters, and neither of us did a very good job explaining our feelings on paper. I tried to keep my letters upbeat because I did not want Jackie to worry about me. That strategy backfired. Separated by several thousand miles, and I unable to explain my feelings well in words, she took my upbeat tone to mean that I was getting gung-ho army again and wanted to go back on my promise and continue with my military career. How could I explain? How could I know her frustration? How could she feel my loneliness and know how much I had tried to keep her from worrying about my physical safety?

I kept on constant alert for any options that would permit Jackie and me to be together once more sooner than later. One day I thought I discovered the possible solution. I heard that Major General Joseph A. McChristian, currently in charge of intelligence for Military Advisory Command Vietnam (MACV), would be returning to Fort Hood on June 1 to command the 2nd Armored Division. His son had been a second-year man at West Point in my company when I was a first-class man. I knew that I could get credit for a one-year tour in Vietnam after ten months, so I asked General McChristian if I could accompany him back to Fort Hood as his aide. I expected a replacement at Dak To soon, anyway. It seemed like the perfect plan. General McChristian questioned me carefully during an interview in Saigon where he told me he would let me know about my request. I later received word at Dak To that he decided not to take me with him because in our interview he learned that I had already spent nine months as a general's aide in the States. It was a devastating disappointment.

In May 1967, ten months after I arrived in Vietnam, I received orders to report to Fort George F. Meade, Maryland, upon returning home. Although I had resigned my commission before leaving the States in 1966, the army had the right to extend my time one additional year through a fifth year of service, and they had done just that. There was absolutely nothing I could do about it. My greatest concern was Jackie's reaction to this news. Her worst fears were being realized, and I did not want to break the news to her. I was heartbroken. I felt that I had done my duty—had even volunteered—and now I must pay an additional penalty because I was a regular army officer. It didn't make sense to me and certainly didn't seem fair.

If my time had not been extended or if I had received the aide's position, I would have been credited with my fourth year of service and a full combat tour after only ten months and could have left Vietnam by June 1, 1967. If I had left on June 1, then I would not have been in Dak To on June 17 when those mortars sprayed shrapnel through the camp. But again, there are no "ifs" in God's kingdom. Instead, this extension meant that I must complete a full year in

Vietnam and not go home until several weeks later. This one military decision changed not only my future, but also my entire way of life.

Reaching Out

Although the trips to Saigon became depressing and lonely, the return trip to Dak To often brought relief and even humor. When I returned with supplies for the villagers, we were always met with wonder and glee. After one such trip, I took several men and went to a nearby village with my load of supplies. We lined up the village children, gave them each a bar of yellow-and-red striped soap wrapped in yellow-and-red striped paper. It was no accident that the soap contained these particular colors. They are the national colors of South Vietnam and the same colors displayed on their flag. The government often used such tactics as propaganda measures, knowing full well that these items would eventually reach even the most remote villages as long as the Americans were present. After giving them the soap, we marched the children to the nearest stream where we showed them how to bathe. The children splashed and frolicked in the sudsy water and seemed to appreciate the new gifts, but we had no way of knowing how long the soap or the new bathing habit would last.

I also acquired a large supply of toys in Saigon—whistles, plastic balls, and so on. On one trip, the Catholic priest from Dak Roleang accompanied me into the village to distribute the toys to the children. To see evident happiness and joy on their faces from receiving just one simple little plastic ball touched me deeply. I often thought of American children with trunks full of toys that are so often taken for granted and sometimes seldom used. The overwhelming contrast made me understand how life can be so vastly different in other parts of the world. The trip was very gratifying, and I left the village feeling like a tropical Santa Claus.

On yet a third trip, I brought back great bales of clothing, Goodwill castoffs from the United States, and passed them out to the Montagnards and villagers. The Montagnard tribes that assisted us were for the most part animists. A primitive race of people, most of the Montagnard women go topless while their husbands wear only loincloths. They believe that all things in nature possess a spirit—air, streams, mountains, trees, people, and so on. Therefore, they were one with nature and felt very comfortable without clothing. Because of this, it was rather humorous to see the Montagnards in full dress. Although a superstitious people, the Montagnards were very outgoing. Their personal warmth and Texaslike hospitality made it very easy to befriend them.

Not all of the Montagnards were as friendly as those we knew, however. Among them are many diverse groups or tribes. "The Montagnard tribes represented a diversity of ethnic Mon-Khmer and Malayo-Polynesian peoples who occupied the rugged length of the Vietnamese western highlands. The tribes included the physically hardy Bahnar in the upper Kontum area, the secretive Bru in the northern mountains, the coastal Cham, the migrating Halang, the betel-chewing lowland and upland Hres, the quarrelsome Jarai in the Pleiku region, the warlike Jehs, the hostile Katu, the slave-holding Koto, the forest-dwelling Mnong, the polytheistic Raglai, the physically strong Rengao, the friendly Rhade in the savanna of the Darlac plateau, the jungle-dwelling Sedang, and the witch-fearing Stieng" (Stanton: 57).

We worked with a number of different tribes in our area, including the Rhade, Jarai, Bahnar, and Sedang. One of the main reasons the Green Berets were so successful in obtaining the support and trust of the Montagnards was because they mixed with them and got to know them on their own turf. Green Berets and different tribes alike all worked together while each spoke a different dialect or language. We had to make interpreters and squad leaders out of anyone who could successfully communicate with members of the different tribes. A short, stocky, and very personable Montagnard named Liu served as my "leader" on patrols. Either by language, kicks, pats, or nudges, Liu usually managed to get everyone to do what needed to be done.

The Montagnards, although they lived very simply and primitively, always found a way to compensate for a loss or make use of an opportunity. They proved to be a very resourceful people. When fishing became poor, villagers would toss grenades into the rivers, thus stunning the large silver carplike fish that inhabited their waters. They would then have to rush to gather the stunned fish that had floated to the surface before they regained their composure and swam away or got carried away by the swift currents. Some of the tribes harvested casings of expended artillery shells from which they fashioned tools such as knives, picks, machetes, and various farm implements.

The lives of the Montagnards seemed to be self-contradictory. In some ways, they seemed very advanced, while in other ways they were extremely backward. Each tribe elected its village chiefs in a democratic process. Women were held in high esteem and were prominent figures within their society, owning all of the material goods within the tribal village. Oddly, however, there was no formal system of education for the children. This lack of education weighed heavily on my mind, so I decided to round up enough cement to build a schoolhouse at Dak To. By begging, borrowing, and scrounging, I managed to get enough materials, and with the help of men in the camp, we had the building up in no time. A sergeant with the South Vietnamese Special Forces became the first teacher of thirty-five Montagnard children.

In spite of such diversions, the reality of the war loomed over us each moment, and we had to deal with the probability of the enemy lurking nearby as well as with daily intelligence excursions into the jungle. The medics from Walter Reed Army Medical Center brought small cages with them in which they sometimes captured animals to study. I often borrowed some of these cages and gave them to an interpreter who in turn gave them to our agents. This became a standard precaution in the event the agents were captured. They were to tell their captors that they were hunting, and the cages were for trapping small game. Although a hastily thought-up cover story, it served the agents well as a reason for walking so deeply into the jungle near old abandoned village sites.

Our frequent medical missions into the surrounding villages gave the Vietnamese sergeant with us an opportunity to speak to the village chiefs about enemy movements. This reliable jungle grapevine enabled the villagers to always know before anyone else whether the enemy was moving into their area. This soon proved to be the case at Dak To. Because the reports of enemy movements became more numerous, my newly recruited agents became so frightened that, one by one, they began refusing to go back into the jungle at all.

We all would have liked to leave the area entirely, but Special Forces camps are never abandoned unless overrun by the enemy. If that should happen and we could not hold off the enemy, we were to escape in pairs and make a run for it. The land mines that encircled our camp as a defense perimeter would make it extremely dangerous for any of us to escape in a hurry. We were there for the duration—whatever that might be.

Because agents left due to their overriding and pervading fears, I once again found myself in the position of training more new agents. It seemed like a never-ending cycle. Once again, I emphasized the importance of secrecy, instructing them to tell no one of their responsibilities once they returned to their respective villages. If the mission were compromised because of a slip of the tongue, the result could be the loss of many lives. If anyone slipped up and made a mistake, we expected it to be the agents, not one of our own people. However, on one occasion, as I ate dinner with four people, the mission was compromised by one of our own. The dinner party included an American lieutenant who was the A-team XO, the Vietnamese camp commander, Lieutenant Le Quang Nhia and his wife, and the senior Vietnamese sergeant. The lieutenant drank too much and bragged that he knew about my activities at Dak To and boasted that I should be sending my agents in another direction.

I urged him to be quiet, but he only responded, "Don't worry, they don't speak English."

An intelligence officer never assumes that a person cannot understand the language, because many times communist plants play dumb when they really understand everything that is being said around them. Because of the severity of the situation, an officer had compromised an important mission, so I had to send a letter through channels reporting the incident. As a result, the lieutenant was summarily removed from the Green Berets and reassigned to the military police in Saigon. But the lieutenant would not be the only person to betray us.

On another occasion, two agents whom we recruited to pose as medics told a village chief that they had been hired for an intelligence mission. The chief in turn told the Vietnamese Special Forces lieutenant, and he told our camp commander, Captain Gossett. He told me that the word was out that I was recruiting agents to go into the jungle. The agents had blown my cover. The time had come to make a crucial decision. I had only two choices: I could shut down the operation and discipline the two village medics, or we could act as if nothing had happened and leave that one village alone and concentrate on the other fourteen villages in the area. The latter choice involved great risk. Anyone labeled as an intelligence officer became an immediate target of the Viet Cong assassination teams. To help with my decision, I solicited the advice of the two Green Beret sergeants on my team. I first asked them if we should discipline the agents who had broken their pledges of silence.

"We ought to kill them," one of the sergeants snapped. "I'll volunteer to take care of it."

"No!" I exclaimed. "I don't want to take their lives. That's murder, and it's wrong."

"Then, if we can't do that, let's beat them up and break their legs."

The war was brutal enough, and I found it unthinkable to act so barbarically to civilians who had only made a mistake while trying to help us. Reports suggested that the enemy was closing in. If that were the case, I would soon be shut down anyway. I refused to take such action and instead decided to overlook the incident and ignore the village instead. I decided to discuss it with my commanding officer when I returned to Saigon a few days later.

The Enemy Moves In

May and June 1967 were months of heavy enemy activity in our area of operations at Dak To. In early May, a South Vietnamese Army battalion stationed three miles from us at Tan Canh ran into a strong enemy force in the jungle. Rather than fight it out, the battalion called for help. Captain Gossett led a patrol of Green Berets and Montagnards into action to assist the battalion. Gossett's unit made nine separate frontal assaults on the North Vietnamese regulars but could not crack their position. Angry that they could not budge the NVA, a Green Beret major from Kontum wanted to take all the remaining Americans at Dak To and plunge them into battle, even though intelligence officers are not supposed to go into combat. He proposed that we fly over in helicopters and drop on the enemy positions. This was an absolutely insane idea. He actually ordered us armed and at the ready when calmer and more rational minds finally prevailed. Fortunately, at the last minute we were ordered to back off from what would have certainly been a suicide mission. Two weeks later, I discussed that insane order to go into battle with Major Nandor, my commanding officer in Saigon.

"Allen," he said, "you're assigned to me. Never accept anyone else's directions. You're an intelligence officer. If you're ever captured, you could endanger many other lives because of what you know about this operation. I don't want you to ever get into a position where there is a possibility of your being captured."

Additional Special Forces soldiers were sent in to assist the battalion that was fighting the NVA in the jungle. As the fighting proceeded, our helicopters began bringing the dead and wounded back to Dak To, where the choppers landed on the airstrip just outside camp. While helping offload the dead bodies, I recognized one of our own among the dead, a senior sergeant in the Green Berets. Only the night before, he had had a reunion at our camp with his son, also a Green Beret serving in Vietnam. His son had already left camp by the time his father's body arrived by helicopter. We unloaded body bags until I thought I would be overcome with nausea at the sight and smell of so many dead young men. The mourning of Montagnard families who wailed and cried throughout the night and for days afterward is still a vivid memory to this day.

This action was northeast of our camp in an area called the Toumorong. Apparently, it had always been the scene of heavy enemy activity, because the previous June (1966) it was in this area that the story was well publicized in the media that Captain Bill

Carpenter, the celebrated "Lonesome End" of West Point football fame, found himself in a situation wherein he made the decision, surrounded by the Viet Cong, to call in napalm on his own positions.

In 2004, when I was in the veteran community of North Texas, it was my privilege to meet a member of West Point's class of 1962. He had been the cadet battalion commander of my battalion when I was in my last year at West Point. We had not known each other then, but in my incessant questioning of Walter "Ron" Brown of Chattanooga to find out about my fellow Vietnam friends, I slowly drew out of Ron his involvement in the 1966 Battle of the Toumorong, which was so near to my camp at Dak To.

The simplest way to begin Ron Brown's story is to quote from an undated 1967 article written for UPI by Leon Daniel upon his departure from one year of combat reporting: "War reporter says Captain Ron Brown of Chattanooga 'Bravest Man I Met' cites 'Unsung Hero in Jungle Fighting'."

> I believe that a stocky young captain from Chattanooga, Tennessee, named Ron Brown was the bravest man I met in Vietnam. Brown led his company into a jungle hell to rescue the company of Capt. Bill Carpenter, a former West Point football star and one of the army's outstanding combat heroes.
>
> Carpenter and his paratroopers got the headlines they richly deserved, but because of the general confusion and the pressure of deadlines, Brown's heroic role was somewhat obscured and he became one of the war's relatively unsung heroes.
>
> Seeing Brown and Carpenter and their men walk out of the jungle carrying their dead and wounded was one of the most inspiring things I have ever witnessed.
>
> There are some stories I would like to have another crack at. For example, the story of Captains Carpenter and Brown. If I could do it over again, I would not let Brown's heroic role get lost in the story of the heroism of his friend Carpenter.

Ron Brown's Citation for the Distinguished Service Cross
Company A, 2d Bn (ABN) 502 Inf, 1st Bde, 101st Abn Division

For extraordinary heroism in connection with military operations against an armed hostile force in the Republic of Vietnam. During the period 9 June 1966 to 11 June 1966, Captain Brown, the company commander of Company A, had the mission of reinforcing a company that was surrounded by a Viet Cong battalion near Dak To. Upon receiving the mission, Captain Brown immediately assembled his company and began the 3,000 meter move through darkness and treacherous terrain to the battle area. As his company reached the top of the mountain overlooking the beleaguered company, it received intense hostile fire. With complete disregard for his safety, Captain Brown led a squad to the flank of the insurgent positions and initiated an assault that killed nine Viet Cong and forced the remainder of the insurgents to flee. During the assault, Captain Brown charged a machine gun emplacement and personally killed three Viet Cong. Although the situation was extremely tense, Captain Brown positioned himself with the lead element and continued to advance toward the stricken company. Upon entering a valley, the lead element again received Viet Cong fire from the surrounding high ground. While the rest of the company continued forward, Captain Brown maneuvered his machine guns into a position where they placed suppressive fire on the insurgents. As his unit reached the perimeter of the beleaguered company, the rear element was attacked by a determined Viet Cong force and one trooper fell seriously wounded. Captain Brown immediately raced 30 meters down the slope to the wounded trooper and carried him to safety. He then assumed command of the perimeter and positioned his men to repel the repeated Viet Cong attacks. Throughout the next 30 hours, Captain Brown continuously exposed himself to carry ammunition, call in air strikes, and adjust artillery fire. During a mortar attack on 10 June 1966, Captain Brown moved about the battlefield helping move wounded soldiers from exposed positions. Working against superior odds, he organized his company and rallied his men to successfully fight their way through the Viet Cong encirclement. Although confronted with the arduous task of transporting 45 litter casualties over rough terrain to an evacuation point 1,000 meters away, he never relented from his determined efforts to accomplish his mission. While moving toward the landing zone, they were again hit by a Viet Cong element. Despite the fact that he was wounded by a grenade explosion, Captain Brown ordered a charge that overran the insurgent position. After reaching the landing zone, he returned down the mountain to help his comrades carry the litter patients to the extraction point. Through his courage and outstanding leadership, he contributed immeasurably to the defeat of the Viet Cong force. Captain Brown's extraordinary heroism and devotion to duty in close combat against a numerically superior hostile force were in keeping with the highest traditions of the military service and reflect great credit upon himself, his unit, and the United States Army.

This story of Ron's would not be told by a very humble and self-effacing Ron, but as his friend, I have taken license to tell it as an example of the essence of the extraordinary leadership and valor of our warriors in the Vietnam War.

CHAPTER 8

HEALING OF BODY, SOUL, AND SPIRIT

And the War Goes On
Fall/Winter 1967–1968

The fighting in Vietnam had raged on during the fall and winter of 1967. Wounded soldiers still poured into Brooke Army Medical Center each day. We reluctantly watched daily news reports of the fighting of which we had once been a part. North Vietnamese regulars were still entrenched near Dak To during the first week of November when 236 communists and forty-five Americans were reported killed. In mid-November, American artillerymen lowered their 105mm howitzer barrels and fired four-inch shells directly over the American paratroopers' heads into the onrushing enemy. UPI reported that the North Vietnamese lines crumbled.

In a later two-day enemy attack at Dak To, however, 150 mortar rounds blew up two $2 million C-130 transport planes and an ammunition dump containing 1,250 tons of rockets, mortars, dynamite, grenades, and plastic explosives. Observers noted that the glare from the explosives turned night into day. I watched television news films of the battle and saw one of the blown-up C-130s. As the television camera panned the area just outside my old bunk building, a strange, eerie feeling swept through me. It had been only four months earlier when I was caught in a similar battle at the very same spot. Perhaps I was one of the lucky ones after all. At least I managed to get out with my life before the really heavy fighting began.

At the beginning of the last week of November, after three weeks of fighting, official tallies of casualties listed 277 Americans killed, 946 wounded, and 1,377 North Vietnamese dead. B–52s flew raids late on Thanksgiving as the communists finally retreated. That was, at least, a small reason to be thankful on that particular day. The massive and bloody battle that occurred on Hill 875 was one that Jim Hill had wanted to reconnoiter the previous June.

In the fall of 1967, it was a source of great comfort and satisfaction to be visited daily by Captain Abe Stice, a wounded helicopter pilot also brought back to Brooke General Hospital for rehabilitation. He had been assigned to C Troop, 9th Cavalry, 1st Air Cavalry Division. On September 5, 1967, the unit was in a night position at forward Landing Zone Two Bits. He too was wounded in a mortar attack followed up by infiltration of the Viet Cong into their positions. He managed to reach a bunker where he detonated a claymore mine to help repel the enemy.

Abe Stice

I remember during the day, there was a lot of cutting up. Wheelchair races through the halls and down the ramps were a norm. However, when darkness fell and the lights were off, reality would set in and crying from all directions would make you want to bury your head in your pillow to escape the sounds.

It was a bad time for all of us, but we found strength in one another. We played the cards that were dealt, and we were a "band of brothers," like those in the Shakespeare play, *Henry V*, "for he today that sheds his blood with me shall be my brother." We will always carry with us a membership deservedly earned as a "Band of Brothers."

Just before Christmas 1967, reporter Jim Brigance of the *San Antonio Light* visited our ward. He was writing a feature story about what the wounded veterans at Brooke would be doing on Christmas Day and how we felt about the war. I gave him the following statement, which he quoted in the article: "No, I'm not bitter. I paid the price, and it was worth it. I'm just thankful I'm alive. I don't care what they believe over there. I was needed in Vietnam. I volunteered, and I knew what I was up against. I've got everything to live for, and it's worth dying for, too."

I meant what I told Mr. Brigance when I uttered those words way back then. But, I have to admit that, after forty years and with 20/20 hindsight, I do not feel the same way now. I have twinges of conscience about the real value of my sacrifice due to how the war was conducted, especially after the revelations in the 1990s from Secretary of Defense Robert S. McNamara, and the release of the tapes that President Johnson had made in 1964.

The first few months of the New Year in 1968 proved to be historical, tragic, and even earth shaking. The Tet Offensive in Vietnam struck forcefully and without warning, causing casualty lists to mount. The extreme burden of the war pressed down on our national leaders as they were forced to make monumental decisions. President Johnson, haggard and drawn from the toll the war had taken on him and the lack of support for the war at home, went on television to announce that he would not seek re-election. In the spring and summer, two national heroes and leaders, Dr. Martin Luther King Jr. and Senator Robert F. Kennedy fell victims to assassins' bullets. And angry antiwar protestors disrupted the Democratic National Convention in Chicago. Our national fabric seemed to unravel before our very eyes.

The atmosphere in the hospital seemed little different than the events occurring in the outside world. My own life had unraveled, too, and the possibility of putting it back together seemed eons away. Watching the antiwar protests on television planted seeds of resentfulness and bitterness, but I couldn't let it affect me. I just couldn't think about it, so I buried those seeds deep within me where they would germinate and sprout for me to deal with years later. But for now, I only knew that my legs were gone, and my first and foremost worry was rehabilitation so I could learn to walk again. And by 1968, rehabilitation had turned into a long and painful process. In addition, I had yet more school looming ahead of me. And although I knew it could never happen, I desperately wanted my old life back; I longed for the world to return to what it once had been. But I had to earn a living; I had to start a new life and a new career. I faced my future with great uncertainty and trepidation and with a low confidence level that needed rebuilding. I just couldn't think about the domestic turmoil in America in 1968. I was engulfed in my own deeply emotional problems.

Healing of the Body

I continued to make progress in my physical healing through the fall of 1967, past the Christmas and New Year holidays, and into 1968. The healing of my body required the physical mending of my legs so that I could wear prosthetic devices and be able to get around again without a wheelchair. My physical healing had progressed as well as expected and I was prepared to walk out of the hospital on my new legs. I attribute much of my recovery to the strong faith that my parents had instilled in me as a child, although I had fallen away from the intense faith I had felt during the first few weeks and months after my return from Vietnam. Slowly, I began once again to rely on God for my recuperation and ultimate physical healing.

For some time, I had been lifting weights twice a day at my bed to build up my arms. By October 1967, my stumps were sufficiently healed to enable me to get into my wheelchair and go to the rehabilitation room for an hour twice a day where I lifted weights on mats and performed exercises to strengthen my upper leg muscles. Therapists brought my first artificial legs to me in early October. They consisted of plaster casts that fit over my stumps with a one-and-one-half-inch-thick steel rod built in for stability that attached to the artificial foot in a shoe at the end of the leg. These legs attached to my body by means of elastic extending from the plaster casts over my stumps to a belt around my waist—not unlike a lady's garter belt!

Holding onto two parallel bars, I placed each of my stumps into a prosthesis and took my first steps on October 5. Once I placed my full body weight on my extremely sensitive stumps, excruciating pain raced through my legs, and I realized at that moment that learning to walk again would not be a quick or painless experience. It was very frightening. How could I walk on what seemed and felt like stilts? But I knew from the beginning that I could and would master it. I had to. One of my physical therapists, a female lieutenant, watched my first unsteady and awkward steps that day. She walked along beside me and cushioned my falls each time my legs gave way.

The next step in the recovery process required that I be fitted with very rough, unfinished and unpainted prostheses. The foot had an open area at the ankle so the therapist could readjust the pitch and set the tilt and height of the legs.

"How tall were you before you were wounded?" one of the therapists asked.

"Five feet nine inches. But, I've always wanted to be six feet two inches and tall and dark and handsome like my father."

"Well, Allen," he said, "unfortunately, we can't make you taller. If anything, you should be shorter because the shorter you are, the better you will walk."

That settled it. I would be five feet eight inches. However, always in the back of my mind I thought that I would eventually master those stilts, and if I ever got refitted with new legs later on, I could get taller ones and master those as well. In time, I might even make it to six-two!

Although I often saw men on the ward walking around on artificial wooden legs, I still couldn't believe that a person could keep his balance on them. However, I eventually learned that it was somewhat like riding a bicycle; I just had to learn how to balance on something new beneath me. In addition, I wondered if I would have any strength while standing on my new legs—if I would be able to carry anything, or if I could even lift a baby. I took my concerns and questions to a double amputee from World War II with twenty years of experience who had once visited our ward.

"I can pick up my brother who weighs 175 pounds," he answered sympathetically. "Does that answer your question?"

Surgery continued to slowly make small improvements in my legs. On October 23, doctors performed the Ertl operation, named for a German doctor who developed the procedure during World War I. They took a piece of rib and placed it across the bottom of my left leg for extra stability and created a flap of calfskin to pull over it. Two weeks later on November 9, doctors performed the same procedure on my right stump, using the remaining part of the rib that had been cut in half for the first operation. In addition to these two operations, I continued to experience severe pain caused by a bone spur in my right leg, which inhibited my ability to walk on my prosthesis. Doctors later whittled that away in another operation on Valentine's Day in 1968, resulting in a definite decrease in the pain.

My walking ability progressed slowly, day-by-day, step-by-step. No one gave me instructions nor told me the obstacles I would face. I was pretty much on my own. Each morning I set goals for myself for that day—goals such as walking across a particular room once, twice, and then three times. Steps and ramps proved to be extremely difficult at first, and taking slopes straight ahead proved virtually impossible. When I tried to walk down a ramp, I always tumbled forward. It would take me two years to learn to walk sideways down an incline. As my walking ability slowly progressed through those first few months, I managed to graduate from the metal crutches that fit around my wrists and forearms to two canes, and then to one. I thought that walking with a cane would be impossible, but I was mistaken. Each day I saw slow, but steady improvement.

What I did not realize at the time is that physical healing is also a miracle of God. In the days of the early church, Christians knew where healing came from. They witnessed the healing power of Christ while He walked the earth and continued to see those miracles in the years to come. However, the slow advances of civilization led man to look to himself for answers, and "the successes of science . . . have led to a decline in religious beliefs and given birth to a new humanism as man has looked to his own skills, rather than to God, to solve his problems" (Dearing: 185). Although Christians believe in Jesus' miracles of healing, there is a tremendous skepticism that the power to heal was transmitted to believers beyond the early church. From my military training, I know that authority is delegated to fulfill responsibilities entrusted to us. And I believe that Christ "delegated to His subordinates, the children of the kingdom, His unique and wonderful spiritual authority. He (has) done this by giving us the right to use His name as we obey His commission to preach the gospel, heal the sick, and cast out demons . . . Divine healing is ministered through a power which emanates from Jesus and by an authority vested in the use of His name" (Dearing: 88).

Today, I know that we can appropriate the gift of healing in the world. But we must first have the faith that James taught in 5:15: "And the prayer of faith shall save the sick." At this time in my life, I wasn't praying that prayer of faith. I was asking God for what I wanted. When we pray in faith, Matthew 21:22 tells us that whatsoever we ask in prayer, we will receive. But we first must have faith that God will answer within His will for us. This requires persistence and perseverance to PUSH (Pray Until Something Happens) through to receive an answer. We must begin with a will and a desire to be healed, and who among us does not desire that pain and suffering end?

I accepted that it was God's will that I be well, and I definitely wanted to be well. But sometimes it is self-condemnation that enters the picture and inhibits our healing process. Sometimes people are inhibited by diversions and distractions and, "Instead of praying with faith, instead of quietly trusting His promises, instead of reading God's Word and growing in strength, instead of committing their futures to His keeping—most lonely people watch TV, read junk magazines, and grow spiritually dull. Their faith is weak because they are spiritually crippled. They pray only in quick snatches. They wallow in self-pity and self-condemnation" (Wilkerson: 126). I believe that we constantly question whether we are good enough to merit healing, and that is where I found myself as I began to heal physically.

For the next twenty-five years of my life, I needed healing in other aspects of my life besides the physical—I also needed healing in my soul and spirit. I didn't know how even to begin to heal either emotionally or spiritually, though, and I would not learn until much later when I would intensely study the Scriptures and eventually teach others about healing. But even so, I still knew that I had deep emotional and spiritual scars that needed the Master's touch.

Healing of the Soul

In January 1968, I received an encouraging letter from Sandra Chilcoat, a Dallas resident who worked with Jackie's aunt. This letter looked back on the past—on the sacrifices made not only by the Vietnam soldiers, but also by American soldiers throughout history.

> I am a stranger to you, so you won't know me. Your aunt, Mrs. Bellah, works with me at Volk [department store], here in Dallas. It was through her that I first learned of you. I just wanted to write to you and say a great big "THANKS" for all that you have done for our country and the people all over the globe. To me, sir, you are much more than just a soldier who is doing his job—to me you are a hero, like one I read about in my history books. You are a brave man and a great man to have given of yourself to people who seem as ungrateful as we do. The work you have done is much more than just a job; it's a very worthy cause—your country's freedom and the freedom of all peoples.
>
> To know you would be a truly great honor. Brave men like yourself are what made this country what it is today—a place where all men may walk the streets and speak freely and without fear, a place where you can make of yourself whatever you wish.
>
> To me and many other freedom-loving citizens, you are a living symbol of what freedom and courage are all about. Thank you, sir, for the unselfish giving of yourself to keep all of us alive and free. As long as I live your memory will live on in my heart and my life. God bless you, sir, for a job well done.

Ms. Chilcoat's loving and kind words gave me courage then and continue to encourage me today. Her letter and others like it not only helped me begin an inner healing process, but it also captured the essence of why we fought in Vietnam. Its repetition of the words *free, freedom, freely,* and *freedom-loving* best sums up how I felt about my own sacrifice at the time—words that brought back the memory of a song that I had heard at a patriotic "Up with People" concert nearly two years earlier at Fort Hood and quoted at my Dallas going away party in July 1966.

> Freedom isn't free;
> You have to pay the price;
> You have to sacrifice
> For your liberty.

The beginning of the healing of the soul began when hospital therapists introduced patients to occupational therapy. This seemed a somewhat ironic term because none of us actually had an occupation anymore. Although mundane and sometimes tedious, I suppose this therapy was intended to both keep our minds occupied and to prove to us that we could still be useful and productive people. One of my first projects was to make a leather purse for Jackie. Occupational therapists brought all the necessary materials to my bed, and I worked steadily each day. Apprehensive at first because I never thought I was very good with my hands, I managed to produce what I believed to be a very nice purse.

After leather work came decoupage, a process that places pictures on wooden items, such as furniture or plaques, by covering the picture with a coat of a substance that serves to both glue it to the wood and dry into a smooth, clear finish, giving the appearance that the picture is blended into or painted on the wood. In my first efforts, I arranged pictures from the covers of old church programs that the chaplain had given me. I enjoyed this work much more than working with leather and began to turn out decoupage projects as if I were working on an assembly line.

One day a therapist approached my bed and said, "Captain Clark, we have a policy that you must change your occupational therapy from time to time. Decoupage is okay for a while, but we want you to move on to weaving or silverwork. You need the change."

"Decoupage is what I like to do and what I want to do," I responded defiantly, "and it is what I am going to do."

I obviously felt rebellious and defiant, but I had grown tired of the hospital boredom and tired of taking orders. The military system and discipline that I once thrived on began to irritate me. I guess that mentally I was already slowly becoming an independent civilian who spoke his own mind. It was a way to begin "spreading my wings." And, in spite of the warning, I kept turning out decoupage pictures.

To further spread my wings, I received and accepted an invitation to speak at a special patriotic ceremony at Bandera High School on George Washington's birthday in February. I welcomed the chance to go to Bandera, located just northwest of San Antonio in the beautiful Texas hill country. However, fresh from surgery and unable to walk on my prostheses, I had to return to my wheelchair for the trip. That small obstacle did not deter me, however. This would be my first public appearance in full uniform, and I welcomed the chance to represent my country once again. The people at Bandera gave me a warm reception and applauded my speech. Their extended applause caused my heart and my spirit to swell with pride.

Because of this positive reception, my host, a retired air force colonel, suggested that perhaps I should consider a career in politics. This seed of an idea implanted itself in my thoughts and began to germinate. The demons that had already instilled fear and anxiety within me now appealed to my pride and vanity—that same pride and vanity that entered the hearts of Adam and Eve so very long ago and brought sin and death into the world in the first place.

Two of my weakest traits have always been pride and ambition. Satan always attacks us at our weakest points, and I was not prepared for what would follow. In military terms, war was being waged on me by an attack on my strongholds—the things I could not surrender to God. These strongholds were obstacles that Satan purposely directed at me and were meant to keep me off balance and spiritually unhealthy. Author Liberty Savard said we all have such strongholds that provide access for the enemy's assaults and that protect wrong attitudes, beliefs, and patterns of thought we have learned to trust more than we trust the truth (*Shattering Your Strongholds:* 48). Christians have protection from such attacks, and it is outlined in Ephesians 6 as the full armor of God. This is a powerful military image. "In every battle you will need faith as your shield to stop the fiery arrows aimed at you by Satan" (Ephesians 6:16). I was not aware of this protection, so Satan was able to attack me with a vengeance at my weakest points.

The interruption of my progress with my prosthetics and struggle to walk again, constant agony and uncertainty for my future academic plans, and now this short-lived "acclaim" for my speech each presented a major roadblock in my life that resulted in many sleepless nights. Two days before the speech in Bandera, I went without sleep as I planned for my new post-army and post-hospitalization life. In addition, I had pushed all my feelings down to a place deep within me where I would not have to deal with them. Inevitably, they began to simmer and build until they finally rose to the surface and demanded attention. I did not even realize what was happening, and no one at the hospital had discerned my problem either. On February 24, just two days after the Bandera speech and a total of four days now without sleep, I cracked. Heavily sedated, I was transferred from the orthopedic ward to a closed psychiatric ward in another part of the Fort Sam Houston military post where individual and group therapy were the order of the day. Thus began what was a literal fourteen-week nightmare as I fought to deal with my demons and find my way back to the real world.

Originally, I was assigned to a huge room where perhaps forty of us lived and slept on metal army cots. Only prison could have been worse than this—the strictest environment in which I had ever been placed. What I had thought to be totally confining cadet life at West Point had been total freedom compared to this place, which offered only a highly structured existence that reminded us daily that we were still in the army. Reveille, lights on, lights off, occupational or group therapy, and mealtime each had its own specific time or schedule during the day.

While I was in the closed psychiatric ward two, classmates who were in law school at the University of Texas in Austin, Jim Armodiga and Ben Benjamin, came to visit me.

Ben Benjamin

I believe Jim got word of your wounds and arranged for us to go to San Antonio to visit you. Even though he was in law school, he was still in the army and had some contacts who kept him up to date. We didn't know what to expect, but we sat under a tree on the hospital grounds and talked. You were positive and resolved to go forward and to have a useful and productive life, which you surely have done. There was no "Woe is me" or any sign of a search for sympathy—only a desire to get well and to move ahead. No doubt those were very tough days, but you didn't show it. At that point in time, all three of us had been to Vietnam, and I'm sure I had a strong feeling of regret for your ordeal but also a question of whether I could have shown the courage and resolve you displayed that day—qualities that carried you far after that day.

Every type of imaginable patient populated the psychiatric ward—alcoholics released from active duty, new recruits who cracked under the pressure of basic training, combat-traumatized Vietnam veterans, "druggies" boarded out of the military, and just plain and simple nervous breakdown patients. While all of them had valid reasons to be there, I felt different and had difficulty relating to them. After all, I felt that my problem was vastly different than most. Yet amazingly, while I felt like an obvious oddity among all of them, I actually related to each of them in some basic way. And many of them began to discern that I had a reason to be there as well. Eventually, they began competing to push my wheelchair, whether to the mess hall or to different counseling and therapy sessions. Several patients were even genuinely concerned by my condition, feelings that elicited different emotions from each of them. In one group therapy session, a young man said something negative about me, bringing feelings of anger and hurt to the surface. As I wheeled from the room in an effort to get away, the group leader stopped me and used the situation as a teaching point for us all.

I began to slowly improve as the days and weeks wore on. The therapy team assigned a patient to me who apparently had washed out of basic training. A little "offbeat," he had had trouble submitting to the structure of the military and should probably never have been inducted in the first place. He had a truck that he parked in the lot outside, and, when I was well enough to leave the ward from time to time for orthopedic appointments or prosthetic fittings, he served as my chauffeur. We became good friends, and years later he came by my office to visit—still as offbeat and eccentric as ever.

Eventually, I moved to a five-man room as I continued my transition to the real world. But what was the "real" world? My real world had changed dramatically. What had once been real for me was no longer my reality. West Point, the army, and even Vietnam seemed so very long ago—almost as if they had occurred in a dream—or in some cases a nightmare—that had never actually happened. It all seemed so surreal now. So much had occurred in the intervening months and years that sometimes the memories seemed like only distant, cloudy images that floated dreamlike through my consciousness. Then, at other times, they were as vivid as if they had just occurred only hours before, and a flood of emotion would pour over me. Life in therapy became a virtual rollercoaster ride of emotion. As I worked through the daily sessions, it became necessary to reflect on the events that had brought me to this place. This time of personal trauma and turmoil in my personal life forced me to examine the truth about my real world of the present—my situation, as it now existed.

When something such as this happens to a person, no one knows how long it is going to last, how deep the scars will run, or for how long pills and therapy must continue. The final diagnosis upon discharge from the neuropsychiatry service after my treatment read thus: Paranoid state, chronic, moderate, in partial remission, manifested by episodes of delusional thinking, agitation, insomnia, and depression, severe external precipitating stress . . . no evidence of incapacitating emotional illness prior to entrance into service. This describes the classic onset of post-traumatic stress disorder (PTSD) and its cause.

In later years I worked in a medical center operated by the Veterans Affairs Department and learned much about PTSD, which has affected so many Vietnam veterans, and most likely many other war veterans even though it had not been identified in earlier wars. Even the problems that I suffered during my hospitalization would not be diagnosed or classified as PTSD until long after I had been discharged from the hospital when it would finally be more understood by the medical community. I had come a long way since the summer of 1967 when I saw a psychiatrist for the first time. I even balked at the idea because I considered therapy a sign of weakness. In reality, people who feel that way just don't understand the inner workings of the human psyche and how the events of our lives play such an important role on our minds. Although therapy proved to be a very painful experience, it became a necessary and integral part in the equation of ultimate healing of body, soul, and spirit. And, as I later learned, we cannot be effective soldiers for Christ until we are healed in all three areas, "for God did not give us a spirit of fear, but spirit of power, of love, and a sound mind" (II Timothy 1:7).

The time I spent in psychiatric treatment proved also to be a horrible time for Jackie and my family. They were fearful that I might never recover from such an emotional trauma. My failure to be strong and succeed and even overcome the loss of my legs without this emotional roadblock has always been a special source of regret for me. However, it is through my loving and supportive family and their consistent prayers that my recovery was slow but sure. Healing is often brought through the intercession of others when we are so ill that we can no longer pray. And it is by the grace of God that I have been healed from all elements of that episode and have gone thirty-four years without any further medication or psychiatric therapy.

This part of my life has always been a deep dark secret, which I have shared with only a few intimate friends. As a society we are seldom able to cope with, much less understand, this type of illness. Thirty-nine years later, we are more open and sensitive to this disorder, not only among war veterans, but also among all who experience extremely traumatic events such as the tragedy of September 11, 2001. Perhaps my experience will give hope to others who can heal from PTSD, emotional disorders, traumatic events, losses of all kinds, and even substance abuse. Because of my own healing, I was not only able to consider my future and focus on what I could do (not on what I could not do), but also look for ways that I could reach out to others to help them in their healing journeys. Perhaps this is the purpose of my experience after all. God often allows us to experience traumatic events in order to have a testimony and help others in similar circumstances. One who has already "been there" can better understand the suffering of others. That is why Christ, who took the pain and suffering of the entire world for all time during His three hours on the cross, understands our pain like no other.

The Beginning of the Healing of the Spirit

For some of us, it takes tremendous trials and trauma in life before we finally begin examining ourselves so we can try to sort out what life really means. This became such a time for me. As I completed treatment, and my soul began to heal along with my body, I also began to realize that it took being an embattled soldier—a wounded warrior—for me to fully understand the spiritual battle being waged on battle fronts daily all over the world to capture the hearts, minds, and souls of every individual. Spiritual "healing" can be a lifelong journey for most. I realize now that my own spiritual healing could not begin until my soul and body were healthy and whole.

My four years as a cadet included extensive studies of the wars of the world. We studied lessons from all the great battles and wars of history. I learned about the weapons of warfare in my military training, but it took other battlefields in future years for me to learn of the spiritual weapons available to me that are intended for spiritual warfare. I had no idea as a cadet or even as a young officer what the ultimate battle of all mankind was to be. I had no idea that Christ's coming the first time was really in a spiritual sense a part of the "war for the world" in which Christ would descend "into hell, (where he) totally and irrevocably defeated and disarmed Satan both legally and dynamically" (Billheimer: 71). However, the battle continues because God allows Satan to conduct guerrilla warfare or a "rear guard" action until Christ's second coming. We have a fierce enemy whose original force of one-third of the angelic host has proved a formidable opponent for God's people.

The Australian songwriter, Eric Bogle, captured the feelings of many wartime amputees in his song, "And the Band Played Waltzing

Matilda." Senator Bob Kerrey, also a Vietnam veteran and leg amputee, often quotes from its touching lines to which all disabled veterans can relate:

> So now every April I sit on my porch,
> And I watch the parade pass before me.
> I see my old comrades, how proudly they march,
> Reliving old dreams and past glories.
> And the old men march slowly, old bones still and sore;
> They're tired old heroes, of a forgotten war.
> And the young people ask, "What are they marching for?"
> And I ask myself the same question.

I never could just sit on the porch. I had to get into the parades of life, which some would term the games of life—possibly even the serious struggles or wars of our lives. There is no question in my mind but that the spring of 1968 constituted my introduction to the battles of life, not on faraway battlefields with bullets and shrapnel that can hurt one, but in the spiritual warfare realms of the soul and spirit. In future years, I learned much about this arena where we humans do battle, sometimes not knowing in what battle we are warriors. This was a battlefield totally alien to me. My preparation for physical battle on the battlefields of earth could never prepare me for this type of spiritual warfare, "A multilevel conflict between good and evil initiated on the supernatural plane with the prehistoric rebellion of Lucifer, and transferred onto the natural plane with the fall of man. Satan, man's adversary, continues to work to deceive and divert people from salvation in Jesus Christ, and to harass and hinder Christians through enticement to sin and exploitation of weaknesses" (White: 23).

I certainly had my weaknesses in the spring of 1968, and my adversary definitely exploited them. Depression and despondency had hit me dead center. I provided the target, and my adversary hit me hard right in the center of the bull's-eye. My thinking became tremendously distorted, and satanic forces worked within me. My paranoid state had moved me past the first level of demonic oppression to literal obsession. It was a serious attack, but I survived and hope my words may help others do likewise.

In his classic book *The Screwtape Letters,* author C. S. Lewis describes exactly what happened to me. In this story about spiritual warfare, the devil writes to his minion, Wormwood, who has a human assignment: "Did the patient respond to some of your terror pictures of the future? Did you work in some good self-pitying glances at the happy past?" (page 13). This defined my circumstances in a nutshell. I had been given "terror pictures of the future," I had been filled with self-pity because of the past, and I had become consumed with fear, anxiety, vanity, and pride. Remember, Paul's letter to young Timothy says that God does not give us a spirit of fear. That leaves only one place for its origin. A diabolical attack had driven me into psychiatric treatment, and I didn't have the weapons with which to fight it—weapons given all Christians with which they can counter such attacks. I didn't understand any of this while lying in the hospital, but I learned later to put on the full armor of God each day for my protection, which included the shield of faith that Paul writes about in Ephesians 6:16.

I must make it clear, however, that I do not ascribe to demonic involvement all that ails or afflicts or torments us or that divine healing is always God's will. Our bodies realistically get worn out from age, abuse, disease, accidents, genetic defects, or the consequences of wrong choices. However, only divine healing from God can fully restore, and we have the freedom and faith to ask for it. God *can* work miracles if we ask. But it is His choice, not ours, if He *will.*

I am reminded of a line from the 1970s *The Flip Wilson Show* when comedian Flip Wilson would quip, "The devil made me do it," whenever he did something wrong. There is great truth in this in that it is possible that the devil can make us do things, but if we follow God's rules, pray, and seek His will, we can do battle with these unseen forces of evil that inhabit our world. The fact is that man lives constantly torn between two worlds, the world of our Creator and the world of sin controlled by the devil.

As I proceeded through both physical and psychiatric therapy, mental tapes of sadness and pain played through my mind every day—tapes of that fateful day at Dak To when my life took such a tragic turn. But I did not have the luxury, or even the possibility, of rewinding and rerecording those events for a different outcome. My physical recovery proceeded very well, but I would never have any possible means of knowing how many hurdles would still face me in my future, many in their own way rivaling that of my battlefield wounds. However, I had to look forward. I could not live in the past. I had to begin the long years of mental, emotional, and spiritual recovery and healing.

My challenge as I recovered from the baggage of war and wounds was to remove myself from evil influences and pray in Jesus' name for the powers arrayed against me to be broken and for healing in all situations. And, although the war in Vietnam was over for me, spiritual warfare would not end until my time on earth is over. To remain healthy in body, soul, and spirit, I had to put on the full armor of God and prepare myself for a new battle. Total healing had only just begun.

CHAPTER 9

REBUILDING A LIFE ON EARTH FOR ETERNITY

Dallas, Texas
1968–1973

In January 1968, I received a letter from Major General John Kelly, for whom I had worked as an aide at Fort Hood, that gave me hope and encouragement regarding my future. My physical healing was still progressing well, my emotional and spiritual healing had begun, and now I needed to look to the future and what I would do with the rest of my life. The possibilities for me seemed unclear, but General Kelly's letter assured me that at least there were possibilities out there.

> Allen,
>
> I was at a cocktail party in Washington, and I chatted with a gentleman who is very active with the Disabled American Veterans. The DAV is aware of a program that Johnson & Johnson Pharmaceutical Company in New Brunswick, New Jersey, has for hiring, training, rehabilitating, and working with disabled veterans. So, I am going to put this gentleman in contact with you.

I immediately forwarded a copy of my resume to William McCord, then director of corporate management development for Johnson & Johnson. Mr. McCord made a special trip from New Brunswick to San Antonio to visit with me.

"You wrote a very impressive resume," McCord told me. "You laid it all on the line—what you can do and what you think you can't do. We want someone who has served his country like you have; we want someone with a background like yours. If you want to get a graduate degree in night school, fine. If you want to go to graduate school first, that's okay, too. Either way, we want to hire you, and we'll find a place for you in our company. Our offer is open-ended as far as you're concerned."

This "no strings attached" offer to me, a disabled veteran, served as a tremendous confidence builder. However, ever since returning to the hospital, I had made plans to attend law school. Only a few weeks earlier, I had traveled to Austin to visit attorney Joe Kilgore, my parents' friend and former congressman. He related the wartime service disabilities he lived with each day. Kilgore spent an hour talking to me about my interest in law school and told me he would help me in any way he could. I decided to put the Johnson & Johnson offer on the back burner while I applied for admission to the law schools at the University of Texas, SMU, and Harvard. However, my education plans had to be put on hold as I faced the toughest challenge yet, recovering confidence after my psychiatric problem.

Sprouting Wings

The father of my Exeter friend John Gepson lived in Boston and had good contacts at Harvard. Shortly after my application there, Mr. Gepson wrote to me to say that I probably would not get admitted to Harvard Law School because my admission test scores weren't high enough. After graduating in the top 10 percent in my class at West Point, that news was a huge blow to my proud ego. I had taken the test at St. Mary's University in San Antonio while in psychiatric treatment and under a great deal of stress and pressure because of the circumstances. In addition, I had had little time to prepare. I had to swallow my pride and admit the fact that I simply had not done well on the test.

On the advice of John's father, I withdrew my application to Harvard but received acceptance notices from both the University of Texas at Austin and SMU in Dallas. When the time came to actually make a decision, I just could not face law school. I suddenly felt burned out. After the strenuous rigors of West Point, vigorous military training and service in the army, I didn't want to face another three years of demanding law school curriculum at the age of twenty-six. I just wanted to get on with my life. Therefore, I decided instead to enroll in the masters program of business administration at SMU, which would take only three semesters instead of three years to complete. In addition, this schedule would give me more free time during classes. The prospect of going back to school didn't thrill me, but it was something I had to do— one more step in the long journey to recovery and restoring my life back to normal.

It was during this time that the West Point Society of North Texas decided to make me a life member. Norry Longaker and his wife, Cele, made the three-hundred-mile trip from Dallas to present me with the membership plaque at the hospital, something that really boosted my morale. I could always count on my West Point friends to come through when I needed them most—friends like Tom McNiel (class of 1945), who had spent many long hours teaching me how to cope in the civilian world—a world I would have to face very soon and one I had never really known.

The proverbial "lazy, hazy days of summer" best describe the summer of 1968. That's exactly how I felt as I relaxed, got accustomed to my new legs, and slowly eased into a routine of gradual preparation for a return to civilian life. In late August, I walked away from Brooke Army Medical Center for good. Then in September, as I left my beloved army through medical disability retirement, I carried with me the final "recommended findings of physical evaluation board," which deemed me "medically unfit" for further military service. The findings further recommended that I obtain a psychiatrist for continued individual psychotherapy. So, very grudgingly, I attended individual psychotherapy during the two years of graduate school that followed and took an antidepressant and sleeping pills intermittently—but everything else was looking up!

Graduate School

A new sense of optimism and hope arrived in the fall of 1968. Finally discharged from the hospital, I moved to Dallas with Jackie into a small wood-frame house on Goodwin Avenue near the SMU campus. There we resumed our married life and began our new careers: she as a math teacher at Stockard Junior High School and I as a graduate student at SMU. Although located in the hot Texas climate, the SMU campus somehow reminded me of those gorgeous cool autumn days at West Point where I had enjoyed campus life and a disciplined academic routine. After fifteen months of hospitalization and numerous surgeries, I finally had new goals for my life toward which I looked with eager anticipation. Jackie and I had finally begun a new and wonderful journey back to a normal life together. My hopes and my spirits soared.

In March of that year, several months before I left the hospital, Jackie and I had purchased a new gold Chevrolet with an automatic transmission and newly installed hand controls so I could drive once again. I felt as if I were sixteen years old as I slid behind the wheel of a car for the first time in well over a year. It didn't take me long to master the instruments that controlled the horn, brake, accelerator, and headlight dimmer switch. Although it would be a while before I felt comfortable driving with my hands, I had it mastered by the time we moved to Dallas six months later. Being able to drive again helped me regain a sense of independence that I had lost during those long months of hospital confinement.

Attending school as a twenty-six-year-old veteran made me self-conscious at best. Not only was I older than everyone else, but I also had to get around the business school on two canes that made me stand out as different. I did manage to secure a permit to park in the disabled parking area next to the business school as well as a key to the elevator so I would not have to tackle the long flights of stairs. That made the daily physical routine much easier for me. As that first semester gradually progressed from days into weeks, my confidence began to slowly return. During that first semester, I took only two morning classes; however, after realizing that I could manage school well, I signed up for four courses the second semester. By the end of the first year of graduate school, my old self-confidence had returned, and I dared to go out and secure a summer job with Schneider, Bernet, and Hickman, a regional brokerage house in Dallas.

That same summer, retired army brigadier general John Torrey Jr. (West Point 1936), whom I had met at Fort Hood in 1965, and John Plath Green invited me to head a special subcommittee that would encourage schools to recognize state and national holidays in a more patriotic manner. The subcommittee worked with schools to sponsor essay and poster contests. The winners' essays appeared in the newspaper, and each winner received a U.S. savings bond. Each of the then two major Dallas newspapers provided writers William Murchison and Bronson Havard to help us obtain publicity. In addition to working on the subcommittee that summer, I recruited high school students interested in West Point by attending college nights at Dallas area high schools. The committee I developed for the West Point Society at North Texas also became the prototype for the Texas A&M recruiting committee when I served on the development council of the Corps of Cadets in the 1980s, upon the recommendation of Davis Ford of Austin, president of the former students association.

During the fall of our two years at SMU, Jackie and I attended the SMU home football games at the Cotton Bowl on a special pass. We parked very close to the stadium and walked from the car to our seats. It proved to be an excellent way for me to test my new legs and provided me with a real source of satisfaction when I actually managed to make it without incident. However, it was during one of those football games that I first experienced what is known as phantom pains. It felt as if someone were sticking needles in my toes, the tops of my feet, my ankles, and calves—parts of my body that were no longer there. Although surgeons had cut the nerves in my legs and closed them underneath the stumps, the brain didn't know that the legs were gone and continued to send and receive signals from the nerves going to the legs as if they were still there. Therefore, I continued to feel pain in the parts of my legs that were missing. The pain often became excruciating, and I continue to have it to this day, although with less frequency

During this period of my life, I also experienced recurring dreams in which I still had my legs. In one dream, I could do things that required extraordinary physical ability. In another, I had a flat tire on my car and had to walk a long distance to a service station. That dream was more like a nightmare, because since I lost my legs and learned to drive again, I've always worried about having a blowout on a remote highway where I could not get help. Fortunately, I've never had car trouble of any kind on the road. The only flat tire I had occurred only two blocks from my house. Fortunately, I was able to contact Gene Smith, an SMU classmate, who immediately came to my rescue.

I completed graduate school in June 1970, and Jackie and I flew to Hawaii for a much-deserved three-week vacation. We stayed at the Reef Hotel next door to Fort DeRussey, the military R and R center in Honolulu. While attending the show of famous Hawaiian entertainer Don Ho, we observed a number of American soldiers there on leave from Vietnam. It became evident that the show had been especially designed just for them. An ugly war had become an integral part of the tourist business in Honolulu—an ironic twist in a world full of irony and mystery.

For Jackie and me, the trip to Hawaii was very special because, unlike the reunited couples all around us, we had not been able to meet at any time during my tour of Vietnam. While there, we sailed along the shore in a sailboat belonging to classmate Gordy Waugh and enjoyed the peace, beauty, and tranquility of that wonderful tropical paradise as well as each other. This trip was our R and R together—the trip nearly three years overdue—and we carried memories of it with us for many years.

After returning to Dallas, I began a job with Ross Perot's Electronic Data Systems, a company with a good history of hiring military veterans. Four people, including Perot himself, interviewed me for the job.

"What would you like to do in my company?" Perot asked.

"I think I want to be a financial analyst," I answered.

We talked about that job among many other things such as West Point, the Green Berets, and the naval academy, from which

Perot had graduated. As we talked, I could not help but notice a large carved eagle that commanded one wall of Perot's spacious office. Underneath, a printed caption stood out: "Eagles don't flock. You have to gather them one at a time." I often thought about that quote and its meaning during the ensuing years.

Eventually, Tom Marquez made me an offer to work for EDS. Perot hired me to serve as his financial assistant and initially made me responsible for his stock portfolio. He set up a one-year training program in which I would learn to sharpen my skills in stocks, bonds, short-term money market instruments, real estate, tax shelters, taxation, investment banking, and special investments. He gave me an office just two doors down from his own and next to his private secretary. Each day I scoured the *Wall Street Journal* for articles I felt he should see and worked on an analysis of his stock portfolio and real estate investments. Perot called me into his office to discuss financial matters two or three times a day.

My military and civilian psychiatrists had told me my condition would be precariously fragile for several years and I was to avoid stressful situations and jobs until I healed. However, being hardheaded, stubborn, and obstinate and overwhelmed by the opportunity to work for a business luminary such as Ross Perot, I foolishly ignored that medical advice and thrust myself into a pressure-filled job in a pressure-filled small but growing company where life became a pressure cooker for a guy still healing from wartime trauma and hospitalization ordeals.

During the summer of 1970, Perot sent me to New York City on a day's notice. I was to assist in the audit of the Francis I. DuPont investment banking and brokerage firm, Dupont Glore Forgan, which Perot planned to buy. During the eleven days I spent in New York City on the team working on Perot's eventual purchase of this firm, I pushed myself into all hours of the night every day and started again to go without sleep. When I finished my assignments for Perot and started back to Dallas by plane, I found myself becoming extremely disoriented. Jackie had been talking to me from Dallas every day, and she could tell that I was slipping emotionally. She met my plane in Dallas accompanied by my psychiatrist who gave me a sedative and returned me to the hospital for a week of rest and therapy. Then he called Perot and told him what had happened. Perot was very understanding and kept me on the payroll for six weeks, after which I returned to EDS for my exit interview. I told him that I just could not work in such a high-pressure job at this time in my life.

"I understand, Allen," Perot said. "Some people can, and some people can't dedicate themselves to a high-powered corporate existence. Your job will be here a year from now, or a year-and-a-half from now if you want it back. For now, where would you like to work?"

"I would like to interview with Republic National Bank's trust department."

"I'll do what I can down there," he answered.

Perot kept true to his word. He spent an hour talking with Edmund Mennis in the trust investments department at Republic. In addition, Tom McNeil, my ever-faithful West Point friend, worked behind the scenes to help me get the job. Their work for me paid off when the bank eventually hired me into a job that didn't carry as much stress or demand such a hectic pace as did EDS. Life finally began to slow down, and I settled into a well-ordered routine balanced between work and family. The position at Republic Bank eventually led to the position of chartered financial analyst, which lasted eight years as I helped people preserve and build their investment assets.

Living with Embarrassing Moments

My life since the amputations hasn't been without its moments of embarrassment and humiliation and sometimes even humor. And, even though I know that children possess a natural and honest curiosity, it took me a very long time to get used to them staring at me when I swam in public swimming pools without my legs. However, it is much easier to accept the innocent curious stares of children than the overt, insensitive comments of adults. There have been times when I've been both angry with narrow-minded people who don't seem even to try to understand the problems of the disabled and grateful to those who do. Once, while attending a

Dallas Cowboys football game at Texas Stadium, my legs began to hurt so badly that I took off my prostheses and put them underneath my seat. A man sitting next to me reached down for his soft drink and noticed my legs lying there.

"With fifty thousand people in this stadium," he remarked to his wife in a tone loud enough for me to hear, "we have to sit next to this guy."

Later during the game, he exchanged seats with his wife and then joked about her sitting next to "the guy with his legs off." Of course, it bothered me, but I've learned to live with comments from people like him over the years. After a while, I even grew to expect it.

Another evening Jackie and I went to the Carswell Air Force Base Officers' Club in Fort Worth with some of her high school friends. Watching the others inspired me to dance—something I had not yet tried on my new legs. When I lost my balance during the fast-step jitterbug, Jackie reached out to stop my fall, but I only pulled her down with me. There we lay, flat on the floor—not drunk, just flat, in spite of what others may have thought. Two friends helped us up, and we continued to dance the evening away. This glorious experience helped me realize that I could do most of the things I had done before, but perhaps with not as much finesse!

I continued to have embarrassing moments with my legs long after I got used to them and long after I left SMU. Years later I took a trip to Chicago for a mini-reunion with several West Point classmates. When they decided to go for an outing of golf, I volunteered to drive the golf cart and went along for the ride. As we approached hole number three, Steve Best asked me why I didn't try to play.

"Well, I've tried it a few times, but never seemed to do well," I replied.

Homer Holland, who had graduated first in our class, used some clever psychology on me and convinced me to try. So, even though I wore slick-soled street shoes, I picked up Steve's club and took a swing. Both of my legs popped off and flew five feet across the fairway. I'm not one to accept defeat easily, so I got up, put my legs back on, and tried again. I managed to get on the green in five strokes. Not bad. On number four, it took me six strokes, and on number five I fell again and hurt my knee. That evening my friends, led by our class golf captain, John Woods, presented me with a trophy for the golfer with the "highest handicap." Their amiable good humor made all the day's difficulties worthwhile.

My embarrassing moments continued to occur in front of scores, and sometimes hundreds, of people in very public places. During President Carter's term in office at a "peanut stomp" at a Republican state convention in Houston, I started across the dance floor toward the refreshment table when I slipped and one leg came off and sailed across the floor like a low-flying missile. Several good people also came to my rescue that evening. After a few moments, I got my leg back on and continued my journey to the line at the refreshment table.

"Are you ready to dance again?" Cathy Smyth, a long-time Dallas friend asked good-naturedly.

"I sure am," I replied.

Although I have learned to live with the insensitive remarks of ignorant people, I am also so very grateful for those who understand disabilities and tend to make people comfortable with them—people like my golfing buddies and Cathy Smyth. Not long after moving to Dallas, Jackie and I developed a good friendship with Doug and Ginger Simmons. Ginger taught school with Jackie, and Doug had served in the navy with service in Vietnam. We had a lot in common and hit it off right away; they still remain two of my dearest friends. Their true friendship was put to the test early on, however, when they dropped by our house unexpectedly one evening. Normally, I came home from school each day and removed my prostheses to rest my legs and used my wheelchair for the rest of the day. I had never allowed any of our friends to see me without my legs because I didn't want to place them in an awkward or embarrassing situation.

However, on that evening when Doug and Ginger dropped by, they found me sitting on the sofa with my ugly stumps protruding through the legs of my Bermuda shorts. Self-conscious and embarrassed, I feared their reaction when they saw my legs. After all, my stumps always seemed ugly and grotesque to me, so I thought they must appear the same to other people as well. To my surprise, Doug and Ginger had no reaction whatsoever. They acted the way they always had when we were together. That evening with Doug and Ginger, and many other evenings afterward, helped relieve my self-consciousness about my legs. I am eternally grateful to them and others like them for their understanding and unconditional friendship.

And the War Goes On

The Vietnam War continued to lay heavy on my mind throughout 1969 and 1970 during my graduate school program. I guess it wasn't unusual for me to want my sacrifice to count for something, but nothing seemed to change. As the war raged on, the battles became bigger and more severe and men, women, and children continued to die. In Asia U.S. forces moved into Cambodia. At home student protestors were shot and killed at Kent State University in Ohio. SMU students placed crosses in front of the main building on campus to call attention to those who had died in protest of the war. I just went to class and tried to ignore the unrest around me as best I could. I continued to push down those seeds of resentment and bitterness toward those who opposed the war.

In 1969, a counselor at Bishop Lynch High School in Dallas asked me to speak to a class during Brotherhood Week. I talked to the class about Vietnam and showed them slides taken during my tour of duty there. However, I did not tell them that I had resented the fact that President Johnson had not allowed us to aggressively move into North Vietnam earlier when the public was more support-ive of the war. Perhaps it might have ended then. Now it had become a no-win situation, and we weren't even doing all we could to get out. By this time, the administration had begun troop withdrawals based on a specific timetable rather than need.

When I mentioned the timetable for troop withdrawals, a young boy raised his hand and asked, "Sir, is a timetable worth dying for?"

"No," I answered. "A timetable is not worth dying for. Do you recall those little children in the mountains that I showed you a moment ago? Those children are worth dying for."

The room grew quiet.

"You handled those kids perfectly," the counselor told me afterward, and I wondered if he really understood.

In the midst of all the protests and negative publicity, these high school students who were supposed to be learning about our own history and how this country came about through war and revolution had no idea that we were fighting for the freedom of an oppressed people—a people not unlike ourselves in a situation not unlike our own some two hundred years ago.

Operation Cherry Comes Back to Haunt Me

There was no shaking the war. I dreamed about it and thought it through a thousand times. One morning during spring 1970, the war hit home especially hard. I picked up a copy of the *New York Times;* it reported that the Khmer Serei had been used on covert missions in Cambodia in 1967. This was according to testimony at the trial of a Green Beret captain convicted in 1968 of killing one member of the sect. The Khmer Serei, the article said, were Cambodians dedicated to the overthrow of the "legitimate" government of that country. Sworn testimony by witnesses and the defendant, Captain John J. McCarthy Jr., revealed that Detachment B-57, 5th Special Forces Group, used Khmer Serei during project Operation Cherry outside South Vietnam.

I searched my files and found a February 1968 Associated Press clipping that my father had sent me. It reported that McCarthy, twenty-five, of Phoenix, Arizona, had been sentenced to life in prison for the murder of Inchin Hai Lam, a Vietnamese national. Scribbled across the top of the newspaper clipping were the words, "Did you know him?" I did not know Captain McCarthy, but I certainly knew Lam, the small, frail Cambodian spy whom had presumably grown up in the court of Prince Sihanouk and who I had interviewed extensively in 1966. The original 1968 article said that Lam had died on November 24, 1967, and that much of the testimony at the trial in Long Binh, South Vietnam, had been taken in closed sessions for what the army cited as "security reasons." The prosecution and defense agreed, however, that McCarthy had been present in the car in which Lam had died, and that the captain's weapon, a .38-caliber pistol, had been fired. (Frank Lennon, who had been a debate partner at West Point, was later in B-57 and told me personally once that McCarthy borrowed his .38-caliber pistol on the day of Lam's murder.) Small world!

A non-commissioned officer who had served in McCarthy's Saigon-based detachment testified for the army. He stated that McCarthy awakened him early on November 23 and told him that Lam knew too much. He had to die. According to the article, another non-commissioned officer confessed to driving the car that carried Lam and McCarthy into the country, about ten miles outside of Saigon, where Lam was killed. Together, they tossed Lam's body into a ditch near Ho Ngoc Tau, another Green Beret camp where I first heard of the B-57 mission of espionage in Cambodia.

I remembered having my own questions about Lam and his eagerness to join our cause. I also remembered being hesitant to use him as an agent because we did not know enough about him. The *New York Times* reported that defense lawyers still maintained three years later in 1970, as did military counsel at the time of the trial, that the Khmer Serei wanted to kill Lam because they believed him to be a Soviet spy working for the Cambodian government. That would make sense since he had trained at Patrice Lumumba University in Moscow as he had candidly told me.

An August 1969 *New York Times* article quoted "reliable sources" as saying that more than 150 double agents had been caught and executed by allied forces in South Vietnam. A later 1970 article quoted State Department sources as saying the United States never had anything to do with the Khmer Serei except to hire Cambodians living in South Vietnam who were members of the group. That was a double-sided statement that could mean just about anything.

Obviously, I knew as much, if not more, about Inchin Hai Lam and Operation Cherry than possibly anyone else in the free world. The world of intelligence gathering is indeed shadowy. As intelligence operatives, we always mistrusted our agents because of the possibility that they might be working for the enemy. This possibility obviously placed all our lives in jeopardy every day.

I did not know if the information I had obtained from Lam four years earlier would affect the case or not, but I wanted to talk to someone about it. I called my father in El Paso for advice. Four hours later I received a call from McCarthy's defense attorney, a young army lieutenant from Washington, D.C., who flew to Dallas the next evening and interviewed me at my home.

"Some of what you've told me is new information," he said. "It will be helpful."

On October 29, 1970, three judges of the army Court of Military Review set aside McCarthy's murder conviction. The court indicated that the key factor in its decision was a statement by the examining medical officer that he may have been mistaken in his testimony at the original trial. The army was given the option of ordering a new trial, but they did not.

Although McCarthy had no comment, the *Norfolk Virginian Pilot* later quoted McCarthy as saying that he had taken part in a secret mission (Operation Cherry) designed to aid in the overthrow of Cambodia's Prince Sihanouk. By this time, Sihanouk had been ousted by a Cambodian army coup in March 1970, about a month before American and South Vietnamese troops entered the country to hit communist supply bases. According to the Norfolk paper, McCarthy said that the clandestine operation was directed from South Vietnam by the Central Intelligence Agency. The Associated Press, which transmitted the *Virginian Pilot* story, said that the Pentagon denied any knowledge of Operation Cherry. Contacted at his new post at Fort Huachuca, Arizona, McCarthy refused to elaborate on the newspaper article. The paper, however, quoted McCarthy as saying he was leaving the army because the government had suppressed defense evidence at his trial.

"I have come to the conclusion," he said, "that loyalty, silence, and faith are to no avail."

Officials apparently found sufficient evidence to convict McCarthy of Lam's murder. Any killing is highly unfair, whether in war or otherwise. In war we are forced to make hard choices, which many times lead to a blind following of orders, resulting in situations such as this. When things go wrong, higher officials sometimes back off the unfortunate consequences of certain actions coming to light, and the lesser officers and enlisted men must bear the brunt of it all.

Because I had formed Operation Cherry, I could have been in McCarthy's shoes on the date Lam was murdered. I have to be candid, however. I could not have killed another person in cold blood. Had I been ordered to kill him, as McCarthy possibly was, I would have refused the order and suffered the consequences myself—whatever that would have meant.

The memoirs of Prince Norodom Sihanouk were published as *My War with the CIA* in 1972. Prince Sihanouk learned all about Operation Cherry and the murder case through trial testimony printed in U.S. newspapers. He argued in his book that this was but one of many attempts by the CIA to undermine and overthrow him (page 67). One interesting sidelight to this story is that Prince Sihanouk never mentioned in his book that Inchin Hai Lam grew up on his palace grounds and had been his son's childhood friend and possibly even his son. The enemy could have planted Lam as a spy from the very beginning, and it could have been that Detachment B-57 learned of his true reason for helping them out.

The horrors of war sometimes necessitate drastic actions in order to accomplish the common goals of allied nations and their security. In defense of using indigenous agents as intelligence operatives, Shelby Stanton wrote, "By early 1969 . . . detachment B 57 Project GAMMA had developed into the finest and most productive intelligence collection operation the United States had in Southeast Asia. Much of the success resulted from the fact that its indigenous agents served an intelligence gathering network that operated without South Vietnamese awareness" (Stanton: 211–12). I partially planted the early roots of the formation of B-57 and its ability to eventually be successful, although by the time I was wounded, I had seen very little fruit of my efforts. Reading this caused me to be proud.

My old unit B-57 became quite controversial in 1969 when another double agent murder case made headlines. *A Murder in Wartime,* a book by Jeff Stein published in 1992, told me much about the overall picture for B-57 to which I had not been necessarily privy at my low-level agent handler level. Our mission was Project Gamma.

Our unit was evolving in 1966 as I was assigned to it. Stein described it in 1968 as "buried deep inside the headquarters of 5th Special Forces Group in Nha Trang. In South Vietnam U.S.-only or 'unilateral' intelligence operations were routine in any allied country. But in South Vietnam they were mandatory only because the Saigon Intelligence Services had become riddled with Communist spies" (Stein: 43).

Obviously the mission of the B-57 was significantly broadened after my "reassignment."

"One of Gamma's principal missions was to confirm or elaborate on photos taken by U.S. satellites and U-2 spy planes streaking over Cambodia; its spies were given miniature cameras to photograph supply trains running north from the Cambodian port of Sihanoukville. But agents were also dispatched to put wiretaps on telephone lines to gather evidence of collaboration between supposedly neutral Cambodian officials and the North Vietnamese" (Stein: 44).

The 5th Group commander in 1969 was Colonel Robert Rheault, who had attended both my schools, Phillips Exeter Academy and West Point. The group had become a semi-autonomous U.S. Army unit that was spread all over Vietnam, with many special units conducting reconnaissance on the Ho Chi Minh Trail, grabbing NVA and allied country officers for secret interrogations (Stein: 58).

Special Forces, which had always been viewed with distrust by the regular army, became even more suspect due to its close ties with the Central Intelligence Agency. Project Gamma (through the B-57 agents) had become very successful in penetration of Cambodia through wiretaps and photographs, providing strong evidence to the complicity of Royal Cambodian army officers with the NVA (Stein: 73).

Eventually, several officers and men in B-57 were implicated in the murder of another B-57 agent by the name of Thai Khac Chuyen. The question always loomed for us in covert intelligence,

Who could we trust? This case brought down Colonel Rheault and B-57.

Stein's investigative reporting developed that "Detachment B-57 provided administrative cover for other intelligence units. One was Project Cherry, tasked to assassinate Cambodian officials suspected of collaborating with the North Vietnamese, and in some cases, the Soviet KGB" (Stein: 361).

My original Operation Cherry had transformed from dropping off young Cambodian Khmer Serei members in impenetrable jungle!

Grim Reminders

In the fall of 1970, I received a phone call from the Pentagon. The voice at the other end asked me where I would like my Silver Star presented. The award ceremony for that medal of valor, the third highest decoration the army can bestow on a soldier, offers a small picture of just how the army operates.

Captain Larry Gossett had recommended me for an award for gallantry shortly after I was wounded at Dak To three years earlier. In the interim, I had received a Bronze Star for Achievement, a Purple Heart, a Combat Infantryman's Badge, the Air Medal, and the Vietnam Service Medal with two battle stars. I had never pursued the issue for the higher award because I thought Captain Gossett's paperwork had been destroyed in a mortar attack at Kontum. My official discharge paper, a DD214, indicated an award of a Bronze Star for Valor, but I never wore it; I assumed it was an error because I had no award orders.

Dad, however, related the story to his boss, a colonel in the judge advocate general's office in El Paso. The colonel later transferred to Fort Bragg, North Carolina, where he just happened to move next door to Colonel Francis J. Kelly, who had commanded the Special Forces in Vietnam during my tour of duty. During their conversations with each other, Kelly learned that I had been nominated for an award, and he brought it to the attention of the new Green Beret commander in Vietnam, Colonel Ernest Ladd, who proceeded to initiate the proper paperwork. It was only through this bizarre series of circumstances that I received the Silver Star at all.

Brigadier General Harold Parfitt, a West Point graduate and division engineer of the southwestern division of the army Corps of Engineers in Dallas, presented the medal to me in his office in Dallas in the presence of my dear friends Tom McNiel and Norry Longaker. (General Parfitt's daughter, Karen Parfitt Hughes, became an adviser to President George W. Bush in 2001, and in his second administration, an undersecretary of state). To my deep regret, Jackie did not attend the ceremony. She still stood firm in her belief that medals could never equal the sacrifices of the men who fought in Vietnam or anywhere, for that matter. The combination of Jackie's absence and the familiar words spoken at medal ceremonies dredged up all the old memories of my early dedication to the military, the personal conflict over military life in our early marriage, and the horrible memories of the amputee ward in San Antonio. Unlike the physical scars, the deep emotional scars caused by the war had not healed—scars that my family had to bear as well.

Jackie Clark

During Allen's recuperation, I tried to stay upbeat and do what needed to be done each day. I would not allow myself to get down because I felt the happier and better adjusted I was, the happier Allen would be. Just before the medal ceremony, I had a delayed case of depression, and I did not think anything—any medal, not even a medal for valor—would ever make the war worthwhile for me.

Medals and awards like that have never meant a whole lot to me because I have never really been around them. Later, knowing how much it meant to Allen, I wish I had gone to the ceremony. I should have gone, but Vietnam had caused me so much mental anguish that I wanted to live in the present, work for the future, and forget the painful past.

All my life I had strived for perfection—for self-worth, for proof of my manhood, proof of my courage, and for some great intangible something inside all of us to reach satisfaction. On June 8, 1960, at West Point graduation exercises, the army chief of staff, General Lyman L. Lemnitzer, spoke these words:

When a man's heart sinks into the pit of his stomach with fear, and all men experience fear; when the supporting air strike or artillery barrage, which you counted on, and was such an important function in carrying out your plans, fails to materialize; when ammunition does not come through as scheduled; when there are no rations; when the enemy is beating the living daylights out of you; then you will need one other quality, and unless you have it, you will still not be a good leader.

That quality is self-sacrifice, and as far as you are concerned, it means simply this; that you will put duty, honor, and the interests of your country first. Next, you will put the safety, well-being and security of the men you lead . . . and last all of the time, you will put your own interests, your own safety and your own comfort. Then and only then, will you be a good officer. (Lemnitzer: 20)

Through it all, I had been true to my upbringing, training, dedication, and discipline. My Silver Star citation indicates that I asked that the other wounded be treated before me. When that Silver Star was pinned on me, I felt as I forced the tears away, that I finally was that "good officer." In a way, the Silver Star brought closure to my participation in Vietnam, a culmination of the long journey begun at age eight with the desire to be a soldier. Although my military career evolved at a time when the Korean War was so real to me, perhaps it was really just a way to play childhood war games. But the boy once desiring to play soldier had, by definition, become the soldier I had always dreamed of becoming.

Fatherhood

While still at Pleiku Hospital in South Vietnam in June 1967, I impatiently waited one afternoon for a nurse to give me another shot for pain as I suffered through one of my recurring pain cycles. As I lay there in agony, a tall, thin, bespectacled army chaplain approached my bed. A white sheet and blanket covered me. At that point, I had not checked out my body yet, but only heard what the doctors told me about my wounds, so I had a few unanswered questions.

"Chaplain, would you raise the sheets and tell me if I can still have a baby?"

Without raising an eyebrow or batting an eye, the young chaplain lifted the sheet, took a look, and responded calmly, "You're okay, Captain," and then replaced the sheet.

Although Jackie and I had no children then, we often dreamed of the family we would have together someday. A flood of relief ran through me when I knew that, apparently, I could still sire children. My doctors and that young chaplain had not steered me wrong. In fact, they were proved right on July 9, 1971, when, after a long labor, Jackie gave birth to our first child, a beautiful redheaded daughter whom we named Sharon Elizabeth. I was so grateful that my wounds did not preclude the joys of fatherhood. Jackie and I truly felt that Sharon Elizabeth was a gift from God, who saw fit to bless us again three years later with our second daughter, Christina Adell, born on July 16, 1974.

I enjoyed fatherhood tremendously, and Jackie was at her best as a mother—warm, kind, sweet, and patient. It has been a blessing to watch the girls grow through their various stages of life. If I have any regret at all, it is that I didn't give them both more of my time. They were small at a time when I was gone from home much of the time trying to reestablish a new identity for myself and rebuild my self-confidence through political and community involvement.

As with most people, becoming a parent brings on all kinds of pangs of consciousness about what one should or should not do now that there are children in the family. Our reactions were no different. After Elizabeth's birth, we felt that because we had a baby, we simply *must* go back to church—for the sake of the child, of course. We said it often, but seldom did anything about it. Having a newborn baby in the house required special discipline to get to church on Sunday mornings. Therefore, Sundays, more often than not, found us staying home.

Spiritual Renewal and Continued Healing

Raised in a Christian home, I was active in church functions most of my life. I considered myself basically a good guy, and herein lies the essence of the conflict: misunderstanding and contrast between my good works and lack of true faith. During those years of attending church and participating in religious ritual, one thing stands out clearly in my mind: I prayed only at bedtime or when I wanted something. I never *talked with* God or ever really had a *relationship* with Him.

When I went to Vietnam, I felt as if I grew closer to the Lord because I prayed more often—usually while under pressure, lonely for Jackie, or when in need or hurting. The isolation and loneliness of the war made me seek out comfort often, and I soon began attending chapel in Vietnam whenever I could. I continued to seek comfort from God while recovering from my wounds in the hospital in San Antonio. However, when the pain began to subside and more immediate problems occupied my mind, I would turn away and forget about Him again.

In the fall of 1972, a West Point classmate, Andrew Seidel, and his wife, Gail, moved to Dallas. I called Andy after reading in the alumni magazine that he had resigned from the army after nine years, including a tour in Vietnam as a combat engineer officer. He told me on the phone that he had moved to Dallas to attend the Dallas Theological Seminary in order to prepare for the ministry. Jackie and I visited with Andy and Gail often. Their faith in the Lord was obvious and evident, but they did not give us any hard sell on religion. They simply conducted themselves above reproach in every way and opened their hearts and home to us. I saw in them a sweetness, kindness, and love that I seldom saw in anyone in my travels around the world during my lifetime, and I wanted to know more about the source of their inner strength and peace. As we socialized with the Seidels, we slowly inched into various religious subjects—topics of conversation that I usually initiated. I had many unanswered questions, and I knew Andy would be able to help me work them out. I had questions such as "Why had I been spared in Vietnam while so many others had not?" and "Why was I alive, but my legs were gone?"

After a while, Andy and Gail invited Jackie and me to attend services with them at Fellowship Bible Church, a local Protestant and non-denominational, evangelical church. My first inclination was to look for any excuse not to go, such as the church was too far from our home. (It was actually all of six blocks away!) I finally relented, however, and one Sunday Jackie and I took two-year-old Elizabeth and went to church with the Seidels. The casual informality of the service struck me immediately. I was used to wearing a dark suit and tie to very traditional and formal services. I looked around and saw many of the men in open-collared sports shirts as they enjoyed guitar music played by a woman at the front of the auditorium. This was not the traditional service I was used to.

After the service, we walked outside to the front of the church and talked for a few minutes. I had been moved by the service, but too proud to admit it, so I stood there nervously not knowing what to say.

"You know," I finally said to Andy, "after sitting through this service and seeing what it's all about, I've come to a decision."

Andy's face lit up, and he looked at Gail and smiled. By the looks on their faces, they must have thought I had "seen the light." Letting the suspense build, I let them enjoy the moment for a few more seconds, and then I finished.

"I'm going to take guitar lessons!"

Their nervous and polite laughter told me that my joke had obviously disappointed them.

Nevertheless, impressed by the loving spirit of the people, the Bible teachings, and the knowledge of Pastor Gene Getz, I began to attend Fellowship Bible Church more often. Also a professor at Dallas Theological Seminary, Pastor Getz taught and talked *to* his congregation more than he preached *at* them. One of Getz' sermons made a distinct impression on me and changed my life forever.

"The real war in this world," he said, "is the war between good and evil—Satan and the Lord. They are fighting for the very hearts and souls of all people."

I could certainly relate to war. Getz' words got my attention and made me think. Here I was a dedicated citizen and sincere patriot. I loved my country—I always had. I had given time to community and civic endeavors. I had almost given my life to fight the communists who, in my mind, represented the ultimate evil. I had not, however, given all of myself to the ultimate Provider—God and His son, Jesus Christ.

I sat in church and listened to Getz' words while hot burning tears formed in my eyes. One by one, the tears trickled down my cheeks as I remembered the many battles I had fought—both on and off the battlefield. They seemed small now in comparison to the battles I was hearing about and understanding for the first time—the battles waged each and every day for the forces of good and evil—battles with more lives at stake than all the wars of history put together.

During that service I heard, believed, and reaffirmed my acceptance of John 3:16, "For God so loved the world, that he gave his only begotten Son, that whosoever believeth in him should not perish, but have everlasting life." As a teenager in the 1950s, I had really believed in Jesus Christ and became a born-again Christian. However, at that time, not only had I not understood what it all meant, but I had also not surrendered my life to Christ. In 1973, at age thirty-one, it all began to come together. That evening I began my mature walk in faith.

God meets us where we are and brings people into our lives who can help us understand. He met Peter the fisherman where he was when He talked to him about becoming a fisher of men. He met Thomas where he was when He showed Thomas the nail scars in his hands, because He knew that Thomas had to see for himself in order to believe that the Lord had actually resurrected. He met me where I was when he inspired Pastor Getz to preach on spiritual warfare. I had dedicated myself to being an American soldier, I knew military tactics and strategy, and I understood warfare. God met me where I was and brought His Word alive through someone who could help me understand its truth. I had dedicated myself to being an American soldier in a far superior manner than I had ever been motivated to being a soldier for Christ.

Cadets in military academies of all branches of the armed forces undergo intense and rigorous training in preparation for warfare. "Our military demands that our leaders spend their whole lifetime studying, improving, and perfecting military strategy. The point begins to become obvious doesn't it? If earthly military needs demand such study and careful preparation, how much more our preparation to meet our enemy demands our most diligent effort. The believer who does not become familiar with spiritual warfare will indeed be a poor soldier of Jesus Christ" (Bubeck: 23). Now I had new wars to wage and new battles to fight.

The Beginning of Christian Growth

After that experience, I wanted to know and absorb everything I could get my hands on about Christianity. In the weeks following, I talked frequently with Chuck Lamb, another member of Fellowship Bible Church and my co-worker at Republic Bank. Because Chuck also shared my carpool, we had ample opportunities to talk. I asked many spiritual questions, and Chuck always had the answers I needed to hear. For the first time, I learned about the true meanings of Armageddon and the second coming of Christ. I hung eagerly onto every word and learned everything I could.

I began discussing these new revelations with Jackie, and in talking with her about my conversations with Chuck, I was amazed to find out that she knew about these things all along. She gently reminded me that she had grown up in the Baptist church where such things are taught from early childhood. She had been a member of First Baptist Church in Dallas, pastored by the legendary W. A. Criswell.

"Why didn't you tell me about the second coming and all?" I asked.

With a smile on her face, she responded, "I didn't want to frighten you."

Jackie often expressed her faith through her actions, but she had never really evangelized me. I instinctively knew that she was good and faithful, but we had just never discussed her faith. Now she would help me grow in mine.

The people Jackie and I met at church seemed to have their lives so together. They all seemed mature in their faith—so much more mature than I was. They prayed publicly and openly, responded to questions with ease, and appeared to have a special self-discipline about their religious commitment. I wanted to have all that, too. In the beginning, I prayed silently that I wouldn't be called upon to pray aloud during Bible studies—something that would embarrass me at the time. Of course, that shyness about my newly found faith slowly subsided, and I later became perfectly comfortable praying in front of others.

In addition, I attended a couples Bible study led by Andy Seidel to which I invited several of my West Point friends. One of the more remarkable evenings I ever spent occurred at a dinner at the Seidel's when they also invited as their guests a popular professor from Dallas Theological Seminary, Howard Hendricks, and his wife. Before dinner, I talked to Professor Hendricks and related how Andy and I had had similar paths of life until now: a Texas upbringing, the same classes at West Point, the army Corps of Engineers, and Vietnam. But now our paths had diverged as I entered stock and bond investments and he headed for the ministry.

I could see that Professor Hendricks was more than likely popular with Christians because of his wisdom when he responded, "You really are both in the investment business, but his dividends pay off long term."

My newly discovered faith was always on my mind, even in my dreams. One night I awakened with a start, having dreamed that I was laboring mightily up a hill at whose crest apparently God or Jesus was to meet me, and just before I reached the top to be greeted, I awoke. In anguish, I told Jackie how disappointed I was in not making it to the top.

She had a simple but startling explanation: "They didn't want you."

I soon became a regular at Fellowship Bible Church, and for the first time, I paid attention to sermons and Bible readings. I also tried to apply the lessons I learned to everyday life. Jackie was delighted that I now shared the faith she had held for so long. She also expressed her joy in knowing that I would become active in a church. By now, I had realized that there is a distinct difference between being active in church and actively practicing one's faith.

In striving to be a good Christian, I first thought that I should, perhaps, stop seeing my friends who were not Christians or who were not as "religious" as my new friends at church. However, after discussing it with Jackie, we very quickly concluded that, just because our lives had taken on a new direction, we should not give up our past relationships. As a matter of fact, we decided it was more important than ever that we keep our old friends and share our new relationship with the Lord with them without wearing our religion on our sleeves. That is just what we have tried to do over the years. I understand that 80 percent of new believers become so through one-on-one contacts with Christians. I have tried to stay true to the decision Jackie and I made that day and continue to attempt to be an example for Christ to everyone I meet.

Being a Christian in a world controlled by Satan is an extremely difficult task. We are besieged from every side with temptations and opportunities to "fudge" on our ethics and morality. I soon learned through reading the Bible, and through attending the Bible study led by Andy Seidel, that the Bible is God's inerrant truth, written by individuals who were inspired and led by God and preserved over the centuries so Christians can have a daily guide for practical living as well as a storehouse of spiritual knowledge. God's Word has allowed me to develop more trusting relationships with my family and become more stable in my career. The Bible is also a problem solver as well as a source of divine inspiration. Through God's Word, I have found a special armor with which I can fight the battles of everyday living in a secular world.

I attempt now to bind myself to the will, purposes, timing, truth, character, and attributes of God, the mind of Christ, and the control of the Holy Spirit (Russell, A. J.). Most importantly, I have gained through the Word an enormous confidence in knowing that when I pray for forgiveness for my sins, the slate is wiped clean. It is comforting to know that if I go to sleep and die tonight, I will be with the Lord tomorrow, because Christ won the final battle for me by defeating death on the cross. Because of that victory, I have achieved eternal life.

With my renewed Christian faith, I felt back on track again and more equipped to handle life and whatever it may bring.

Although I could always carry the weight of the war and continue healing, with God as an integral part of my life, I felt as if I was preparing myself to be a soldier in another army, maybe even to become strong enough to be a warrior in God's army.

Paying Tribute

Already on a high from my new religious awakening, my mood intensified in the spring of 1973, when I received an invitation to represent all the veterans wounded in Vietnam at a Cotton Bowl ceremony and show honoring Vietnam veterans and especially the returnee POWs. Overwhelmed by such a request, I gladly accepted. I learned later that David Pickett, a young Dallas lawyer and Vietnam veteran, had submitted my name. The events of that evening would, indeed, prove to be enough to assure me that the Lord really does move in strange and mysterious ways. The memories of the war were again too much for me as I prepared to participate in the grand ceremony, so I saw my psychiatrist, who placed me on tranquilizers for the night's events.

The night of June 2, 1973, turned out to be one of the greatest and most rewarding nights of my life. Four convertibles with tops down began the program by first entering and then circling the stadium. The first car carried Admiral James Stockdale and General John Flynn, the two senior-in-rank returnee POWs who represented the POWs of the Vietnam War. The family members of a man killed in action rode in the second car. They represented the more than fifty-eight thousand men and women who died in Vietnam. The third car carried the family of a man missing in action—the number of which would eventually rise to more than 2,400 unaccounted for. Jackie and I rode in the last car, proudly representing the war wounded.

After alighting from our car and being introduced to the forty thousand people in attendance, Jackie and I walked arm-in-arm between two rows of a Marine Corps honor guard to our front row seats. Our photograph, taken from the back and showing me using my cane, appeared in the *Dallas Morning News* the next day, Sunday, June 3, 1973. Several friends from around the country sent me clippings of the photo that appeared in their local papers as well.

The show following the opening ceremony featured Bob Hope; Tony Orlando and Dawn, who popularized the song, "Tie a Yellow Ribbon 'Round the Old Oak Tree"; singers Gloria Loring and Barbara McNair; former Texas governor John Connally; and then deputy secretary of defense William P. Clements Jr. Even though it brought back many painful memories, the program proved to be a grand, glorious, and unforgettable experience.

During the program, I reflected on the war and the more than 3 million men and women who served in Southeast Asia. I listened to the speeches, heard the tributes, and reflected on the meaning of it all. So many had sacrificed so much. Of the wounded whom I represented that evening, seventy-five thousand were severely disabled and would never be able to do all the things they had done before they went to Southeast Asia. I could see the faces of the incoming wounded at Dak To, and I continued to wonder why I had lived and some of them had not. The ceremony and the memories it revived in me left me shaken and depressed for days, and the demons came back for a while.

Putting the War Behind Me

In 1973, my life was good. I felt good about my renewed religious faith as well as my job. However, old questions about the war still lingered. Although I had never questioned whether we should have fought for the freedom of an oppressed people, I often questioned whether my sacrifice was worth it, given the way the war progressed. More and more soldiers died every day, and we seemed to be going nowhere and accomplishing nothing. In addition, I didn't really harbor hatred for any of the presidents in office during the war or our military leaders; instead my questions were more from a military strategic viewpoint, Why didn't we bomb Haiphong Harbor? Why didn't we send troops into North Vietnam? Why didn't we earlier attack the privileged sanctuaries that Nixon attacked in 1970?

It was during this time in my life that Bill Moyers, former press secretary to President Johnson, happened to cross my path. The meeting with Moyers only stirred me up all over again about Vietnam. Moyers then served as a political adviser on a board of consultants for a major Wall Street firm. One of his trips for this company brought him to Dallas where he visited the investments division of the trust department at Republic Bank, the same department in which I worked. That day happened to be one of those rare days when I found myself in my wheelchair because of sore legs. My boss brought Moyers by my desk for a chat. I knew that Moyers did not have much time, so after a brief exchange of pleasantries, I got right to the point—my point.

"Bill, you and I were on opposite ends of the pipeline in the Vietnam War. You were in the oval office with the president, and I was near the Ho Chi Minh Trail at the tri-border point. With all your background and understanding of the war, why didn't we win it?"

Somewhat taken aback by my bluntness, Moyers recovered quickly and graciously and generously shared his thoughts with me as to what he thought was on President Johnson's mind. He reviewed the history of the early 1960s when a major split occurred between the Soviet Union and Red China. According to Moyers, President Johnson was deeply impressed by Secretary of State Dean Rusk's views of that split. He said the apparent strained relationship of those two communists' giants limited the military power the president wanted to bring to bear against North Vietnam. Too much power might force them to unite against the United States. Moyers went on to say that, generally, the military advice given to the president by his advisers was good, and the military leaders were considered first rate. Given my military background, perhaps he said the latter for my benefit. I don't know.

Moyers went on to relate the three options that President Johnson considered at the time. Those options were as follows:

> Option 1: We could invade North Vietnam. This was politically not feasible because international public opinion would swing against the United States. Such an invasion might also result in Russia and China forming a common alliance against us.
>
> Option 2: We could commit a million American troops to the war and hope we could win within ten years. Public opinion about the war had already split the nation, and the administration's thinking had been that the American people would not be that patient.

Option 3: This last option became the compromise. We would send a half million troops to Vietnam and give the South Vietnamese five years to build its military forces to withstand the Viet Cong and North Vietnamese onslaught. The only problem was that there was no way to predict whether that would be successful.

I, like so many other veterans, had been concerned that we had tried to fight a war with one arm tied behind our collective back, so Moyers' explanation of the administration's analysis of the war helped me a great deal. Some thought had gone into the decision-making process after all. Knowing this information helped dilute my bitterness.

Two years later, I wrote to Moyers after hearing his *Listening to America* program with former Secretary of Defense Clark Clifford. Clifford mentioned that one of the reasons for our involvement in Vietnam was to check on intelligence assessments that Russia and China were probing all over Southeast Asia.

"Vietnam is a past chapter in my own book of life," I wrote. "I am now in a new chapter."

Moyers returned my typed letter with a handwritten note that said, in part, "I can understand your disillusionment over events in Southeast Asia. Frankly, the military was asked to do an impossible task. But, were the sacrifices in vain? I don't think so. If everything had fallen ten years ago, I wonder what the map would look like today!"

Perhaps he was right.

CHAPTER 10

THE SEDUCTION OF POLITICS

Pursuing a Childhood Interest

With my military career behind me, I felt a strong desire to restore my self-confidence and perhaps feel valued again. All of my life, I had always been cause-oriented, public service–minded, and helpful to others. So it was only natural that, undergirded by a new direction due to my newfound spiritual awakenings, I gravitated into the political arena. My mind filled with endless causes and uncounted opportunities for public service as well as many opportunities to help others and make my world a better place. However, with my energies now directed toward these new endeavors, my attention was naturally diverted from my wife, my children, and the career that provided financial security for us. This diversion soon sowed only more seeds of discontent in my marriage. After my dedication to the military, restoration, and healing, I had found a new idol. And, in spite of my spiritual awakening, a life in the spotlight of politics was not only attractive, fun, and interesting, but also nourishing to my vanity and pride.

My sudden interest in politics did not begin as a replacement for military service. It actually began in 1948, when, at the tender age of six, I spoke at a local political rally in Mission, Texas. Speaking in Spanish, I told people that although I would soon leave to join my dad in Japan, I still supported Lloyd Bentsen for the U.S. House of Representatives. I even gave a short speech encouraging people to vote for him. The next day the front page of the local newspaper carried a photograph of me at the Bentsen rally wearing short pants and no shirt or shoes. It embarrassed my mother that I had not been better dressed in front of all those important people. (My mom, as most, was always a stickler for propriety, manners, and appearance.) As a child, what did I know about propriety? My mom was not home to properly inspect me when the campaign manager picked me up, so I left with him dressed as I was. To me, it was simply a "come as you are" rally! In spite of my dress, I would like to think that my amateur campaign speech that day had something to do with launching Lloyd Bentsen on his illustrious political career. After all, he later became Texas' senior senator in the U.S. Senate and ran for vice president on the Democratic ticket with Governor Michael Dukakis in the 1988 presidential race.

My next political effort took place four years later in the summer of 1952 when my family visited Mission. The presidential election had gone into high gear by then. Excited by the heat of the campaign, I donned my Cub Scout uniform and campaigned on behalf of General Dwight D. Eisenhower by giving a speech on the loading dock of the C. G. de la Garza warehouse. My mother breathed a sigh of relief to see that I was more appropriately dressed that time. Each of these early childhood attempts at politics served as a forerunner of more to come.

Local Politics

In 1974, my West Point company commander and friend, Nick Rowe, crossed paths again with me. Nick had been captured October 29, 1963 near Tan Phu Special Forces camp in the U Minh Forest and held for over five years before making a dramatic escape (Rowe). He ran for Texas State Comptroller on the Republican ticket. I had always felt a special obligation to Nick for the role he played in convincing me to stay in school, so I decided to help him by raising money for his campaign. After my earlier childhood attempts, this became my first step back into the political arena.

Although Nick lost the election to Bob Bullock, who eventually became lieutenant governor, the atmosphere of politics excited me, and I remained active, soon becoming the president of the Dallas County Republican Men's Club in June 1975.

In late 1976, Charles Pistor, president of Republic Bank, suggested that I compete for a White House fellowship. This program allows several people from the private sector to compete in a grueling process for a one-year position at either the White House or as an assistant to one of the cabinet secretaries. At the end of that year, each person returns to his or her normal career endeavors. This sounded like an exciting venture, so I applied for the program and soon learned that I was one of 1,400 applicants who would be screened for a position on first the regional and then on the national finalists' list. To my delight, my name appeared on the list of 110 regional finalists, and then finally on the list of thirty-seven national finalists who would travel to Washington, D.C. in the spring of 1977 to compete for the fellowship. Fourteen of the thirty-seven finalists would be chosen to receive a White House fellowship.

I should have sensed how the selection process would be handled as soon as I got to the competition site near Warrenton, Virginia, when I was asked to remove references of my wife and children in the official preliminary biographical sketches we brought with us. But I didn't begin to get a taste for the true political process until the first lunch held with committee members where I learned that newly elected President Jimmy Carter had personally appointed the selection committee to determine the winners. A fellow finalist seated at my table asked a committee member what the committee would look for in the candidates during the selection process. She very bluntly and candidly answered that the committee members reflected the political philosophy of the chairman, John Gardner, whom President Carter had personally selected, and it was most likely that the winning candidates would reflect that same philosophy, which I knew to be more liberal than was mine. As a person who had worked so hard for the Republican Party and conservative philosophy, I should have packed my bags and left

Washington right then, but I stayed through the weekend and hesitantly went through the motions of the interview process anyway.

With great trepidation, yet with confidence, I entered the auditorium where the results were to be announced. In spite of the political games being played, I felt confident that I would still be selected. After all, several of the competitors had commented that I had the most-impressive, well-rounded resume of all the candidates. As we sat down, we were given a written note that said, "yes" or "no." My note said, "no." My heart dropped to the bottom of my artificial legs. Filled with disappointment and wounded pride, I sank deep into my chair to contemplate my loss.

My roommate, Nelson Diaz, a wonderful man of Puerto Rican descent from Philadelphia, was a very outgoing Christian. I had advised him during the selection process to tone down his Christian rhetoric in such a secular setting. The night before the selection results were to be announced, he told me that his wife had prepared two envelopes for him—one to read if he won, and one to read if he lost. He opened his note. It said, "yes." He was so excited that he jumped up and asked me what he should do.

"Read what's in the 'yes' envelope from your wife," I replied.

As he read the very private words from his loving wife, I wondered if her words in the "no" envelope would have been any comfort to me. However, I knew I could not ask to invade his privacy by asking to see a personal note from his wife. So, instead, I sat there, sad and dejected, while at the same time feeling joy for him.

I learned two major lessons about politics during those few days in Washington. First, I witnessed firsthand a winning presidential candidate allowing his political beliefs to influence his appointment of judges to oversee a supposedly nonpartisan governmental program. Those judges were, in turn, influenced by the political philosophy of the president who appointed them. That philosophy permeated throughout the selection process and was somewhat reflected in the final choices of the people who were to receive the fellowship. In all candor, I must admit that four of the fourteen selected candidates were officers and, thus, supposedly apolitical. In addition, all fourteen were also absolutely outstandingly well-qualified citizens. I also learned that a person of high political position holds power and propagates his or her beliefs by appointments and selections of people who oversee political decisions. I had been so naive. I know now that there was no way a Democratic administration would have wanted a highly partisan Republican to be an assistant in the office of a Carter-appointed cabinet secretary.

In spite of my bitter disappointment of not achieving the White House fellowship, I can see now that God's hand was very active in this part of my life as well. If I had received the fellowship and lived in Washington for the last half of 1977 and the first half of 1978, I would not have been able to become involved in what would prove to be another very interesting political endeavor that would lead to even greater opportunities for service in my home state with the governor's race the following year.

State Politics

In October 1977, Jackie and I attended a fund-raising dinner for our local congressman, Jim Collins. Jackie served on the seating committee for that dinner. The following day a newspaper article suggested that Collins might seek the Republican nomination for governor. Former state GOP chairman and Dallasite Ray Hutchison seemed a natural for that nomination. Newspapers also reported that former Houston legislator, Hank Grover, sought the office as well. In addition, Bill Clements, returning home from the Defense Department in the Nixon-Ford administration, was considering throwing his hat into the race. The field was ripe and full for an interesting 1978 gubernatorial election.

Wanting to get back into active politics, I felt a need to pick my candidate early. Many of my friends would support Hutchison because most of us knew him. One evening I discussed the possibilities with Jackie. She had attended high school with Clements' children, Gill and Nancy, and remembered him as a warm, caring father who had been active in the Boy Scout program. Jackie recalled that when she seated Clements at the

Collins fund–raising dinner, he had been very gracious, sent his regards to her brother, and asked about her family. Jackie's family thought highly of him as well.

"Personally," Jackie said, "I think he is a capable man with a big heart. I'm for him."

After conferring together, Jackie and I decided to support Bill Clements for governor. As it turned out, Hutchison and Clements were the only candidates who competed for the Republican gubernatorial nomination that year.

I called Clements in December and again in January to offer my help in his campaign. When I did not receive a response from his staff, I decided to do something on my own. I invited Clements and fifteen young Dallas businesspeople to lunch at the Baker Hotel on a cold, icy day in January. The people who attended that luncheon, some of whom were meeting Clements for the first time, became the nucleus of the Dallas County Committee for Clements. I also contributed to the campaign by organizing three "leadership" luncheons where Clements was introduced to many of the grassroots Republicans in the more conservative factions of the Republican Party.

By March, Clements' Republican primary campaign had gained strength and momentum. I was honorifically titled chairman of the Dallas County Steering Committee, and when I introduced him at a reception at the Hilton Inn in Dallas, approximately one thousand people greeted him enthusiastically. It was evident that Clements enjoyed a lot of popularity among Texans. The next two months brought increased support, and by May he led the field. Clements won a big victory in the May primary over his opponent. His toughest job, however, would be to defeat the Democratic nominee, Attorney General John Hill, in November. Hill was an extremely popular candidate who had unseated incumbent Democratic governor Dolph Briscoe in the spring primary election.

The state general election took place on November 7, 1978. The Clements-Hill race was so close that no one knew the outcome until 1 p.m. the following day, Wednesday, November 8. Texas had traditionally been a powerful Democratic state for more than a century, and to have such a close election not only sparked hope in the hearts of Republicans, but it struck fear into the hearts of Democrats. When all the votes were counted, Clements realized a narrow victory by a slender margin of twenty thousand votes. He had become the first Republican governor of Texas in 104 years!

On Wednesday evening after the election, Clements returned to Dallas. He and his wife, Rita, flew into Cooper Airmotive at Love Field. Still riding high on the bandwagon of victory, I joined many of Clements' loyal and festive supporters at the airport and walked out to the plane's ramp to greet him on his victorious return.

"Allen," Clements said as he gave me a giant bear hug, "we did it. I couldn't have done it without you. You made it all happen."

He probably said that to thousands of people over the next four years, and I suppose he was right to an extent. Every contribution, no matter how small, became a part of the bigger picture. Without those individual contributions, whether monetary or in the form of work that added up statewide, we would not have enjoyed victory.

Clements' wife Rita also hugged and kissed me and said that the margin of victory in Dallas made the difference in the election. A feeling of personal fulfillment swept through me. I had worked for five candidates in my short political career, and Clements was actually the first to win an election. To win such a big and important victory made that accomplishment all the sweeter. My efforts had paid off, and I now realized that the "political bug" had bitten me. However, even though our candidate had won the governorship of Texas, Dallas County campaign chairman and close friend Bill Elliott and I agreed over a lunch soon thereafter that neither of us would follow Clements to Austin when he took office in January of 1979.

Only five days after swearing off any job on Clements' staff, Elliott called and asked if I would reconsider going to Austin. He had recommended me to Clements for a staff appointment. My friends had speculated that I might end up going, and their speculation excited me and fueled my desire to continue in politics. Elliott's words over the phone persuaded me to change my mind and at least talk to the governor-elect if he needed me. Two weeks later I received a call from someone on the governor's staff who invited me to meet Clements in a suite in the Vaughn Building near the capitol in Austin. After an initial interview, Clements offered me the job of special assistant for administration. My head spun. It had all happened so fast. I told Clements that I would need to discuss this with Jackie and would let him know within a couple of days.

After the interview, I went to the coffee shop on the ground floor where Jackie waited. As I rode the elevator down, I said a prayer of thanks to God for allowing me this fabulous opportunity. I told her that Clements had offered me a job. We decided that we needed to think it over and discuss all the possibilities before committing to such a drastic move and career change, but the idea of moving to Austin excited us both.

Jackie and I went back upstairs where she waited in a reception area while I spoke with George Steffes who was in charge of Clements' transition office prior to the inauguration. While I visited with Steffes, Clements happened to come upon Jackie in the outer room.

"We're going to love Austin," she told him, giving away the direction in which we were leaning before I had a chance to say yes.

Several nights later I went to Fellowship Bible Church and thanked Pastor Getz, who had meant so much to me in my spiritual development as a Christian. I would miss his leadership and spiritual guidance. I also asked the church members to pray for me as I undertook a new and exciting career in public service in Austin.

Inaugurating a New Career in State Politics

The weather on inauguration day, January 16, 1979, was pleasant and cool with overcast skies. We began the morning with the traditional inaugural prayer service at First United Methodist Church before going to the swearing-in ceremony on the south steps of the state capitol building. As Governor Clements began his speech, the sun broke through the clouds, casting its warm rays on all of us. The governor's usual exuberance was evident. It had turned into a perfect day, and I stood proud and tall beside the governor. I literally *stood tall*—three inches taller, in fact.

When the doctors fitted me with my artificial legs in 1968, they told me I needed to be slightly shorter than my original height in order to get the best use out of my prostheses. I ended up being five feet eight inches tall from 1968 to 1978. That year the Veterans Administration authorized a new set of legs, giving me a golden opportunity to grow in height! Without my doctors' permission, I told my prosthetist in Dallas to make my next set of legs long enough to put me at five feet ten inches tall, one inch taller than my original height. I picked up the legs a few days before I left for Austin. They were not two, but *three* inches longer than my first set, placing me at five feet eleven inches tall. I had wanted to be taller all my life and was happy to be three inches taller. However, this new and much welcomed height posed two problems.

First, I could not rise to that new height until I got some new clothes to fit my new legs. I immediately went out and bought five suits, picking them up the day before I left for Austin. I was so busy during the transition that I couldn't get the suits cuffed until 5 p.m. on the eve of the inauguration. I had heard of people growing in their jobs, but I had not even started mine, and I had literally grown three inches overnight. Second, standing at five feet eleven inches placed me an inch taller than the governor, when I had previously been two inches shorter! What would he think? I remembered from my army days that generals frequently picked shorter aides, and I hoped my new height would not make any difference to my new boss. One day while riding down the elevator with Clements, I told him about my new legs. The broad smile on his face said it all. He was happy for me. (Ten years later, in 1989, I would again "grow" two more inches when I got another set of legs that placed me at six feet one inch tall. I had finally realized my dream of standing over six feet tall. Then in 1995, I went to six feet two inches tall, proving that one should never give up on their goals and "grow in all their jobs.")

Inaugural festivities continued throughout the day. Viewing stands were erected along Congress Avenue in front of the capitol building so all the invited dignitaries could view the inaugural parade. Fortunately, an acquaintance, Gene Fondren, was in charge of seating in those areas. When he spotted Jackie and me on the sixth row behind several other people who were also standing, he immediately proceeded to move me to the front.

"Allen," he said, "we have one empty chair behind the governor. It's supposed to be for security. I know you're secure, so why don't you come up near the front so you won't have to stand up to see."

Fondren's thoughtfulness made it possible for me to sit and relax and have a very enjoyable afternoon. As we looked around at the dignitaries seated around us, Jackie and I had to pinch ourselves to see if we were dreaming. I sat behind Governor Clements and his wife, Rita, and right next to Governor and Mrs. John Connally who, as the different bands and marching units passed by, proudly gave me a Texas geography lesson. In addition, future president George H. W. Bush and his wife, Barbara, were in attendance. (I would later meet George's son, the future governor and president, George W. Bush, when I joined the governor-elect's transition office in December 1978 when he came to Austin from Midland to meet with Governor Clements.) Also seated nearby were Ambassador Anne Armstrong and her husband, Tobin, Congressman and Mrs. Jim Collins, and Mrs. John Tower in the senator's absence.

After the parade, I took Jackie to the capitol building, where we checked out my new office for the first time. The high ceilings, red carpets, and flowing drapes reminded me of the old historical monuments in Washington, D.C. The quiet halls echoed with the sounds of our footsteps as well as the silent ghostly footsteps of men and women of the past who had walked the halls before us and who had changed the course of state history. It was very exciting to know that I would now have a chance to be a small part of the history-making process as well.

The inaugural ball that evening was held at the Austin Convention Center, where the arena was transformed into a fairyland of flowing ball gowns, tuxedos, excellent food, and beautiful music. Jackie and I dined and danced into the wee hours of the morning. I enjoyed myself so much that I wasn't even aware until later that I had done all this on a new set of unproved artificial legs that had increased my height by three inches. So I awoke the following morning to find my legs totally worn out. One night's rest was not enough to relieve the toll that all the standing, walking, and dancing had taken on them. As a result, on January 17, my first full day in my new position at the capitol, I had to report to work in a wheelchair. Governor Clements was so busy and preoccupied with affairs of state that he made no comment when I wheeled into our first staff meeting and parked my chair right behind him at the conference table.

During the day, however, he turned to me at one point, placed his hand on my shoulder, and said, "Allen, are you okay? Are you hurting?"

"I'm fine, Governor. Thank you very much for your concern. All that dancing last night wore a little sore on one leg, so I am going to stay off it for a few days. I'll be back in shape by Monday."

During those Austin years, I would cross paths with many of the people who surrounded the governor, including Karl Rove who worked at the Governor Clements Committee. By 2000, Karl Rove would become the political strategist masterminding Governor George W. Bush's successful campaigns for the White House and would eventually become a counselor to President Bush in 2001 and deputy chief of staff by 2005.

Healing Old Wounds

Doctors had told me in 1968 that I would need to have constant revisions to my stumps over the years. I was very pleased that I had been able to go eleven years without a problem. However, in September 1979, I had to enter Scott and White Hospital in Temple, Texas, for an operation on my left leg. Jackie told Elizabeth, then age eight, that they would have to rush to Temple right after school on the day of the surgery so they could be with me and I wouldn't be lonely.

When assured that I would have a TV and newspaper, Elizabeth said, "Daddy won't have any problems. He has two things that mean a lot to him."

That small comment made me aware of just how observant her little eight-year-old eyes were and served as an expression of the future good sense that would serve her well in the corporate world.

I had to use my wheelchair for about a week while the surgical wound healed on my stump. When I returned to work on Friday, September 21, Governor Clements had left for a three-week trip to eastern Europe and Russia. He phoned while in Amsterdam, and the first thing he asked about was my leg. I will always be grateful to him for his solicitude about my recovery as well as the welfare of others on his staff. It was a pleasure to work for someone who I know cared about people and their well-being.

Hard Work Begins

Although all on the governor's staff were burdened with work, deadlines, and pressures from outside interests, Governor Clements' enthusiasm, exuberance, dry wit, and sense of humor went a long way in alleviating the stress and tension that built up from day to day. We never knew what to expect or what he might say next. For example, once when the governor was returning from the Southern Governors' Association meeting in New Orleans, his driver did not show up at the airport to pick him up due to a misunderstanding about his arrival time. Therefore, George Bayoud, the governor's personal assistant, offered to drive him home. While climbing into the car, Bayoud lost a contact lens. Everyone pitched in to help search for the lens, but that took even more time. When the governor finally arrived home, he met his driver leaving to go to the airport.

"Did you have a good nap?" Clements quipped with a grin, and just kept on walking as if nothing had happened, leaving the driver gaping in astonishment.

Another time, one of our staffers tried to explain some complex legislative maneuver that none of us could grasp. Governor

Clements went over it several times, only to receive as many questions as the time before. Finally, he cut off the discussion by saying, "We'll just let that one develop," and moved on to other things.

Besides all the hard work, there were memorable events and highlights during the two and one-half years that I remained on the governor's staff. On June 6, 1979, former governor Price Daniel was honored at an appreciation dinner given in Houston. Governor and Mrs. Clements flew to Houston in the governor's plane, and I joined them and other dignitaries that included Jim Innes who worked for the Texas Department of Community Affairs. Jim and I wanted to attend the dinner to honor Governor Daniel, because he and I had been instrumental in helping Jim found the Austin Christian Men's Association when we first moved to Austin.

The fact that the six living Texas governors at the time were together that evening for the first time made the dinner historical and especially memorable. Those governors, some of whom are no longer with us, included Allan Shivers Sr., Price Daniel Sr., John Connally, Preston Smith, Dolph Briscoe, and Bill Clements. One could sit and look around the room and view Texas history in person. Evenings like that are not often repeated. I later ordered a photograph of the six governors together and got each of them to autograph the photo, which I will probably someday donate to a museum.

On the "Speaking Tour"

The American Coalition of Citizens with Disabilities held a solidarity day on October 20, 1979, when they presented state officials with a bill of rights for the disabled. They conducted the ceremony in the magnificent rotunda of the state capitol building, and the governor sent me down to speak to the group. I gave a short speech in which I pointed out various physical improvements to the capitol complex that had just been completed for the benefit of the disabled—long overdue improvements such as widened restroom doors, ramps, and special parking spaces.

Gathered there that day were polio, muscular dystrophy, and stroke victims as well as people with physically disfiguring birth defects and other varying disabilities. They were the maimed, the malformed, the disabled, and I was one of them. As I surveyed those who had assembled for this event and took in the massive obstacles they each had to overcome, I realized that God had blessed me with only a minor inconvenience. Their cause stole my heart, and I knew that from then on I must work for the cause of this group and dedicate myself to use the powers of my position to improve conditions for the disabled everywhere.

A White House conference for the disabled had been held the previous year in the spring of 1978. By October of 1979, the Texas legislature had not yet acted upon the recommendations of the conference. I called this to Governor Clements' attention, explaining the necessity of pursuing the implementation of as many of the conference recommendations as possible. Clements, a very caring and sensitive man, was very receptive and gave the effort a great deal of support. Through his support and a lot of hard work, we strengthened the scope and influence of the Governor's Committee for Disabled Persons. We hired Virginia Roberts, a severely disabled person, to be a full-time administrative assistant on Clements' staff. Part of her responsibilities included supporting a planning committee appointed by the governor that would develop a long-term policy for the disabled in the state of Texas.

In my opinion, this is the single greatest accomplishment of my service to the state of Texas and the one of which I am most proud. Although the initial idea was mine, Governor Clements had the authority and motivation to make things happen. I was simply fortunate enough to be in a position where I was able to get the ear of a compassionate governor who listened to a disabled staffer with an idea that could initiate change. The two of us, along with many other hard-working people, carried the idea and the dream to fruition. The words of my dear friend Justin Dart Jr., Clements' chairman of the Governor's Committee for Disabled Persons, express better than I just where this initial effort led. Justin served later as the vice chairman of the National Council on the Handicapped, and in 1989 was appointed by President George H. W. Bush as chairman of the President's Committee on Employment of People with Disabilities.

On June 20, 1984, he wrote:

> Most significantly, (Allen Clark) took the lead in creating a mechanism to develop a comprehensive long-range public and private disability policy for the state of Texas. The resulting policy statement, developed by a bipartisan blue ribbon panel, which included several prominent leaders of the disabled community, was highly respected both in Texas and on the national level as an historic achievement. The Texas legislature acted favorably on all its preliminary recommendations and established a permanent body to ensure its long-term development. Utilizing the Texas plan as a model, the National Council on the Handicapped created the National Policy for Persons with Disabilities. Early this year, the Congress passed, and the president signed, PL-98-221 making the National Council on the Handicapped an independent federal agency and requiring that it undertake a comprehensive evaluation of all federal disability laws and programs and make recommendations for new legislation to maximize the independence and dignity of disabled people.
>
> Thus, the planning initiative promoted and advocated on all levels by Allen Clark has resulted in the first comprehensive federal policy on disability in the nation's history. . . . I have no doubt that the benefits of Allen's initiative will eventually extend to most nations of the world—international distribution of the national policy is already underway.

In January 1980, Elizabeth and I went home to Mission, Texas, to meet my mother for the activities of the Texas Citrus Fiesta, which would provide a nice time of celebration and relaxation with family and friends. However, even this brief respite did not relieve me of my official duties. While there, we attended the mayor's brunch where I read a proclamation from Governor Clements. Afterward, the three of us rode in an open convertible in the Fiesta parade where many people lined the streets.

Mom didn't say much about the activities that day. She had grown up on the south (Mexican-American) side of town during the 1920s and 1930s. I had heard many stories of the discrimination she had witnessed firsthand. I knew it must have been a personal triumph for her to return to her hometown riding in a parade in an open convertible with her son, who represented the governor of her state. I felt proud for her. She sat in the front seat; I sat in the rear on the right and waved to the right. Elizabeth, age nine, proved to be a real trooper, waving and smiling at everyone along the left side of the street. At one time, I forgot and waved my left hand, crossing her right in the process.

"Daddy," Elizabeth quipped, "this is my side. You take care of your side."

The children in my life seemed to always have a pure and honest way of putting everything in perspective as well. Once I went to Montgomery, Alabama, where my sister's husband, Alan, was an instructor, to speak to an air force officers' career class on leadership. While there I stayed with my sister's family, including her older children, Chuck, Chad, and Charlene. One evening we were all relaxing in the living room while their six-year-old daughter, Cheryl, played on the floor before us. All of a sudden she playfully reached over and hit my leg—my wooden leg! She jumped back in wide-eyed surprise at the feel of this unusual leg. I patiently explained to her that I had lost my legs in a war and now I walked on artificial legs.

"Did you kill anyone in the war?" she asked me with the innocent curiosity that only children have.

When I answered that I had not, she responded, "Bad shot, huh?" There is nothing like the candid remarks of family and friends to bring a person back down to earth and keep him humble.

That same summer the American Legion invited me to be a speaker before 975 high school boys at Boys State, which was held at Hogg Auditorium on the University of Texas campus in Austin. Standing before those young men, I truly felt like a soldier again. Looking out over the crowd of fresh eager faces, I realized that my words could possibly make a difference in some of their lives. I hoped that my military service and my presence before them that day would help preserve a free world for all young people everywhere. My sacrifice was worth it if it enabled young men like them to live in a free country.

Whenever I spoke to groups such as this, I always tried to remember to say, "The true heroes cannot receive your applause and accolades. They are buried. I only represent them."

In January 1981, I spoke in McAllen to the forty-four adjutants general of the U.S. National Guard, another branch of our nation's military. Although seldom given much credit for their service, the National Guard has always played a strategically important role in national defense. If one has seen the movie *Saving Private Ryan,* he can never forget the heroism of the men of the 29th Infantry Division (a National Guard division) at Omaha Beach. The Guard serves as the protector of the home front, responding in a timely and professional manner during times of domestic unrest and national and local disaster. In addition, it has always been at-the-ready to be called upon for service during disputes in foreign countries as well. Members of the National Guard have flown combat missions in Vietnam and fought against terrorism in both Afghanistan and Iraq. Many of them have given their lives in the cause for freedom. All Americans should be proud of these fine men and women.

I spoke to many groups and organizations during my years with Governor Clements. I can honestly say that those experiences proved to be of personal benefit to me. In each case, I felt personally involved in the ceremony or the cause, whether the group consisted of disabled Americans, veterans, military personnel, minorities, people with patriotic and history-making ancestors, or simply fresh-faced young men just beginning their journey in life. I could identify with all of them, and I am pleased that I had the opportunity to meet them.

Lifelong friends were made on the governor's staff. Military service, political campaigns, spiritual endeavors, and important public service ventures forged alliances and relationships that are deep and strong, and we typically weaved in and out of one another's lives for years to come. In the governor's office, I became close to George W. Strake Jr., the Secretary of State, and Janie Harris, the governor's secretary, who usually was there with only me each evening to close the office upon the late-working governor's departure. Janie later married a widower, Lieutenant General James F. Hollingsworth, USA (Ret.), unarguably the most highly decorated graduate from the Corps of Cadets of Texas A&M University.

A dedicated member of my staff who went on to bigger and better positions of responsibility was James Cicconi, who followed James Baker to Washington in 1981 and eventually became White House deputy chief of staff in the Reagan administration. One of the most valuable members of the 1978 gubernatorial campaign and later General Counsel and also Secretary of State was David Dean. Fifteen years later our lives would intersect in a way that could only have been orchestrated by God.

Eyes Turn Toward Washington

National elections were held on Tuesday, November 4, 1980. Governor Clements invited Jackie and me to join the rest of the senior staff and other friends in his suite at the Sheraton Crest Hotel in Austin to watch election returns. At 7:20 p.m., as Jackie and I were driving to the hotel, we heard a radio announcement that California governor Ronald Reagan, the Republican presidential candidate, had already acquired the electoral votes from twenty-seven states. The radio announcer intimated the possibility of a landslide Republican victory. That seemed too good to be true, so we decided to wait it out without getting too excited. As we entered the hotel dining room, we spotted H. R. "Bum" Bright, director of Republic Bank and chairman of the Governor Clements Committee, seated at a nearby table with his wife, Peggy. They asked us to join them for dinner. We had scarcely finished dinner and made our way up to the governor's suite when Jimmy Carter, the incumbent and Democratic presidential candidate, appeared on TV to give his concession speech at 8:50 p.m. The polls had not even closed on the west coast. We couldn't believe our ears. It was over so quickly.

At 7:30 the next morning, Charles Pistor, the president of Republic Bank and the brother of Jackie's best friend, Ginger

Simmons, called to congratulate me for having the courage to step out years before in a predominantly Democratic state and break the ice with heavy political involvement in the Republican Party—the party that had no real previous power in Texas but that eventually became the vehicle for the conservative surge in the state. Although that breakthrough for the Republicans required the hard work of many dedicated and hard-working people, I felt proud to know that I had a small part in it.

An opportunity for a position in Washington emerged one month after the national elections. In the spring of 1980, Governor Clements had spoken to me about possible career options with a new Republican administration in Washington if I chose not to return to Republic Bank after a two-year leave of absence. As a result of that conversation, I told him that I would like to follow up on that idea if the Republicans won in November. I even went so far as to give him my choice of positions. My first choice would be to head the Veterans Administration, and my second choice would be to serve as one of the assistant secretaries of the army. Admittedly with little humility, I felt my intense military training, background, service, education, and subsequent experience in state government qualified me for either position.

Although Governor Clements had originally suggested the option of a position in Washington, D.C., the election came and went and we did not pursue the issue further. However, unknown to and unsolicited by me, several of my friends recommended me to incoming president Ronald Reagan. As a result of their recommendations, my name was placed in the "hopper" as a possible candidate for a national post. The best and strongest recommendation most likely came from Justin Dart Jr. whose father, a California industrialist, was a longtime friend of Reagan's and a member of his "kitchen cabinet."

After the election, there was a lot of speculation about who would be chosen as the head of the Veterans Administration, and my name kept surfacing. I tried to be patient, secretly kept my fingers crossed, and prayed a lot, but never really lent much credence to the rumors circulating around me. When Clements heard that my name appeared on the list of people to be considered for a senior appointment, he expressed surprise but remained totally supportive.

Although one collective eye remained on Washington in anticipation of changes that would certainly occur, the governor's staff tried to meet the day-to-day challenges of state government and events that would affect the people of Texas—events such as those that had occurred within the previous two years. In April of 1979, the people of Wichita Falls had suffered great personal and property loss in a series of severe tornadoes that cut a wide swath through that north Texas community. The following summer oil spills plagued the Gulf of Mexico, leaving its bordering beaches and oceanfront property bathed in black ooze washing in from the sea. One year later in August 1980, Hurricane Allen slammed into the Texas coast, causing millions of dollars in damage and destruction.

In January 1981, only four days after my National Guard speech in McAllen, Jackie and I excitedly left Dallas on the Texas inaugural charter flight headed for President Reagan's inauguration in Washington. We sat next to Ebby Halliday Acers and Maurice Acers on that flight, where we began a friendship that has lasted to this day. When he served Governor Allan Shivers, Maurice had occupied the same office in the state capitol that I occupied, and he regaled us with stories of his time in Austin. That flight turned into a 1,500-mile-long party, and the celebration had only just begun.

We arrived in Washington to a flurry of activity that began with the black tie and boots Texas State Society party at the Sheraton Washington Hotel. Initially, we could not enter the ballroom when we got there because the fire marshal had said the room was filled to capacity. There were six other people with Jackie and me: Doug and Ginger Simmons, Charles and Regina Pistor, and Ray and Kay Bailey Hutchison, who was then general counsel at my old Republic National Bank and eventually served as U.S. senator from Texas. Luckily for me, the governor's security section chief from Texas walked by and, after I explained our predicament, the eight of us wound our way circuitously behind the Texas trooper standing guard, through the kitchen, and eventually into the ballroom. There is always a way.

Jackie and I were awed to be in the same room with so many politically "elite." We visited with Congressman Phil Gramm and his wife, Wendy; Ray Hunt (son of Texas oil man H. L. Hunt) and his wife, Nancy; and our old friends Congressman Jim Collins and his wife, Dee. In addition, we all got to shake hands with newly elected Vice President George H. W. Bush of Texas. Staying at the Holiday Inn across the street from the Watergate complex, which had been the scene of historical events in 1972, became one of the highlights of our stay in Washington.

The following day, Sunday, we picked up our tickets at Union Station and enjoyed all the sights and sounds of the nation's capital. Then it was off to the hotel again for a special reception where I had the privilege of meeting one of my great heroes, General Omar Bradley. Age had taken a visible toll on the general. He sat very quietly in a wheelchair, watching the activities around him.

As I took General Bradley's hand to shake it, I whispered to him the words others had spoken to me—words that mean much to anyone who has served in the military, "Thank you for your service to our country."

Governor Clements stood at the end of the long receiving line greeting people as they filed through. One of the guests, upon reaching the governor, asked him why he was so popular.

"I'm not popular," the governor responded with his usual wit, "I'm just a curiosity."

Inauguration Day, Tuesday, January 20, was cold and mainly overcast. January weather in Washington is very unpredictable, and we hoped for a dry and comfortable day. Jackie and I joined our longtime Dallas friends, Doug and Ginger Simmons, who came from Atlanta, and other people headed for the ceremony, most of whom were dressed well and warm. Red, white, and blue bunting and American flags draped the west front of the capitol building. When President Reagan spoke about the men and women buried in nearby Arlington Cemetery and the sacrifices our veterans have made for this country, my throat tightened and my heart swelled within my chest. His words made their sacrifices—indeed all of our sacrifices—seem essential to the freedom of our great land.

As I listened to the familiar strains of "America" and "Faith of our Fathers," I realized that this was indeed a red-letter day for me. The little skinny ten-year-old Cub Scout from Mission, Texas, who had stood on the loading dock of the C. G. de la Garza warehouse spouting campaign clichés for Dwight Eisenhower, never dreamed that at age thirty-nine he would attend a presidential inauguration. I had come a long way, God had been good to me, and life couldn't be better.

Jackie and I attended several inaugural balls and then, exhausted, headed back to our hotel. Along the route we passed the Veterans Administration building that stands next to the Church of the Presidents where an ancestor of my West Point roommate, Jim Dickey, had been a priest. It is one of those historical sights that I have always loved so much. In hopeful, yet hesitant, anticipation that my appointment to the VA would go through, I thought to myself, "What a great place to work someday." We drove farther and passed the Christmas tree that stood on the circular ground south of the White House known as the Ellipse. It had been relit in celebration of the release that very day of the fifty-two American hostages held in Iran for nearly two years. Yes, indeed, this had been a red-letter day.

Jackie and I returned to Austin and tried to resume our daily routines, but it was difficult because we both felt as if we had just returned from Wonderland on the other side of the looking glass. Life with our daughters was eventful and always full of surprises, and we tried to carry on as best we could. One evening, I sat in my wheelchair and watched a John Wayne war movie on television while my youngest daughter Christi, then six, played next to me. She soon crawled into my lap. Prompted by the pictures she saw in the television screen, Christi asked me if I had ever been in a war.

"Yes, when I was younger," I told her.

"Next time you go, Daddy," she said, "I'll go with you, but I'll wait in the car. Okay?" Like little Cheryl's remark about my being a bad shot, Christi's humorous perspective served to keep me balanced.

Rumors continued about the candidates under consideration for the VA post. My hopes would rise with one rumor only to be dashed by the next. On March 3, I heard that Lieutenant General John Flynn, a former Vietnam POW from San Antonio, was under consideration. I also heard at the same time that my name was still in the pot. That, at least, was a temporary relief.

The following day, March 4, a reporter from CBS *Evening News* interviewed me about a problem that had plagued Texas coastal communities for several years. Vietnamese refugees had settled along the Texas coast where they could fish for a living—the only living some of them knew. This did not set too well with Texas fishermen who viewed the Vietnamese as a threat to their own livelihoods and fishing territory. An emotionally charged situation soon erupted. Small fishing communities along the coast swelled with unrest, protest, and frequent personal attacks against these displaced people. I had been involved in negotiations with various groups for almost a year in an effort to settle their differences and accommodate both sides. The negotiations were extremely delicate because we had to be careful not to offend people in such a way that we would spark retaliation against either side. I felt that we had been successful because, up until that time, no serious violence had erupted.

By the spring of 1981, all the major agency posts had been filled with the exception of the VA administrator's position. There were approximately nine men whose names appeared on the list of possibilities. Apparently, the top four people considered, but not selected for a variety of reasons, were Representative William Ayres (R-Ohio), New York state assemblyman John Behan, James H. Webb Jr., and General John Flynn. When these four did not work out, the administration, supposedly upon the suggestion of a senior California staff member, chose a "safe and known quantity" from California, Robert Nimmo, on April 30. Nimmo's name supposedly had not even appeared on the original list of nine.

Robert Nimmo had a long record of loyal service to our country as a World War II bomber pilot, a retired colonel in the California National Guard, and service as a California legislator. However, quite a stir arose after his nomination because there were those who felt the Vietnam veterans had been passed over for an older World War II veteran. My selection as deputy administrator by President Reagan was to have supposedly quelled that criticism.

I had just left the hospital after additional surgery on my leg when I received an invitation from the White House to come for an interview. Although I knew I would have to once again attend an important event in my wheelchair, I experienced an emotional high just thinking of the possibilities. My former West Point roommate, John Dunn, drove me to the White House and let me out at the southwest gate. I wheeled myself up to the office of the White House personnel director, Pen James.

At the time, Robert Nimmo temporarily occupied an office in the old executive office building. James invited Nimmo to join us in his office after he and I visited for a while. When Nimmo arrived, the seeds of impending problems began sprouting as soon as James told Nimmo that I was under consideration for the post of deputy administrator of the VA.

"Are there any other possibilities?" Nimmo snapped in my presence.

Responding with a firmness that left no doubt as to the administration's intentions, James answered, "Allen is the president's choice to be your deputy!"

After a brief ten-minute meeting, James suggested that I accompany Nimmo back to his office so we could get better acquainted. He seemed rushed and too busy to talk to me, but I wouldn't be dismissed that easily.

We visited for a while and then Nimmo remarked, "We are different personality types. You are much more outgoing than I." Was he trying to tell me from the beginning that we would not be able to get along? That remark did not bother me much, however, because I had worked with a lot of people who had a different personality type than me. However, his response to my next comments began to trouble me a great deal.

"I realize that I was supposedly in contention for the number one slot at the VA," I said, "but wasn't selected. You were. I pledge to be a hardworking and loyal deputy to you."

I leaned forward in my wheelchair and paused, waiting for a response, but received only silence. Not a word was forthcoming. Already disappointed in my new boss after less than an hour with him, I pressed forward.

"I hope you appreciate what I just said."

Again, no response—only a perfunctory mumbling came from his lips. That was enough for me.

I left his office and soon thereafter left Washington and returned to Austin to await the administration's decision. On May 29, 1981, the announcement of my selection by President Reagan to become the eventual nominee became official. I would become the deputy to the administrator of the Veterans Administration when nominated and after confirmation hearings before the Senate Veterans Affairs Committee. As I moved from one area of public service into another, Governor Clements issued the following generous statement to the press:

> I am pleased that Allen Clark, who has served as my assistant for administration since the early transition days, has been selected as Deputy Administrator of the Veterans Administration. Allen is an outstanding individual, and his contributions to state government during these last two and one-half years have been enormous.
>
> His distinguished military background, his education, and his even-handed administrative skills will prove a valuable asset to the federal government as he moves into a management position with an agency that has a $25 billion budget and 220,000 employees. As a West Point graduate and a combat veteran, he brings a deep personal commitment to the programs he will administer.
>
> Allen's departure will be a great loss to my staff, but he certainly has earned the opportunity for greater service to his country. We will miss him very much. I thank him and compliment him for his many accomplishments in state government and wish him every success in his new assignment.

It was imperative that I send to the governor my feelings about my time with him and the following went in a letter to him:

I depart your staff with positive professional expectations of the challenges of federal services, but with a heavy heart, personally, due to leaving your Administration. Without a doubt, the past thirty months with you have been the most professionally rewarding of my life. I have learned so much from you and I will use your leadership, management, and people techniques the rest of my life.

My original reasons for supporting your candidacy have all been fulfilled and you have exceeded all my expectations for your statesmanship.

Building upon the success generated by Texas Republican senator John Tower, the governorships of Bill Clements laid the groundwork for the future immense success of Republican victories in Texas. He truly was a man who helped build the Republican Party of Texas at the grass roots.

My real political baptism of fire had begun. Being a Republican in a Democratic state was nothing compared to being a Republican in a Republican administration and working for a man in my own party who I neither admired nor respected and who, in turn, did not respect me. I knew that my work would be cut out for me from the beginning. But determined to do my best, I returned to Washington prepared to work hard and get along the best I could.

The differences in the management styles of my new boss and me began to clash early on. Not only did he not like my presence, but also he would not give me any responsibility at all. In most agencies, the deputy is the line manager and the administrator oversees the total operation. Nimmo planned to delegate no direct management authority to me. It seemed obvious to me that, as far as he was concerned, I was to be a figurehead deputy—a token to be trotted out whenever Nimmo wanted to impress people that the Vietnam veterans were represented in the VA, which was giving attention to their problems.

After being slighted by both Nimmo and his chief of staff, Nick Longworth, I decided that I had to leave the VA. I could not work for someone with such an extreme lack of sensitivity, ability, and leadership after working for Governor Clements, one of the great leaders of our country. I contacted Ron Mann, my liaison at the White House, to tell him I intended to pack up and leave Washington as soon as possible. Immediately, Mann arranged for what he hoped would be a conciliatory meeting with Nimmo. During that meeting, Nimmo offered me line management authority for the VA hospitals. What he did not know was that I had done my homework. I politely thanked him, but told him I knew that by law the VA administrator could not delegate the authority for the hospitals to anyone in the VA except the director himself. Nimmo was, by law, personally responsible for the hospitals, and he knew it.

At this point, I had just quit caring altogether. I had never felt so mistreated in my life. I had been a dedicated soldier, public servant, and patriot. I had left Governor Clements, uprooted my family, moved to Washington, and made a commitment to serve my country again in a job that could benefit fellow veterans. And, all for what—to be a token, a figurehead to appease the Vietnam veterans? I found the management environment totally unacceptable and withdrew my name from consideration for the nomination. I immediately called Jackie, and we made plans to meet in Washington and then drive home to Austin together.

Because I did not want to cause embarrassment to President Reagan, I made the following public statement that masked the true reasons for my sudden departure: "I found it necessary to decline this specific public service for professional reasons. I have sought and will continue to seek out those public service opportunities where my contribution can be made in a meaningful way for the benefit of this great nation and its people."

At the White House, Pen James, John Herrington (Secretary of Energy by 1988), and Ron Mann were simply wonderful to Jackie and to me, and I will always be grateful for their understanding and continued support. They were determined to find another place for me in the Reagan administration. At the time, the position of under-secretary of the army, normally the number two position at the Department of the Army at the Pentagon, remained unfilled

At the suggestion of Mann, he, Jackie, and I went to the Pentagon in a White House staff car to discuss the position with Jack Marsh, then secretary of the army. During the drive over, I kept thinking how great that job would be as a salvage job—one that could take the place of the number two position at the VA. It had been my second choice all along. Maybe something good would come out of all of this. I felt excited again.

A very charming and friendly Jack Marsh told us that he had promised the position to someone who had civilian experience with weaponry as a contractor. Jack said he really needed that person to fill the slot. However, Ron Mann—bless his heart—kept plugging on my behalf. He reminded Marsh that the paperwork had not reached White House personnel yet, and until that happened anything could be done. I could still become the nominee. I looked Marsh in the eye, realizing what could happen if I allowed political clout to have its way.

"I appreciate your commitment and understand your position," I said. "If you really need this other person to complete your team, I won't allow myself to be forced on you."

I left Marsh's office disappointed but proud that I had done the right thing. Pen James then wanted me to meet with Chief of Staff Ed Meese personally and explain my story of the conflict within the VA. But Meese couldn't meet with me for a couple of days, so I met with his top assistant. Pen James joined us for the meeting in which we were all intent on making one last effort to save me for some kind of service in the administration. However, I did make it clear that I would under no circumstances work for Nimmo. However, in spite of the efforts of all my loyal supporters, there just didn't seem to be another place for me in Washington. Prior to that meeting, I had already made plans to meet my daughters in Atlanta for an excursion to Six Flags. Besides, I had cut my ties with Washington emotionally and mentally, if not physically. I knew it was over. I decided not to wait the extra two days for a meeting with Meese and left Washington with my head "bloodied" but not bowed.

My leaving the VA after only ten days became a media event because Nimmo's supporters at the VA made highly unfair and unkind remarks about me that were summarily carried by the press. Extensive coverage of my departure appeared in medical and veterans' publications as well as the Washington and Texas media. I learned very quickly that involving myself in politics meant placing myself in a position to be ridiculed and criticized. I had to learn to take the bad with the good if I expected to survive. The situation that evolved was very stressful for me, and it took much of my spiritual strength not to lash out in kind.

On Wednesday, July 22, 1981, the *Austin American-Statesman* carried an article by reporter John Henry. The excerpts that follow best sum up and clarify the facts surrounding the debacle at the VA.

> Not only had President Reagan tapped a highly decorated Vietnam veteran, a double amputee, and West Point graduate, he thought he was sending the management-starved agency a proven line officer with a reputation for quickly getting to the heart of an issue and resolving the problems. . . . It wasn't long after Clark's arrival in Washington that veterans and longtime VA employees knew they were dealing with a character different from previous administrators.
>
> "He was refreshing," said one former infantryman who, like many other VA employees, feared for his job if quoted by name regarding Clark's brief tenure at the agency. . . . "He certainly had the management capability to stabilize the agency for the first time in a good many years," the employee said.
>
> Faced with accepting what VA insiders described as "a token role" to appease Vietnam era veterans or bowing out, Clark left the VA July 6 after nine and one-half days. Either way, sources said, substantive issues and front line management duties were to be handled from the VA's number three slot, a job given last week to former army Sergeant Edgar "Nick" Longworth. . . .
>
> We would have loved to have retained Allen Clark in the administration because he's an extremely bright, able fellow," a White House spokesman said. "We've thought very highly of him all the way along. . . ."

VA and White House sources have another version. When the options became clear, sources said, the administration let Clark go rather than face the politically embarrassing prospect of losing Nimmo. Nimmo was the fifth person seriously considered for the VA administrator by the White House sources said.

Marine Corps veteran Jim Webb removed his name from consideration after telling White House officials that "No one could survive in that job, particularly a Vietnam veteran, without having some absolute guarantees for policy and budget access. . . ."

(Ross) Perot, a longtime supporter of Vietnam veterans, called Clark "a top-flight man. Every part of his record makes him the kind of man you want to bring into your business. I was thrilled when he got the (VA) job because I thought we would finally get somebody up there to clean up the hospitals, clean up the veterans' programs. He's tough. He'd get it done. . . . Allen Clark would have looked after the veterans." (Henry).

On July 15, six days after I left the VA, President Reagan wrote me the following letter:

Dear Allen,

Out of my great personal respect for you, I accept your resignation . . . but I do so with sadness in my heart. You should be a part of our team, and I'm sorry there are circumstances that prevent this being so. We will miss you. Please know that.

Nancy and I both send our warmest personal regards and affection to you, to Jackie, and to your daughters. We will always be grateful for the sacrifice you were willing to make for us and what we are trying to do here.

Sincerely,

Ron

One year later, Charles Hagel, deputy administrator of the VA, later senator and the person who replaced me, resigned his position for the same reasons that I had when I left in 1981. Following is a portion of an article that appeared in the *Dallas Times-Herald* on June 30, 1982.

Charles Hagel, deputy director of the Veterans Administration, will leave office by August because of policy differences with the agency's controversial director. . . . Hagel, 35, a twice-wounded Vietnam veteran, linked his departure to differences with VA Administrator Robert Nimmo.

Reagan has been under pressure from a group of congressmen to dismiss Nimmo because of allegations the VA chief misused public funds. Nimmo has repaid the government more than $6000 improperly spent for a personal chauffeur. The repayment was made following a VA inspector general's report detailing Nimmo's use of the driver, the expenditure of more than $54,000 to redecorate his office, and the giving of his old office furniture to his daughter, Mary, who is a public information official at the Commerce Department. (*Dallas Times-Herald*)

Sometime in the spring or summer of 1982, an article by Lou Cannon reported:

Nimmo, a World War II veteran, former California legislator, and dedicated golfer, regards many of the programs specifically directed toward the Vietnam vets as "preferential" coddling not provided for the survivors of other wars. . . . He is particularly scornful of the claim that former Vietnam veterans suffer from what doctors have called "post-traumatic stress syndrome," which affects their attitude and performance in civilian life.

Amid surrounding controversy, Robert Nimmo resigned from his post as administrator of the VA after only seventeen months in the position. It is not too much of a stretch to say it was best for me to leave the VA at that time and not associate myself with the debacle that followed.

I departed Washington with great sadness, but my family joined me immediately for an excursion to Atlanta where we visited Six Flags over Georgia. Elizabeth, then age ten, persuaded me to take her up for the parachute ride. This ride lifts seated passengers up in parachutes for several stories and then drops them in a freefall flight along cables before slowing the parachute just before it reaches the ground. One experiences the same sensation he would feel in an actual parachute drop from an airplane. I had jumped five times during airborne school while in the army, so I thought this would be a snap.

As we started the slow ascent upward, I noticed a bar that we could hold onto with our hands, but there was no bar in front of my legs—nothing to support them whatsoever. If I had lost my legs on the golf course and dance floor, I could not imagine what might happen to them on the way down on this ride. I thought, *Oh, Lord, what have I done?* When the brakeman released the brake and the parachute began its rapid descent (you guessed it!), my legs almost fell off. I had to take my hands off the support bar to hold my legs while Elizabeth held onto me in the seat—and all of this during freefall! Obviously, we both made it safely back to earth, but I haven't attempted anything that risky since. (Later legs were more firmly attached to my residual limbs.) This fun took some of the edge off the VA disaster.

Upon my return to Austin, I could not return to my old position with Governor Clements because he had filled it when I left for Washington. So instead, I entered the oil business, taking a position as assistant to Thomas D. Coffman, an Austin oilman to whom I was introduced by Hamp Hodges (West Point, 1961). By 1982, I was working in Midland, Texas, as president of several oil industry companies owned by Coffman. This change of events led me to meet yet another future president. Tom Coffman had known George W. Bush in Midland and suggested that I meet him. In June 1982, I called him and met him at his downtown Midland oil company office where his secretary brought us sandwiches for lunch. We engaged in a most interesting and long conversation that lasted for an hour and forty-five minutes. I found him to be very well informed about many topics and thoroughly enjoyed our time together. We had gone to rival prep schools— he to Andover and I to Exeter—so we exchanged some friendly bantering on that topic.

Forty-five minutes after I left Bush's office, I received a call from Governor Bill Clements in my Midland oil service company office. He asked me to join the 1982 Republican ticket as our party's candidate for state treasurer. I would oppose the Democratic candidate, Ann Richards. After the bitter disappointment in Washington, Jackie and I agonized over whether I should stay in public service. After careful consideration, I decided to join the ticket and was generously supported by Tom Coffman, who allowed me to work only part-time during the campaign.

Although only four months remained until the November elections, I began my campaign with a willingness and eagerness to do battle and win. When I campaigned in Midland in the fall of 1982, George W. Bush very graciously and generously introduced me at a fund-raiser I held at a private home. I would not cross paths with him again until 1987 at an Austin breakfast where he told me that he had packed up his desk just the day before to prepare for his move to Washington, D.C., where he would assist in his father's campaign for president. While packing, he told me he had found a copy of the New Testament that I had given him at our lunch five years before. The fact that I had given it to him had totally slipped my mind.

John Kraggs was my media and political consultant for the campaign, and he wrote in his 1986 book *Two Party Texas*, "A fast learner and strong organizer, Clark was a steadfast competitor who covered more ground on artificial legs than most people do on their own. He also had the marked disadvantage of starting as a new candidate on the statewide scene only five months prior to the election. Most new candidates who win statewide races start running more than a year before a general election."

The senior Texas senator, John Tower, went that extra mile for me in this campaign. He transported Jackie and me on his campaign plane from Austin on two occasions to fund-raisers in Corpus Christi, Victoria, and Wichita Falls. He was a U.S. Navy veteran and felt a special affinity for me, I believe, as a veteran.

One of the more interesting incidents occurred at a church in Houston during this campaign. It had been my understanding that I would have center stage at the service as a visiting "politico," but during my remarks a well-known political figure entered the sanctuary and sat quietly in the room until my remarks were concluded. There are two different methods to approach political audiences filled with mainly senior citizens. I spoke of faith and commitment and patriotism. The speaker who followed me, Senator Lloyd M. Bentsen (D-Texas), spoke about social security among other topics. I never would get it!

After the November 1982 elections, when all the votes were counted, the Democrats under the leadership of Senator Bentsen swept back into power with a vengeance. Mark White defeated Bill Clements for the governorship, and Ann Richards soundly trounced me for the office of state treasurer. The Democrats won all the statewide offices and reclaimed the power they had lost a few years before. In the six years following that election, Ann Richards' political star rose to the point that she was invited to give the keynote speech at the 1988 Democratic National Convention. She later became governor of Texas.

There were a few redeeming features of that particular race. First, I was supposedly the only candidate who ended his campaign free of debt. My race had cost approximately $649,000, and I had raised $650,000. Marlow Preston, who had worked as a full-time volunteer in my campaign, kept a tight rein on expenditures, enabling me to wind up with the $1,000 surplus. I so highly respected his business skills that after the election in 1983, we formed a business partnership in real estate investments and property management that lasted until 1989. The tax bill of 1986 and all the myriad other challenges of the Texas real estate market of the 1980s had presented us with numerous character-building and learning opportunities. Finally, Jackie, with a new self-confidence developed from campaigning with me in 1982, became a successful residential real estate broker in Austin.

The power of prayer works in every avenue of one's life. One of our investments was an apartment complex in San Antonio where we discovered very bad roofs that were going to cost us all our reserve funds to repair. I prayed for a solution to this problem, and as improbable as it sounds to the secular minds, there occurred a freak storm two weeks later that ripped off several roofs and insurance covered the repairs. *Amazingly* the adjacent apartment complex and a school across the street were *untouched*.

In the 1980s, there were a few political highs. My name was considered for Texas state chairman of the Republican Party, but I suggested the eventual selectee, George W. Strake Jr., of Houston, a much more qualified individual. I attended the 1984 Republican National Convention in Dallas as an at-large delegate from Texas and witnessed the thrill of the second nomination of Ronald Reagan to serve another term.

It took one more run at elective politics before my running for public office in Texas would be over. In January 1986, while at the Texas State archives building of the state capitol grounds, I became engaged in a conversation with Karl Rove, whom I had known from working with Governor Clements. In the course of our conversation, he suggested that I run for Travis County judge against the man who had been the county tax assessor/collector, Bill Aleshire. I guess I was "riding to the sound of the guns" again, so I filed my candidacy for that office.

Democrat Bill Aleshire had selected civilian alternative service during the Vietnam conflict due to a conscientious objector status he claimed when he received his draft notice. This quickly became a heated issue in our campaign. Back then, I quickly passed judgment on and felt a great intolerance for those in my own age group who had chosen not to serve in the military. After all, I had been raised in a family in which serving in the military was the one and only thing to do. Therefore, in spite of the fact that I was a Christian, I did not pass up the opportunity to raise the issue at a public meeting during the race. This was one "trespass" I could not forgive.

"Who was the poor white, brown, or black man who took your place in the army and possibly died?" I asked bitterly during one of our joint appearances.

This confrontation ended up on the 6 p.m. news. In the heat of political battle, I had used a weapon that I thought was a fair one to use. However, my underhanded tactic backfired when Aleshire soundly defeated me at the polls in a county not known for its kindness toward Republicans at the ballot box. I had offered myself twice for office and lost both times.

Two years later, in the summer of 1988, after having engaged in about three years of growing in spiritual maturity through a commitment to conduct my personal relationships as a Christian, I invited Bill Aleshire to a private lunch, where I quickly apologized to him for my bitter attacks on his lack of active military service. He admitted that I had hurt him but appreciated my apology. I am grateful to God that, through His grace, I have been able to develop a spirit of forgiveness and that I no longer harbor negative feelings toward those who did not serve in Vietnam, whatever their reasons might have been. My apology to Aleshire served as a final purging of the venom remaining in my spirit and freed me from years of bitterness over this issue.

In a broader sense, I now realize that wars are an expression of the worst that human beings can inflict upon one another. To maim, hurt, and kill is not the normal course for most of us to take. From time immemorial, however, neighbors have been pitted against neighbors, states against states, and countries against countries in order to achieve some aim, whether that aim is personal, economic, military, or territorial. The ultimate reason, however, always seems to center on greed or selfishness or both. Older men have dreamed, planned, and reacted to satisfy their personal, community, or national goals. They have sent the younger men (and boys) off to fight their battles and do their dirty work. In the Gulf War and especially to Iraq and Afghanistan, we sent even our young women, many of whom were mothers of small children, off to serve the national purpose.

Obviously, in my own mind, most of the United States' involvement in wars has been motivated by basically pure motives such as self-defense and freedom of oppressed peoples. Sometimes, however, these motives have been more obvious or well explained to the masses than at other times. What we did in Vietnam was no different than what so many other people have done in other wars past. Some of us answered the clarion call. I will never again denigrate those who did not serve—whatever their reasons might have been. I can no longer pass judgment on someone for not wanting to die. I did not come to that mindset easily, and

I could not have come to that mindset without the love of Jesus Christ within me.

Satan, the prince of darkness, in order to keep the world in an uproar and keep God's people from living peaceably in our own society, ultimately masterminds wars. Most people don't want to hurt others. All that most of us really desire is to be happily married, take care of our families, own a piece of property on which we can live peacefully, and be fairly paid for an honest day's work. The mission of our political leaders is to strive for a world that allows its citizens—even the Iraqi, Afghani, Palestinian, and Israeli—not to have to bear arms against and kill one another. This may sound like striving for the impossible dream, because history and human nature are not on our side. The Bible tells us that things will not get better, only worse, until our Lord returns once more. However, we must never stop trying to stop war; we must never stop working for peace, especially spiritual peace for our combat veterans.

Saying Good-bye

In September 1980, after my mother had to undergo cancer surgery, we learned that she was dying of a malignant brain tumor. We were blessed to have her with us for three more years, but lost her to cancer in July 1983. Three weeks before her death, I visited her after having given the commencement address at Moody Coliseum on the SMU campus for the W. T. White class of 1983. In my presentation I mentioned how much I owed my mother.

When I relayed that reference to her, Mom replied, "You don't owe me anything."

I am thankful to God that she lived long enough to see me recuperate from my wounds, make a good life for my family and myself, and present her with two lovely granddaughters. She and Dad were proud of me and my accomplishments, just as I was proud of both of them.

Although I returned to the private sector in the '80s, the years I spent in public service led to special occasions from time to time. On September 10, 1984, President Reagan signed a proclamation designating Hispanic Heritage Week. I was privileged to be an invited and honored guest at the signing ceremony at the White House in which the president alluded to me and my family and our Hispanic heritage. My name had been suggested by my friend, James Cicconi. At the time of the ceremony, Dad was lying in a hospital in Dallas, also dying of cancer. I felt that the most important thing about the ceremony in Washington was not the fact that the president singled me out, but that I was able to share it with Dad because he died just two days later. I went to his bedside and shared the honor that President Reagan bestowed on the Clark and de la Fuente families by reading him the president's remarks:

> Within the Hispanic community are a host of heroes to whom this country owes a debt we can never repay. I think of one, Allen Clark, whose mother was Hispanic. He lost both his legs while serving his country in Vietnam. When he came home, his body was broken, but his spirit never faltered. He went back to school, earned his masters degree in business administration, served his state in a high government post, and is now a successful businessman. He's an inspiration to all who know him.

I am so grateful that God saw fit to leave Dad on earth long enough for him to hear those words. He died a proud father on September 12, 1984.

Challenging Years

The 1980s were very challenging in every way. Jackie and I were beset and besieged by tragic family situations—the deaths of three parents, incredible financial pressures with the real estate bust in Texas. The legs were constantly developing sores, which necessitated a return to my wheelchair for weeks at a time. I thought I would have my trusted army doctors look at them one more time in 1987. I returned to Brooke Army Medical Center to have them examined by the amputee specialists there at my old Beach Pavilion. I was pleased to see a new but familiar person serving in that department. I had recruited Kevin Christensen, a U.S. Army physician, for West Point's Class of 1976 while he still attended Pearce High School in Richardson, Texas. But seeing familiar faces didn't ease the stress of walking through those old wards where I had experienced so much pain. The familiar sights, sounds, and odors evoked many unpleasant and ghostly memories. I could still hear the screams of other amputee patients and smell rotting flesh and antiseptics. That day proved to be more traumatic than I had imagined it ever could, and I felt extreme relief when I left. I never could shake the effects of June 17, 1967.

However, as this onslaught beset me beginning in the early 1980s, it was also a time of incredible spiritual growth. I voraciously read many religious books and dove into learning about prayer and spiritual warfare. And although it was a time of many "valley" experiences, as my friend (and later wife) Linda Frost once defined it, the valley experiences can be very refreshing if we wade through the cool streams of water that wash our feet as the Lord ministers to us. These experiences can perhaps be more refreshing in the valleys than on the mountaintops where we constantly strive to reach heights to seek distant views, but with thinner air to breathe.

My attempt at entrepreneurship from 1983 to 1989 in the real estate investments industry ended in disaster, causing great personal and corporate hardship. But, as so often happens to me, God had another place for me to go.

CHAPTER 11

INFECTED WITH POTOMAC FEVER

As a young adult, my newly found faith in Christ gave me an entirely new perspective on life. Since that experience, I have tried to build upon and enhance my sense of community, civic, and spiritual involvement. I once served as a soldier for my country. I always felt that I had a responsibility, as do all people of faith, to be soldiers in Caesar's world, whether it be in business, government, our places of worship, or simply in neighborhoods across this land. Many people of faith have abdicated that responsibility. All who care and become involved in their respective communities can make a difference.

This deep sense of spiritual commitment had a part in leading me into the political arena originally. I believe that committed citizens can make our communities, states, country, and indeed the world a better place in which to live by taking their ethics, morality, and spiritual maturity into the everyday battles of the secular world. These battles are as important as those fought in the hedgerows of France, over and in the waters of the South Pacific, in the jungles of South Vietnam, or in the deserts of the Middle East. We have a special responsibility to occupy and be stewards of the enemy territory and hold it until our Lord's return. We should feel compelled to try to turn this world over to Him in better shape than when we entered it.

In election year 1988, I was privileged to be the vice chairman of the Texas Veterans Coalition to elect George H. W. Bush to the forty-first presidency. With his stellar record as a naval aviator in World War II, it was a simple challenge to stir up veteran support for him.

When he won, I had been working for the Nations Bank main facility in Austin responsible for marketing the repossessed properties that were casualties of the real estate war zone Texas had become in the late 1980s. My position was terminated, but my good and loving provider gave me one more chance in Washington, D.C. to chase my dream of political involvement. One of my friends termed it infection with "Potomac fever." In old cavalry days, it was like "riding to the sound of the guns." Public service called once again.

Elation and happiness were the order of the day when I was asked to be a political appointee in the President George H. W. Bush administration. Washington became a place with high hopes of satisfaction and peace after the tough 1980s in Texas. My responsibility was to be the Assistant Secretary for Veterans Liaison and Program Coordination at the new cabinet entity, the Department of Veterans Affairs. It was a high privilege to serve the president in this political position. Confirmation occurred with a vote of the U.S. Senate on October 6, 1989.

My time in Washington in the Bush administration was filled with incredible highs as I was associated with all the great men and women of our nation's military. The highs were always punctuated with a malaise of spirit in that Jackie chose never to join me for my five years in the Northeast, and a time of estrangement developed.

There were those incredible highs. The movie *In Country* starring Bruce Willis premiered in Washington, D.C., in the fall of 1989, and I will always remember the Vietnam veteran character acted by Bruce Willis saying that "he would always have a hole in his heart" after his Vietnam experience. How true that was in the movie and in the lives of all of us who experienced the horrors of our war.

After the premiere there was a reception, and the highlight for me was a chance to dance with Demi Moore, the actress then married to Mr. Willis. I told her I just did a two-step, one left and one right. She was very gracious and kind-hearted to me and accepted my offer to dance. Elizabeth thoroughly enjoyed meeting the two stars.

A most privileged responsibility in my position was to be the executive director of the National Veterans Day Committee for the Veterans Day celebration held each year at the Amphitheatre of Arlington National Cemetery. I had attended this ceremony in the 1950s as a teenager, and now I was in charge of planning it. The speaker at Veterans Day 1989 was Secretary of Defense Dick Cheney. Nick Rowe, who was responsible for my not resigning from West Point, had been assassinated in Manila the previous spring and his widow, Susan, was to attend the ceremony with her two young sons. I arranged to have her introduced as was the widow of Audie Murphy. After the ceremony Secretary Cheney, VA Secretary Ed Derwinski, Susan, her two little boys, and I went to Nick's grave, which is just steps away from the north Amphitheatre portico. It was especially poignant to pay tribute to Nick with his widow and young sons. Very emotional and touching. Nick had been a real hero in the army, especially in the Special Forces community, after surviving and escaping from the Viet Cong in South Vietnam and then return- ing to Fort Bragg to oversee the survival, evasion, resistance, and escape (SERE) course.

During the afternoon of one of our Veterans Day ceremonies in the Amphitheatre, I was the principal speaker at the annual cere- mony sponsored by the Veterans of World War I at the gravesite of General John Pershing. Beside the famous general's grave was another simple government issue gravestone of the general's grand- son, Dick Pershing, a 101st Airborne casualty in Vietnam and a member of the class behind me at Exeter.

In my remarks I quoted a World War I veteran talking about the enemy as the "Hun." A few short days after my speech, Secretary Derwinski called me to his office to read a letter written to him by the German army military attaché who had been present at the program. The German officer, obviously now an ally of the United States, took extreme offense at my use of the term *Hun*, referring to his German military predecessors in World War I.

I guess I would never have been a candidate for a diplomatic post in the State Department.

In the spring of 1989 when I interviewed for my nomination, I informed the White House personnel people that my financial position in my Texas company was extremely precarious and that I might have to declare bankruptcy later in the year. My interviewer told me that was not a deal-killer because my possible position was not in the financial management arena. Unfortunately, later that year another heavy shoe fell on me. Before I returned to Austin after Christmas vacation, I informed Secretary Derwinski that I would probably be filing for personal bankruptcy over the holidays. He said he appreciated my candor. It happened as I feared.

I declared personal Chapter 7 bankruptcy on December 28, 1989, in Austin. It was Jackie's and my twenty-sixth wedding anniversary. The inevitable newspaper article followed. Actually, the newspaper article wasn't that bad. It was written by John Henry, a political writer for the *Austin-American Statesman* who had inter-viewed me after the debacle in 1981 when I came to the VA. The article was published in several newspapers in Texas and even aired on radio. At that time in 1989, my bankruptcy was more important news than Michael Dell being named Entrepreneur of the Year because my article was placed above his.

One of my investors, Bob Protzman, an orthopedic surgeon in Fort Worth and my Beast Barracks squad leader at West Point, called my partner Marlow Preston in Austin after hearing only the second half of a radio announcement and thought I had died.

With my new life in Washington, I thought the news may not necessarily be known up there, but the world is very small, especially for federal political appointees. On the afternoon of Thursday, January 11, 1990, I was interviewed by Bill McAllister of the *Washington Post* about the filing.

That night I went to a Bible study with Frank Salcedo at the home of air force Colonel Stuart and Debbie Johnson. Betsy North, the wife of Ollie, was also there that night. When prayer requests were named, I asked that the article be "lost" and not printed at all. Frank asked that it be fair. The group prayed with me and I went home really feeling drained. The article appeared the following morning, and it was a concise, fairly and accurately reported story. I spent the day at the VA regional office on North Capitol Street (right across the street from Gonzaga, the high school I had attended), so I didn't see any friends during the day.

Elizabeth was still in Texas and I was by myself until Sunday evening when I went to see Stu and Debbie, who had invited me for supper. That weekend was one of the most difficult in my life. I felt "disconsolate" because I had failed in business. There were no actual negative political implications because my problems were disclosed in February in my White House interview and again in June when my financial report was reviewed by the White House.

Still, I had been trying to build my new life in Washington and put all the past three years' financial strains behind me from Texas. Elizabeth had participated at Thanksgiving in the National Debutante Cotillion and Thanksgiving Ball, and she had been selected as the Cherry Blossom princess for Texas by the Texas State Society. She had only planned on living in Washington for the fall semester, but loved it so much she decided to stay. Jackie and Christi had not yet scheduled their move and were still in Texas. Simply put, I was devastated.

A uniquely timed event also occurred that Tuesday morning after the three-day weekend. I had picked up my new legs, which were being rebuilt over the previous six months, and I wore them to the office for the first time. Whereas, on Friday, when people looked at me, I assumed it was because "That's the guy who was in the *Post* today." On Tuesday I made the assumption that they looked at me at my new towering height of six feet one (up from five feet eleven) and said, "He surely looks tall."

When I returned to the office on Tuesday, I had been helped by God through my hurts. My conclusion was that if my idols were my material possessions and if my self-image was based on my bank balances to give me assurances and security, then I was lost and would stay lost. But, if, as was truly the case, my self-image was based upon my value in God's eyes, and those of my family, friends, and my new VA family, then I still had all I really needed. That understanding and acceptance was a major breakthrough for me spiritually and emotionally. Many of my material possessions were lost, but all I truly needed for strength was still a part of me. I told Assistant Secretary for Public Affairs Ed Timperlake, a good friend of mine, my feelings on this. He told me more people in the Washington arena needed to believe that. So much in Caesar's world had been lost, but I knew who I was and again; I was a survivor.

Lieutenant General Howard Graves joined me for lunch soon thereafter. He was a devout Christian and friend of Andy and Gail Seidel's. He was assistant to the Chairman of the Joint Chiefs of Staff, General Colin Powell. He told me to call him any time I needed to talk to somebody. He was in a Thursday morning Bible study at the Pentagon with twenty-five general and flag rank officers. He later became superintendent at West Point and president of Texas A&M University. Unfortunately, he succumbed to the ravages of cancer at a relatively young age. I never called on him for the prayer, but there were times I should have. But, as is normal with people, we tend to try to handle it by ourselves.

On February 9, 1990, I received a real lesson in taking instructions too far as in speaking too much to the president. It was very embarrassing to me. We had a world affairs briefing at the Indian Treaty room of the old executive office building. Secretary Derwinski was master of ceremonies. Chairman of the Joint Chiefs of Staff Colin Powell spoke, as did President Bush. At the end of brief remarks by the president, I went up to the rostrum as I was to introduce the veteran commanders present, introduced myself, and suggested the president step over to the flag as I announced our veteran group commanders for the "photo op." He said to me, "I know what to do." So much for being a control freak!

The VA sponsored winter sports clinics at Colorado ski resorts, and at one I learned to ski on my artificial legs with smaller skis fixed upon my ski poles. It was a great morale booster.

In my political position, it was a blessing to have an opportunity for involvement in several Washington circles, and the religious community was one that was most gratifying. The Reverend Chuck Swindoll, then pastor of a church in Pasadena, California, led a retreat held in Charlottesville in April 1990 for members of a Pentagon Bible study and another one held at the capitol. Colorado Senator Bill and Ellen Armstrong attended, as did General Howard and Gracie Graves. I was able to dine next to Chuck and his wife, Cynthia, and found him to be approachable, warm, witty, and a perfectly marvelous gentleman.

My father had served in Korea and was there when the armistice was signed in 1953, so it was with a special family memory and sense of pride that I was able to be involved in a very unimportant manner with the Korean War Memorial on the Mall. I went to the White House with several Korean War veterans for a planning meeting that became contentious for some reason or other, and when the meeting was over, I walked down the marble hallway beside a young White House female staff member who commented her displeasure with the seeming "toughness" of the veterans in the meeting. I told her you couldn't expect us to go off and experience the rigors of a combat experience and be expected to be "soft" when we returned to civilian life. So much for White House staffers with no exposure to the military, of which I would find many more during my time in the VA.

Naturally, the Korean War Memorial would cost money, so a fund-raiser was held May 1, 1990, at the Omni Shoreham Hotel. What a night of memories and pleasantries. The master of ceremonies was our Secretary Derwinski and the chairman of the gala was General Richard Stilwell (USA-Ret.), who had been such a source of motivation to me as a cadet when he was commandant. Elizabeth was with me at a table with Bonnie and Ed Derwinski. Joining us at this table were Ambassador and Mrs. Park of South Korea, chaplain of the House of Representatives Jim Ford and Mrs. Ford (he had been chaplain at West Point when I was a cadet), and General and Mrs. Andrew J. Goodpaster. He was chairman of the American Battle Monuments Commission. Small world indeed. One of the Goodpasters' daughters sat next to me in an eighth grade class in Alexandria, Virginia. Not bad company for that barefoot kid from Mission, Texas.

Abigail Van Buren, "Dear Abby," was a special guest, and the entertainment was provided by none other than Rosemary Clooney and Bob Hope. They would leave the next day for a USO trip to the Berlin Wall. After the gala, we mixed with a small group upstairs, and I chatted for short a time with Mr. Hope and Ms. Clooney. What a night!

As VA veterans' liaison to the veterans' community, it was my duty to rally veteran support for administration initiatives. On June 20, 1990, my forty-eighth birthday, we had a vote pending the next day for a flag amendment, and our veterans were invited into the Roosevelt Room of the White House to be lobbied. I checked in with the guard on the Pennsylvania Avenue side west of the Oval driveway and proceeded past the Marine Guard into the waiting room. I rearranged the name cards on the table to ensure proper respect to organizations and titles.

Vice President Dan Quayle entered and sat down and said President Bush would step in for a few minutes. He did and stood right in front of me for about five minutes. In fact, because my legs were stretched out so far, I was afraid he would trip over me as he left. He didn't!

My forty-eighth birthday was celebrated in the Roosevelt Room of the White House after the president and vice president departed with a cupcake topped by an American flag. Mike Duncan of Kentucky had become a friend of mine in his position in the Office of Public Liaison at the White House, and he brought it in. Mike was a banker from Inez, Kentucky, and later ran a college in Kentucky and became treasurer of the Republican National Committee.

The Democrats had pushed through the vote so fast our veterans did not have time to muster our votes, and the flag amendment was defeated in the House despite our efforts.

On July 19, 1990, with a beautiful, cloudless sky overhead, a very special ceremony was held on the South Lawn of the White House where President Bush would sign the landmark legislation for the disabled, known as the Americans with Disabilities Act. My long-time Texas friend, Justin Dart Jr., was on the platform with the president as Justin had shepherded this effort through many obstacles.

Hattie Bickmore, from my office, was in charge of seating in the VIP section and put me in my wheelchair in the center aisle, twenty feet from the president and next to Attorney General Thornburgh and Education Secretary Cavazos.

All the leaders of the national disabled rights community were in the audience, the ones confined to wheelchairs, the maimed, the "little people," the stroke victims, the multiple sclerosis patients, the disabled war vets, all those who would now have the law behind them obtaining access to employment and public accommodations.

As we waited for the ceremony, a Secret Service agent brought me a folding chair and asked me to "guard it with my life" because an agent needed to sit in it and face the crowd. Several people asked for it, but I warded them away. Then Sichan Siv, a deputy assistant to the president in public liaison, whom I knew, asked me for the chair; it took me awhile to understand it was for President Bush's daughter, Dorothy (Doro), who had arrived. I told Sichan my dilemma and asked him to prioritize the chair use between the agent and the president's daughter. He told me to hold onto it and he would bring the president's daughter over to sit on it. I thought, great, no agent, but Dorothy would sit next to me.

Motioning to an usher who worked for me, I told him the Secret Service had been preempted by the first daughter and would he please get another chair ready fast. Then Sichan said Dorothy was going to stay where she was and not move. Drats! The usher showed up with the extra chair. I told him, "Hold on to it," because the way things were going, someone *else* might pull rank on the agent.

No less than two minutes later, John Sununu, the White House chief of staff, moved into my area, and after greeting all the surrounding dignitaries, he and I shook hands. Then it happened! "Can I use this chair?" He pointed, of course, to the one under my watchful eye beside me. Well, let me tell you, you don't say no to a deputy assistant to the president and the chief of staff to the president. What do you think this decorated, supposedly fearless veteran of the jungles of Vietnam said to Sununu, in reference to the chair entrusted to my care?

"Take it, it's yours."

So much for the pecking order at the White House.

Naturally, I beckoned the usher for another replacement chair, folded it, and clasped it tightly under my arm and next to my wheelchair. The agent supervisor came up, and not seeing the chair under my arm, seemed disappointed. I quickly pulled it open and smiled at him, telling him he wouldn't know what I went through to keep it available for presidential security that day. I told him that it almost went to the president's daughter, and I pointed at Sununu whose chair was two feet from me. The supervisor smiled big. Many well-known legislators were there: Senators Ted Kennedy, Orrin Hatch, Bob Dole, Paul Simon, Pete Wilson, John McCain and Congressman Steve Bartlett, my old Dallas compatriot from Dallas County Republican Men's Club days.

President Bush made a short, but very effective and emotional presentation about the act and did the ritual distribution of the pens with which he signed the bill. An armless chaplain had given the invocation and offered the space between his toes to grasp the pen. President Bush was seemingly startled, but I heard him say, "Really" as he placed the souvenir pen between the big and first toe.

It was a special day; starting with my work back in Texas in 1979 when we began the follow-through to the White House Conference on Disabled Persons from 1978, and I began working with Justin Dart Jr. Justin kindly credits me with the initiative that started the ball rolling, which culminated with the ADA. Justin did the work. Governor Clements got him started.

After the ceremony, there was a picnic at the Ellipse. The highlight of that was meeting a short woman with her hair tied in a bun behind her head, wearing a nondescript dress. Nothing especially striking about her. She was a salesperson for some technology company benefiting disabled persons. Only her name was special in our short encounter. She was Donna Rice of the Gary Hart episode. She had apparently become a born-again Christian and blended quietly into anonymity making a new life for herself after being in every tabloid in the country. Fame is very fleeting for some.

At the annual convention of the American Ex–Prisoners of War on October 10, 1990, in Seattle, I had two extraordinary personal conversations that were unforgettable. One of them was with British army veteran, Bill Griffeths, there with his wife, Alice. He had been forced by his Japanese captors in a World War II POW camp in Singapore to defuse mines. For his efforts, he lost his eyes and arms when one exploded. I had the greatest love and admiration for Alice who cared for him so wonderfully as do so many of our spouses (especially Jackie) when we return maimed and broken in our bodies and souls.

Also at this convention, I spoke to Madeleine Ullam from Nebraska, who had been one of sixty-eight army nurses captured at Corregidor in the spring of 1942 after the Japanese invasion of the Philippines. It will never be forgotten to hear her describing the wounded and sick Americans for whom she nursed in the Malinta tunnels. She said that though they were hurting, underfed. and undermedicated, they never complained. These were men and women of America's "Greatest generation."

It was an annual tradition, this reception with the president, typically in the summer, to honor the newly elected commanders of the national veterans' organizations. It was my job to get this scheduled. For whatever reason, when I *began* my efforts in July 1990, it was like pulling teeth to get that scheduled. All of a sudden it was easily scheduled by a White House staff, knowing the veterans were again important after the events of August 2, 1990, when Saddam Hussein invaded Kuwait.

A new sense of urgency permeated everything at the VA, because we assumed we eventually would be in another war and we needed to be prepared for casualties to enter our VA medical centers in unknown numbers. Recalling the rather impersonalized manner in which Jackie had been informed of my wounding and how uninformed she had been of my movements for care back to the States, I visited with Secretary Derwinski and suggested that the VA establish a better line of communication with the Department of Defense for informing families of casualties where the wounded men were and what was the schedule for their return to the United

States. I am delighted that the secretary effected just such a program at the VA with a special operation established at one of our medical centers. I do not pretend that the idea was only mine, but I am pleased it was done for Gulf War I with significant improvements over the Vietnam system of notification.

We began our military build-up in the Middle East and the political effort to explain the administration's position was part of the nation's education and understanding. My part was small but important to me in planning a December 14, 1990, meeting of veterans' leaders in the White House Roosevelt Room. We were initially briefed on the situation in the Middle East by Richard Haase of the National Security Council. He recounted the thrust by Saddam into Kuwait, and, but for our quick reaction to defend Saudi Arabia, indicated Saddam might have kept going into Saudi Arabia. Haase declared the imperative of dislodging Saddam early because of the higher cost later if Kuwait were to be more strongly fortified. Haase had said that Iraq would not be inviolate in an attack on Kuwait and that Saddam must be aware of the devastation he would suffer.

Then the president entered and asked for veteran support. He was masterful. He told the story of two women who were in the hospital in Dharain, mother and daughter, who had been raped by Iraqi "soldiers," while the father watched and then was shot in the head. He said he could not understand how the people who recently were showcased on the *Phil Donahue Show* (who were trying to get out of their service commitment) could do that. He said when he saw that "you had to peel him off the ceiling."

General P. X. Kelley, the Marine commandant during the Lebanon barracks bombing, was present and despaired at all the former high-ranking officers who had testified about giving the sanctions more time to work. He said he, himself, had declined testifying. The president said, "Don't turn them down the next time," and we laughed. The president spoke of the morality, the right and wrong, of the situation. Someone asked him about casualties, and he had told them, "He did not want to accept even one casualty." He spoke about the support he would give our troops.

He said, as he closed his eyes, and then put his hands to his head and lowered his head, "I want to be certain in my heart so I can explain it to the parents who will write me." It was really a very special moment.

After the meeting, he walked around the room and shook all the hands. He stood before me with a firm handshake and I said, "Merry Christmas, sir." I wanted to tell him what was in my heart, but I knew his time was limited and I should not hold him up. I recalled saying too much once before. Ed Timperlake and I then went to work with the veterans' groups for expressions of support for the inevitable war that was ahead.

On January 17, 1991, Operation Desert Storm began, and I heard about the assault on the radio that night as I was driving home to McLean on the George Washington Parkway, literally just opposite CIA headquarters. Thankfully, it was over quickly, by February 28, 1991, and the numbers of killed and wounded were much lower than the original alarming estimates and expectations.

Justin Dart Jr. had called me in the fall of 1990 inquiring of my interest in being the executive director of the president's committee on employment of people with disabilities. It would have been a very satisfying position, which Justin said could be mine for the taking, but as the war loomed evermore, I felt compelled to remain at the VA during a wartime period, and I very gratefully thanked Justin for his support, but declined the opportunity.

As has always been the case, God had other plans for me that would plant the seeds of my future service in the spiritual arena.

CHAPTER 12

ARMOR FOR A HEALING WARRIOR

Augustitle 4, 1991, was a very special day in my life. It was announced that my next VA position would be as the new director of the National Cemetery System, the VA's 113 cemeteries in thirty-nine states. It was the pinnacle of my public service career, a high and distinguished honor with the opportunity to lead and direct that 1,200-person organization.

Another very emotional experience occurred that same day at the memorial tribute at National Cathedral for Lee Atwater, who had died of a brain tumor at age forty after being chairman of the Republican National Committee. He had been a hardball political strategist who was a genius in politics.

After reaching the pinnacle of success, he was felled by this illness. Secretary of State Jim Baker talked about visiting Lee and reading the Bible with him. Doug Coe, the quiet force behind the National Prayer Breakfast, once explained theology to Lee by asking if you wanted to communicate with a cow, what would you have to do? Lee answered, "Become a cow." This explained what God did to communicate with humanity by . . . becoming a man through His Son, Jesus. Lee had accepted Christ as his Savior before he died and attempted to reconcile with forgiveness and through apology to all the people he had harmed in his political career. As the tributes were read, I prayed that the Holy Spirit would touch people in the room and prayed that Lee, in death, could impact them by the example he lived and believed in. It was a very stirring service.

Soon after this, I experienced one of those very disturbing times for those of us who are bold to proclaim our Christian faith. Prior to this time, I had prayed with three VA employees who were seriously distressed for one reason or another. It was my belief that it was always with their permission, with no coercion, and seemed to be appreciated. Apparently, these occasions came to the attention of a senior political appointee in the VA, who mentioned to me that he had heard that I "forced" people to pray in my office, and there was an issue of "separation of church and state" involved. I explained to him in very clear fashion that three people were prayed with in my office only because they had personal or professional challenges that I felt could be dealt with only through prayer. This encounter caused me to become very careful, though, and when an intercessory prayer group was begun by me at the VA in the fall of 1991, I wouldn't let it even meet in my spacious office.

My time at the VA in Washington exposed me in a very decided fashion to the challenges of our combat veterans, especially from Vietnam, who wrestled with the horrific effects of post-traumatic stress disorder (PTSD). In my interview for my VA nomination in 1989, I had noted my PTSD on the health issues, but I had kept my own episodes and issues closely hidden and guarded other than vague references to "suffering many of the symptoms of PTSD." I was still not ready to bear my soul to the world about my own bouts with depression. My heart went out to my fellow sufferers in my visits with veterans at medical centers and vet centers, and in personal occasions. The VA offered me my first opportunities to recognize the potential for a future ministry to veterans who needed healing from their combat traumas.

The first really large audience to whom I could express my own healing process was for three hundred Vietnam veterans from Indiana who were sponsored by the Psychiatric Institute of America at a "forgotten hero" ceremony at the Vietnam Veterans Memorial on June 1, 1991. A follow-up letter to Secretary Derwinski from the organizer said, "It was quite evident through the tears and hugs of the men and women in the audience that Mr. Clark spoke not only to their minds, but to their hearts and souls—which in so many cases are still searching for answers. Mr. Clark was able to offer answers to these people. He shared the lessons he had learned. Lessons, which I know, were not easily acquired. On that day we all benefited without having to pay the price that he has paid."

The seeds were planted for me to minister and assist my fellow veterans. Unfortunately, it would be years before all the elements of my Combat Faith Ministry were able to bear fruit.

The Desert Storm homecoming parade on July 8, 1991, which passed down Constitution Avenue, was a glowing tribute to our military. Secretary Derwinski desired that the American veterans welcome back the newest warriors. The VA was in a power struggle with certain members of Congress who wanted to take political advantage of the event and called a meeting in a congressional hearing room to attempt to take control of the event. Secretary Derwinski sent Ed Timperlake and me to the meeting and said the VA should oversee the parade and attendant events. There was a discussion that became intense at times. I arose four times with veteran leaders seated behind me to debate the case for the VA opinion that would allow veterans to plan and execute the celebration. Vivid was the recollection of the original omission of any commemoration of our sacrifices after Vietnam, and I felt compelled to make the case for the symbolism of veterans being in charge rather than the politicians. Eventually, the senior congressman present conceded that the VA should organize the events. Secretary Derwinski recruited Harry Walters, former VA administrator and fellow West Pointer, to oversee the planning and execution.

It was a brilliantly bright Washington day when General Norman Schwartzkopf led our troops down the parade route and stopped in front of the reviewing stand just south of the Ellipse. In the stands flanking the president and other officials were the leaders of our veterans' organizations. We had made our case, and our newest warriors were welcomed back by our warriors of previous conflicts.

The fiftieth anniversary of the attack on Pearl Harbor (December 7, 1991) found me at one of our VA cemeteries, the Punchbowl in Hawaii. This is definitely one of the more scenic and spectacular settings of all our national cemeteries. About 5 a.m. I left my room at the Hilton Hawaiian Village Hotel with Ruth and Wil Mizell (a deputy assistant secretary and former professional baseball player known as "Vinegar Bend"), and we headed for the National Memorial Cemetery of the Pacific, the Punchbowl, for a presidential visit and address before 7,800 people who were mostly members of the Pearl Harbor Survivors Association.

When President and Mrs. Bush first arrived, President Bush laid a wreath at a memorial and Mrs. Bush stood literally five inches in front of me. The president's speech was magnificent, and he left just as the first daylight came into the sky because he was to attend the ceremony at the Arizona Memorial in Pearl Harbor.

I went up to the rostrum, and because I was to give welcoming remarks to the continuing ceremony of the attendees after the president departed, I sat where the president had been seated. I hoped something great would rub off on me, but nothing happened. I made welcoming remarks to the Bomber Group members who had been at Hickam Field on December 7, 1941. What a two days it was. It was a special sense of pride to be in Hawaii for the fiftieth anniversary of that infamous day in our military history.

Another one of those dancin' opportunities with a beautiful woman (besides Jackie) came on January 11, 1992, when I came to Dallas to attend with Jackie a fund-raiser for the National Paralysis Foundation begun by Kent Waldrep. A letter of greetings from President Bush was carried by me and it was read by the co-master of ceremonies, Gary Collins, married to Mary Ann Mobley, Miss America 1959.

Later in the evening, Mrs. Waldrep, Jackie, and I were talking to Mrs. Collins, and I asked her to dance. She at first turned me down, but later came over to me and accepted after she heard from someone else that I was a double leg amputee. She said her excuse of her shoes not fitting paled into insignificance compared to my condition. The favor of a dance with her was not shared with anyone else during the evening.

Coach Tom Landry of the Dallas Cowboys came to Virginia on April 28, 1992, for a speech to the Fellowship of Christian Athletes. There were probably one thousand people in the audience and two other people from his hometown, Mission, Texas. There was Congressman Kika de la Garza and myself. Before the event I was introduced to Coach Landry and mentioned the Mission connection of my mother's, and he mentioned his early friendship with Pepe de la Fuente, Mother's first cousin. Amazingly, in his introductory comments, he mentioned both me and Congressman de la Garza from Mission, also present from his hometown.

In the summer of 1992, then Major General Charles Krulak, later to become commandant of the Marine Corps, was a guest speaker at a Veterans Affairs Department religious group. General Krulak had been a class behind me at Exeter Academy and was the quarterback of the club football team with which I had limited playing time due to my broken rib. Chuck was responsible (among many other heavy responsibilities) for locating and providing water in the amount of one hundred thousand gallons per day for the coalition assault in Desert Storm the previous year. The area where he was based was typically dry and dusty and many miles from the coastal desalinization plants, and no water was to be found. He said they asked desert tribal members, petroleum engineers, and anyone with knowledge of the area, but to no avail.

He had been accustomed to having prayers as a regular part of his morning meetings with his staff, and he said prayers were sent up to find water so the ground assault would not be delayed. A morning meeting was interrupted one day and a fellow Marine asked the general to follow him as they proceeded down a road heavily traveled every day by the coalition forces.

Off this road about fifty yards, General Krulak came upon an amazing sight. Protruding from the ground was a pipe that had at its base a green generator (already containing one thousand gallons of diesel fuel), a red pump, and four new batteries. No one could explain who dug it nor how it had not been seen before. Krulak did the honors and pushed the ignition switch and you know the rest of the story. It produced one hundred thousand gallons of water per day!

To my mind one of the highlights of my entire life and definitely the peak of my public service career was achieved on the high ground east of and overlooking the Vietnam Veterans Memorial on June 21, 1992, which was Father's Day. An effort of the Vietnam Veterans Memorial organization was called Sons and Daughters in Touch. These were the children left fatherless from deaths in Vietnam. The first annual gathering of three hundred of these children (who by now were all adults) was held in Washington, D.C.

A "Rose of Remembrance Ceremony" was held on that high ground, and I was asked to be the speaker. It was with fear and trembling that I accepted this challenge. It was with much prayer my remarks were prepared. I asked some fellow Vietnam veterans for comments to include. Some excerpts of my remarks follow:

> I recently visited with the medic, Jim Hill, who saved my life in Vietnam. Jim remembers me and that day. And he remembers all the other casualties he treated. He particularly remembers the ones he lost, the ones who died. Every medic I've met has guilt feelings about those who died in their arms. They're hard memories. They're hard memories for all of us who were there—where the war was up close and personal.
>
> I didn't know what to say that would be worthy enough to say to the sons and daughters of fallen comrades from a war that has been the subject of such immense interest to the world. I feel as did Abraham Lincoln when he wrote Mrs. Bixby, who had lost five sons in the war, "I feel how weak and fruitless must be any word of mine which should attempt to beguile you from the grief of a loss so overwhelming."
>
> What I will say to you is a product of much reading, much soul-searching, and a spiritual journey that has brought me my own understanding. We all went to Vietnam for different reasons. Some like me because classmates, Burt McCord and Mike Kilroy, were already killed in action and I was a regular army West Point captain who felt I *had* to do my duty there. Others went because it was their job and they were on orders. Others went because they were drafted and they went rather

than avoid or evade. As George Skypeck said in his poem, "Soldier," "I was that which others did not want to be. I went where others feared to go, and did what others failed to do." None of us wanted to be there, really. It was hot, dirty, lonely, and miserable. Our sense of duty and our commitment to our fellow Americans drove us on each day. It kept us going. Very few of us at the time really understood the strategic purpose of stopping the flow of communism into Southeast Asia. We wondered why Laos and Cambodia were privileged sanctuaries.

I have come to a spiritual view of this world and us: Our God in Heaven created this world, but unfortunately the forces of evil have been preeminent since day one. Some humans have been savage, selfish, greedy, and acquisitive. These human traits have caused our wars. To preserve freedom and goodness and the great traditions of humanity, young men have had to march off to war. Jerry Singleton, a POW for almost seven years, who became an air force chaplain, wrote me with a suggestion to say this to you. Jesus Christ said, "Greater love has no one than this, that he lay down his life for his friends" (John 15:13 NIV). I believe that is what we did in Vietnam. A general from another war, a more popular war, Douglas MacArthur, once said, "The soldier, above all other men, is required to perform the highest act of religious teaching—sacrifice."

It is the young men who have always borne the brunt of the savagery of our wars. It was your fathers who were sacrificed on the altar of war. Many thousands more of us will carry mental and emotional scars with us forever. We are the residue of the wars.

Sons and daughters of our comrades who are on the panels of the Vietnam Veterans Memorial, your fathers did not die in vain. Our casualties from Korea and Vietnam, who so nobly sacrificed, demonstrated the resolve of the United States of America to withstand the probes of communism over the past forty-seven years. We won the Cold War. The Soviet Union gave up. We won. Countless millions live today with much more secure and peaceful futures. Those futures were bought by your fathers.

Colonel Roger Donlon, the first Vietnam Medal of Honor Recipient, wrote that (the men and women whose names are memorialized on that wall) "they are the true heroes in my eyes and heart." Anthony J. Principi, the deputy secretary of the Department of Vietnam Affairs, said, "The names carved in the stone of the Vietnam Veterans Memorial verify that your fathers' death was a part of a current that moved our nation and changed the world!" Many other Vietnam veterans and I echo those words about your fathers.

We love you and the good people of America, and the freedom-loving people of the world will always appreciate America and our fallen heroes, your fathers. I close by quoting again from the Abraham Lincoln letter I mentioned previously. "I pray that our heavenly Father may assuage the anguish of your bereavement, and leave you only cherished memory of the loved and lost, and the solemn pride that must be yours, to have laid so costly a sacrifice upon the altar of freedom."

It was one of the most poignant and emotional times of my life. My heart poured out to these young men and women of our country. Hopefully, my words had meaning for spouses, parents, siblings, and friends of our fallen warriors. After that high the rest of my time at the VA was rather mundane. It was a distinct privilege to have had this opportunity to serve our nation's veterans.

My tenure at the VA ended upon Bill Clinton's swearing in as president on January 19, 1993. In serving our veterans, I felt that I had been a part of something very worthwhile. It had been a terrific ride and I had met up close many great Americans, heroes, and heroines.

CHAPTER 13

"THANK YOU FOR BRINGING MY DADDY HOME"

Once one's public official loses a race, there is an overwhelming sense of regret and sadness, due to the loss itself, but obviously due to another time of uncertainty and turmoil in one's life.

That was certainly the case for me as another downward swing of the sine curve of my life seemed to spiral ever lower, but it was a time wherein my two daughters, who by now both lived with me in D.C. as they attended college, made time for their father. We had quality father-daughter time. There are those occasions that are so simple, yet memorable, that prove God answers even little prayers. I sent up many little prayers.

Christi had reluctantly driven me to a lacrosse game and kept pestering me to go on to some other activity for which she had more interest. It began to sprinkle and we left in a decidedly combative mood that continued in silence as she drove me home. I hate those situations and began to pray quietly that, by our return home, we would be in a good humor. Literally two minutes after my prayer, Christi looked over at me with a grin and said, "You're praying, aren't you?" God answers big *and* little prayers.

After speaking to the fatherless young people at the Vietnam Memorial in 1992, their challenges, lack of closure, and lack of knowledge of their fathers weighed heavily on me. I was planning on attending my thirtieth West Point reunion in the fall of 1993, and the thought occurred to me to take small books to the reunion for classmates to write their memories of our classmates who did not return from Vietnam (twenty in all).

Research unearthed twenty-one names of the sons and daughters of these classmates who had been recipients of education grants from our class fund. Equipped with twenty-one little blank books with the West Point crest affixed to the front, I spent the reunion locating attending classmates to enter their cadet and military reminiscences of our classmates who were casualties of the war. Willingly, but sadly, the entries were made and returned to me after circulation all weekend. The books were mailed in early December 1993 to the young people who lost their fathers who had been our classmates.

Several sent thank-you notes, but the most touching was from the daughter of a classmate who related how she had received the book and began reading it, and ended up on her floor in tears as she learned so much about her father, whose life was cut short by doing his duty. That one letter made the effort all worthwhile.

After remaining a few months in Washington and then moving to Durham, North Carolina, I returned to Texas in the summer of 1994 for the express purpose of attempting reconciliation with my wife. It would not happen.

Notwithstanding the constant maturing of my faith through learning to grow spiritually, my thirty-year marriage to Jackie terminated in 1994. Very simply, however unfortunately, and despite all we had jointly experienced and survived, our life's goals and journeys had diverged, and our union was no longer possible. Partially, she was the victim of the hurts and sorrows we severely disabled war veterans experience. I prayed for changes in us both to make our marriage work, and I prayed for God to change her choice to pursue the divorce. I sincerely believed that anything and everything could be changed through sincere prayer to God. But I had not totally grasped the concept of free will, a concept I learned from a godly pastor who told me that God would not override Jackie's free will to choose separation and divorce. God will not override another person's free will choices despite our concentrated desire to make everything come true for which we pray. If the desired consequence for which we are praying requires that another person go along with our prayers and "do what we want him to do," the prayer coming to fruition is then dependent on their exerting free will to make the choices we desire. God will not make another person do what we want just because we prayed it.

That same pastor also taught me a magnificent lesson in the power of prayer. I had told him how saddened I was that Jackie had never forgiven me for volunteering for Vietnam, and together we prayed a prayer related to Matthew 9:38 regarding the sending of laborers of the harvest: "Pray ye, therefore, the Lord of the harvest, that he will send forth laborers into the harvest." Obviously, this is meant for people to go forth and tell others the Lord's message, but we appropriated this idea that a person, television program, sermon, passage of Scripture, and so forth be used to convey an important message or idea to another person that will affect their free will thoughts and choices. So, we prayed in agreement that something she would hear, read, see, or experience would convince her finally to forgive me for that life-changing decision made so very long ago that had ended up costing us both so much of our carefree youthful years.

Of course, the prayer worked. Two weeks later and several months before our divorce was final, Jackie called me. She said that she had been watching a television program on forgiveness and was impressed with how many times the Bible mentioned forgiveness and how she would not be forgiven if she did not forgive others. Without my bringing it up, she finally forgave me for volunteering for Vietnam. What a relief and closure that was for me. In addition, I got to see the "PUSH" formula (Pray Until Something Happens) actually work firsthand.

Although no longer husband and wife, Jackie and I maintain a very warm and cordial relationship, and together we share the lives of our two daughters. Her father, Jack McAdams, still introduces me as his son-in-law, and I thank him for that. Again, these are examples of God's continuing love and the fruit of the Holy Spirit being expressed through all of us. Despite several devastating years that followed, God bestowed His grace on me, and I went on with my life knowing that my faith had grown even stronger through yet another adversity.

The Family Blossoms

In 1989, Elizabeth moved to Washington to live with me, eventually graduating from George Mason University. She served as a White House intern for eighteen months (one semester in the speech writing office working with Tony Snow, eventually President George W. Bush's press secretary). That experience led to some interesting conversations when I picked her up outside the old executive office building each day. When Christi graduated from Westlake High School in Austin, she also joined me and attended George Mason University for two years before graduating from the University of Maryland in 1997. Living with two college-age daughters was quite an experience for Dad.

In February 1993, my two daughters were presented as debutantes at a society event in Dallas known as the Dallas Symphony Orchestra Ball. Connie Johnson, one of the other twenty-two debutantes, is also a great-great granddaughter of the same Byron Clark who my father felt had abandoned him as a young orphan. Neither of the parents, my second cousin Sally Johnson, nor I would ever have dreamed that the descendants of the two siblings of Byron Clark would have their family trees reach out and again touch after seventy-five years.

Elizabeth Clark became employed by Dell Computer in Austin, Texas, in 1994 and eventually worked for the company in Paris, France. She has become quite the adventuresome one, having traveled to thirty-seven countries, whitewater rafted, gone on safari in Africa, ridden camels in Algeria, scuba dived in the Red Sea, and run with the bulls in Pamplona, Spain. In June 2003, she graduated the Harvard University School of Business with a master's in business administration. She now works for Motion Computing in Austin, a premier tablet computer company.

Christi is now employed as a sales trainer for the Medimmune Company, Gaithersburg, Maryland, after five years with Eli Lilly

Company and lives near Frederick, Maryland. On September 1, 2001, she married Matthew Bieberich, son of John R. and Mary Jo of Severna Park, Maryland. Matthew's father also served in Vietnam. She was married at Hyde Park Baptist Church in Austin, where she had been baptized in 1982 with her sister and me at the same service.

Both daughters know the Christ as their personal Lord and Savior.

New Beginnings

Never one to give up on my goals, in 1996, I went for a new set of legs and finally achieved my father's towering height of six feet two inches tall. This lends believability again to being able to "grow in all my jobs."

The year 1996 witnessed my return to serving veterans of the armed forces at the Department of Veterans Affairs at the Dallas VA Medical Center where my duty was as the administrative officer of the spinal cord injury service and the physical medicine and rehabilitation service for four years. In 2001, I was appointed as public affairs officer of the Department of Veterans Affairs North Texas Health Care System. In addition, I do extensive public speaking to military, veteran, youth, and church groups. During this time in Dallas, I also have been able to cross paths with some wonderful patriots from all our nation's wars.

Expressions of my faith had to be very private and cautious at the Dallas VA. The Medical Center chaplain refused me the opportunity to conduct formal sessions for healing of my fellow veterans, but I took many opportunities in the privacy of my office to help veterans heal. One of the most memorable was when I prayed with a very troubled Vietnam veteran who was distressed about the alienation he had with his teenage son. We prayed for a reconciliation, and he popped in two weeks later to say he and his son were talking to each other again. Prayer always works.

September 11, 2001, and the attacks on the Twin Towers and the Pentagon were devastating to all Americans, but especially to our combat veterans. That day I received a telephone call from one of my friends, Houston James, a Pearl Harbor survivor. He said the television coverage was bringing back all the old horrible memories of his own "sneak" attack. I wasn't sure how to counsel him, but I recall telling him to turn off the television and to listen to some soothing music. I told him his generation had fought their war and that he could rest because the new generation of American warriors would take care of the new threat.

My exposure to future president George W. Bush on very intermittent, nominal, but interesting intervals led me after his election in 2000 to believe there might be a chance to serve in his administration in Washington. In summer 1996, I attended the Republican state convention in San Antonio, and upon seeing me in my wheelchair adjacent to him, then Governor Bush came over to shake my hand. In 1999, I contributed to the George Bush Exploratory Committee and found myself in the front row after he concluded his remarks at a fund-raiser. When he came on the stage, he waved at me (or at least in my direction), but what was really special was when he waded into the audience, he came over to me, called me by name, and "cuffed" my neck with his left hand as we shook hands. With all the people he knew, he remembered my name.

Candidly, I believed I was a slam-dunk for another appointment at the national Department of Veterans Affairs, especially after again I had been elected from my congressional district to be a delegate to the national convention in Philadelphia in 2000.

But, despite fervent prayers to fulfill "the desires of my heart" and "*my* will," it was not God's will.

However, sometime in the spring of 2003 (as the story unfolded and was related by my long-time Texas friend, Bill Mclemore, a political appointee), our VA Secretary Tony Principi was leaving a cabinet meeting at the White House when he apparently was taken by surprise by a reference to me by the president asking how I was doing. It is just the same in the military. Even the slightest mention of anything by the top person precipitates action.

The action that followed was a six-month process in which I was considered for a political position again at the national VA to oversee the homeless veteran outreach, which would have included working with faith-based organizations. The negotiations for the position overlapped a serious medical condition, so I bowed out of consideration, which ended up being another gift from God in that a door was closed but another opened to fulfill "the vision" for my ministry to veterans, which would have been closed back in a government position.

One of my greatest joys is a ministry that I initiated in 2004 that ministers to veterans who are or were substance abusers, homeless, or victims of post-traumatic stress disorder. Through this ministry, called Combat Faith Ministry, I can relate my own firsthand experiences and help them heal both mentally and spiritually. Much of what I teach them I learned from reading Christian authors such as John Dawson. In *Healing America's Wounds,* he teaches us how to heal "dis-ease" of the body, torment of the mind, and attacks of evil on our souls (page 105).

The newest change in my life is that Linda Frost, a longtime friend and sister in Christ, has become my soul mate through marriage on September 11, 2004. That good and gracious God who has always been there for me ordained our marriage. Had I assumed the position in Washington, I would not have been in Dallas to marry Linda.

When I decided to propose to Linda in 2004, I contemplated asking her son, Vincent, for her hand in marriage. The next morning I awoke at 4:30 a.m., and, lying in bed wide awake, I saw a vision of Jesus who took my left hand in his left hand, brought Linda up on His right side, put her hand in mine, and said, "I give her to you." That is the way it happened as incredible as it seems. I was at her home at 7:30 a.m. that morning with my proposal. She said that she had to think about it. Before arriving at her home, I had prayed that she would fall in love with me, and I told her my prayer. It took her a week, but she accepted. I believe that our union was ordained by God.

Linda Frost Clark

It was in the fall sometime in the late 1970s when I first became aware of Allen Clark. My husband, Jack, who died in 1994, was a fellow graduate of West Point, class of 1955. We were attending a West Point function in Dallas at Brook Hollow Golf Club when Jack pointed Allen out to me. I can still recall the vision I have of him smiling as he danced with Jackie on the dance floor. Jack told me that Allen had lost both his legs in Vietnam and that he was walking on prostheses. I was stunned! How could he look so triumphant and happy, and how could he be dancing? Jack went on to tell me how well he thought of Allen and that he was a gentleman of the highest caliber and a true credit to West Point. After that, I only knew who Allen was, but because the "girls" sometimes banded together at West Point events, I became more acquainted with Jackie, and I liked her very much.

I was dealing with a loss of my own in those days as I had recently undergone treatment for breast cancer and had sustained the loss of a breast in a radical mastectomy. I often recalled Allen's smiling, victorious image, and it gave me courage through some dark days. I volunteered for the American Cancer Society after my experience in hopes of helping others face what I had faced. Through a series of events, I was asked to speak to various groups on the subject. I recall that I referred to Allen as an example of courage and victory in at least one of my speeches.

Fast-forward to March 1995, after the death of my dear husband, Jack. My dear friends Bud and Fran Bolling asked me to be their guest to West Point's Founders Day, held in Dallas each March. I had attended this annual event with Jack for the past twenty years, and now the Bollings were kind enough to take me along. It was my nature to stay at our table all evening. In addition, fragile in my grieving, I did not especially feel like circulating. A mutual friend, Howard Coffman, came to our table and said, "Linda, come with me; I want you to meet someone." Desiring to be polite, but feeling a little awkward, I followed Howard to his intended destination. There, he introduced me to Allen Clark. I politely said, "Hello." (I believe that is all I said.) But, I thought to myself, *Yes, I know who you are.*

I believe it was the next day that Allen phoned and asked if he could come to my home for a visit. I said yes, and he came. I thought he wanted to express his condolences about my having lost Jack, and he did. As we talked, we realized that we had a lot in common in that we had both had reason to grieve a recent loss and had sought the Lord in a deep way for our strength. We shared our passion for the Bible and other subjects. Jack and I had begun a couple's Bible study before he became ill, and after a time, it resumed. I invited Allen to attend, which he did, and I became even more convinced of what a fine gentleman he was. I got to know him better and came to love him as a brother. I loved him exactly as that—a brother—until that day he came to my home to propose.

I know that God answers Allen's prayers because he prayed, and I did fall in love with him. To me, that was incredible. I had vowed never to love or marry again. My life was going to be lived out alone and in service to the Lord. My intention was to live a simple, quiet, well-ordered personal life and to invest my energy and efforts in service of the Lord's work. I had to "eat a lot of crow," as the expression goes. I had stated emphatically to my friends that I would never even consider marrying again. But I have learned that the cliché is true: "Never say never," and I believe that I will never say never again!

Linda is such a gracious lady that my former wife, Jackie, was invited to and attended our family dinner and wedding. We were married in Dallas at the home of Jean and David Dean, who had the office adjacent to mine in 1979 to 1981 in Austin on the staff of Governor Clements.

To be candid, David and I had not been close friends at all during our time on that staff. However, in 1996 at a time of a special move of God on David's heart to bring him into a deep faith in Jesus, he was driving up Central Expressway in Dallas on a Sunday to join his mother, Libba, at the 11 a.m. service at Highland Park United Methodist Church, also attended by me. As he drove, he had this inaudible, distinct instruction that went somewhat like this: "Find Allen Clark and apologize to him for the way you treated him when he came to Austin in 1978 to serve the Governor." David thought that he had no way of knowing where I was because the last time he was aware of my whereabouts was in Washington. He parked and joined his mother for the service and entered one of the *five* doors into the sanctuary. Exiting the 9:30 a.m. service through the *same* door was the object of his soon-to-be-launched search. After this very surprising greeting, upon seeing me, he said he had to see me and soon. We met for lunch a few days later. At the lunch he apologized to me for his inaction in 1979 when I moved to Austin, because as a connected Austinite (having served also as general counsel for the outgoing Governor Dolph Driscoe), he had made no efforts to outreach to me to help me become acquainted and introduced in Austin.

He also related that, when I had been on the governor's staff, he recalled how I had my little notebook with pictures of my family and Scripture quotations and how I began each day in personal prayer time at my desk. He said that my allusions to my faith had become bothersome to some members of the staff and he had been "volunteered" to talk to me to tone down the expression of my spiritual dimension. If he did that, it went over my head, because I do not recall that part of any conversation, and I kept talking about my faith when I felt the occasion was appropriate. Of course, he was probably very subtle and I did not catch his drift.

At any rate that lunch conversation launched a close relationship as he began his walk with God and began to catch up to my journey. Today he and his wife, Jean, open their home to a monthly ministry attended by Linda and me. Our close friendship led to the invitation to conduct our wedding ceremony at their home, presided over by the Reverend Andrew B. Seidel, my West Point classmate, who had so much importance to my 1970s beginning walk with God.

Once God is in charge of one's life, he weaves people in and out of our lives for our mutual benefits.

God's Grace Is Sufficient

In 1992 in Florida, I had met with Sergeant Hill, the medic who took care of me immediately after I was wounded at the tragic battle at Dak To. I had been plagued by many unanswered questions ever since the battle. During our meeting, I turned to Sergeant Hill hoping he would have some answers.

"With the mortars hitting so close, why wasn't I killed instead of the others?" I asked.

"Captain Clark," he responded, "it is by the Grace of God that you are still alive." I thought that a very strange answer. I did not understand Sergeant Hill's words at the time. However, after having given my life to Jesus Christ, I can now fully understand God's grace. I now more fully understand why certain things happened to me. I know now that God spared me for the purpose of living my life as He would have me live it by representing Him with honor, by blooming wherever He plants me, and by using my experiences in life to help others in similar circumstances.

A friend passed on a passage to me that best describes the outlook we should have when things happen in life that we don't understand. She likes to call it "the filter."

> There is nothing—no circumstances, no trouble, no testing—that can ever touch me until, first of all, it has gone past God and past Christ, right through to me. If it has come that far, it has come with a great purpose, which I may not understand at the moment. But, as I refuse to become panicky, as I lift up my eyes to Him and accept it as coming from the throne of God for some great purpose of blessing to my own heart, no sorrow will ever disturb me, no trial will ever disarm me, no circumstance will cause me to fret, and I shall rest in the joy of what my Lord is. That is the rest of the victory. (Redpath)

As I write this book in a new century and four decades after serving in Vietnam, I find that I am filled with a faith that has matured to a point of a deep and abiding belief in the power of prayer. For the past twenty years, I have immersed myself in books and study on prayer, and I have finally reached the state of belief that Andrew Murray prays about when he says, "Reveal to us, we pray, how in keeping your commandments and bearing fruit according to your will, our spiritual nature will grow up to the full stature of the perfect man, with power to ask and to receive whatsoever we will" (*The Believer's School of Prayer:* 136).

I've prayed much in my lifetime—mostly for things I wanted or thought I needed. Many times those prayers weren't answered, or so I thought. Now in looking back, I can see times when God answered my prayers when I didn't even know it. He just said no instead of yes, because my loving Father knew better than I what my real needs were (Matthew 6:8). I can't think of one thing that I really needed that I ever lacked. Garth Brooks' popular Country Western song expresses this idea in its title: "Unanswered Prayers." I learned that I must pray for what is in accord with God's will for me, not for my own personal desires. I must always pray the prayer that never fails: *Thy will be done.*

In addition, I can see times when God's loving, protective hand guarded my life even when I turned away from Him for a while. I know now that it was by God's divine intervention that the mortar round at Dak To struck in just the place it did and caused just the wound it did so that I could continue on with my life, have children, and make a contribution in this world. I thank God every day for saving my life on the battlefield at Dak To. Sergeant Hill was right. God was there with me all the time, and I did not even know it.

Through a war, double leg amputation, PTSD, death of both parents, financial hardship, divorce, and political losses, God has truly loved me, protected me, supplied all my needs, and preserved me for a greater purpose. After all, that is why He preserves Christians and leaves them here on earth rather than taking them home to be with Him—so we can minister to others in need and bring His truth to a hurting world. My fellow veterans Roger Helle, Dave Roever, and Bob Wieland found that out. They learned that the sacrifices they made in Vietnam were not in vain and that God had a greater purpose for their lives. And I thank God that my own sacrifice was not in vain. In spite of all the pain and suffering, God did not allow any more to happen to me than I was able to bear. It is my great passion and the desire of my heart to fulfill the purpose for which He has saved me.

Unbelievably, Sergeant Jimmy Hill never had received a Purple Heart medal for that shrapnel shard imbedded in him on that fateful day of June 17, 1967. When we reconnected in late 2004, I asked him if I could pursue the award for him. He said it really was not important to him and actually that he considered my life being saved as a sufficient substitute for the medal.

This award was pursued by me despite his comments. On April 15, 2005, at the Dallas Veterans Affairs Medical Center, the award of the Purple Heart medal was made as a complete surprise to him. Under my direction a special program was organized to honor all Vietnam veterans, but it was scheduled on a date he was to be in the area attending a NASCAR race. He and his wife, Dianne, lived in Florida where he had retired after a career in law enforcement.

We really did up in fine fashion—the ceremony for Sergeant Hill. The date was two weeks before the April 30 anniversary date, signifying the final evacuation from Saigon in 1975. Our ceremony honored the service of all Vietnam veterans, and we had as our guests representing the army: Medal of Honor Recipient Colonel James L. Stone (USA-Ret.). On November 21, 1951, in Korea, Colonel Stone, then a lieutenant, commanded a platoon at Sokkogae that threw back six Chinese communist assaults on his position. His platoon of forty-eight men was attacked at midnight by nearly eight hundred of the enemy. Then Lieutenant Stone fought with his platoon until half his men were killed, but not before they had killed 545 of the communists. Colonel Stone was captured and spent twenty-two months as a prisoner of war (Collier and Calzo). He served in Vietnam as the senior American adviser at the Vietnamese military academy.

The Marine speaker was retired three-star general Richard E. Carey, who as a one star directed the final evacuation from Saigon on April 30, 1975. He had another very interesting assignment as a lieutenant colonel when he was based in Danang in the spring of 1968 as a Marine aviation wing operations officer. He directed the air support for the Battle of Khe Sanh and devised the "penlite" operation by our A-6 planes that did radar bombing. He also was instrumental in effecting the "super gaggle," which was the resupply effort for the outposts and main camp at Khe Sanh during the siege.

The speaker representing the navy was Medal of Honor Recipient Michael E. Thornton, a Navy Seal. On October 31, 1972, Michael, then a petty officer, was on a patrol with one other American Seal and three South Vietnamese Seals. They moved toward a beach that day on an intelligence-gathering mission. Once on land, they were attacked by a unit of fifty enemy. Michael was ordered by the patrol leader, Lieutenant Tom Norris, to head toward the beach. Upon hearing from one of the South Vietnamese Seals that his lieutenant had been shot and supposedly killed, Michael ran back to Lieutenant Norris, who was severely wounded, but living, and personally killed two enemy soldiers hovering over Norris. Michael carried Norris and a wounded South Vietnamese Seal, swimming until the junk that dropped them off received the three. Lieutenant Norris lived after a long stay at Bethesda Naval Hospital (Collier and Calzo).

The air force special guest was retired colonel Dean E. Detar, who as a major on March 21, 1970, led a force of twenty-nine aircraft against one of the most heavily defended locations in Southeast Asia, Mu Gia Pass, to rescue an American airman. In the face of heavy opposing fire, the rescue was a success. Colonel Detar was awarded the Air Force Cross.

My wartime friend, Andy Cottingham, read Jimmy's story at the ceremony and had arrived there that day through an interesting progression of experiences to reunite two long ago wartime friends. Andy and I reconnected in 2003, thirty-seven years after Vietnam, never having any contact in the interim.

Andrew J. Cottingham, M.D.
Finding Allen Clark (Copley)

On my final trip to Dak To in the first half of June 1967, we were evacuating our research team personnel as intelligence indicated heavy NVA units were moving into and around Dak To. We rode a C-130 to Saigon from Dak To, and I went from the airport to my headquarters, 179 Cong Ly, at the corner of Rue Pasteur, directly across the street from the Institute Pasteur. My next days were spent evaluating our year's worth of collected data, writing manuscripts, and longing for my year's tour to finally finish. After all the adrenaline-filled nights in the various Special Forces A-team camps, the combat operations with the Pleiku Mike Force, the parachute jumps, the visits to so many Montagnard villages, the deaths and destruction from disease epidemics and combat, the time I was spending in Saigon seemed strikingly anticlimactic.

I awoke early, and I'm not sure why, but rather than go up one floor to the kitchen for breakfast, I descended the stairs to the first floor where I ran into the assistant XO of our team, Captain Dave Cundiff, MSC. It was around (0700 hours) seven o'clock in the morning, June 17, 1966. Dave immediately said, "Dak To was hit last night. Details are still coming, but St. Lawrence and Davis are okay. Did you know that intelligence captain? Well, he took a direct mortar hit—lost both legs—he's been medically evacuated." He continued, "The NVA tried to overrun the camp." Smiling knowingly, he said, "We brought in the Jolly Green Giant. I'll bet that was a world of hurt." I could not help myself. I may actually have thought it, but my body felt as though I had screamed it: "Oh my God, No!" It was the first time in the war that someone I had so personally known, and had grown so fond of, had been seriously injured. This was not my first combat casualty. I had visited American hospitals in Saigon, Pleiku, and had treated combat wounds in the field, in A-team dispensaries, and on the tarmac at Dak To after their return from combat missions; also combat wounded at the C-team dispensary in Pleiku, and wounded Montagnards in the Montagnard Hospital in Pleiku. This was different. I was hurting, and I tried to blank it out of my mind as I finished the last days of my Vietnam experience. I have always been a very emotional individual, even then I cried and I prayed.

Allen Copley was unique at Dak To Special Forces Camp. I was older—I was thirty years old. I was more mature than many of the SF soldiers with whom I came in contact. After all, I had finished college, medical school, an internship, and then volunteered for Special Forces training. SF soldiers were usually a little older—experienced, well motivated, mature, no nonsense types. During my entire time in the Special Forces, I never saw a Special Forces soldier use drugs except alcohol, and I never saw even alcohol in excess. I was a doctor, not a combat arms soldier, but I was always treated with respect and acceptance. Actually, I was always more than welcomed—"Always great to have a doc in camp"—and I was in reality somewhat revered for my bravery by the A-team members. Not many doctors actually went to the real outpost camps where the action happened. At most of the various SF A-teams, I was informed of intelligence concerning NVA in the area and of possible contingent escape plans from the camp in case of a massive attack or should the camp get overrun. I was informed of the various mortar pits, other heavy artillery, detonation of devices, and the radio operation. I was included in the nightly security roster (the individual who stays awake each night watching the perimeters). Of course, I always got some midnight to morning two-hour shift, but I didn't mind—I was glad to receive their confidence and to help them in any way I could; after all they were there for an entire year, and I could leave anytime I wanted, or at least hopefully so.

At Dak To it was different. Dak To was an A-team near the Cambodian border and on the Ho Chi Minh Trail, but because of the extremely good runway for small and large aircraft, it was a camp with a lot of activity of various operational units coming in and going out. It was a staging center for operations in II Corp. I was always available, but I was never asked to participate in the security duty roster, and I was never briefed by the camp commander. I think they felt too secure, and, after all, I think to them I was "just a doctor"—even though I was Special Forces qualified and had undergone the same training, maybe more than some. Allen Copley was different. He had a certain flare, a certain swagger. He was assured, self-confident, and he was a West Point graduate. Education had always been important to me. He seemed smarter than many others in the camp. I respected Allen's education and, besides, I liked him because he paid attention to me. He seemed to like me and asked me to participate with his team on some Med Cap missions (medical missions to help the indigenous Montagnards with whatever medical help we could provide) to the various Montagnard villages in the area. Maybe he was using me, but I didn't care—I was glad to help and glad someone paid attention to me and my team. We had our own job and priority, but we were SF soldiers and we were proud to serve. All SF soldiers were volunteers; there was never a no answer or a hesitation. It was always volunteer, whenever for whatever.

I remember well the last time I saw Allen Copley—it was a warm late May night in Saigon. I had returned to Saigon from Dak To for after-action reports, debriefing and planning for our continued missions. My day was boring and I was tired; I decided to go out to dinner. Local Vietnamese restaurants were a little too risky for me when alone. The Rex Hotel was a high-rise hotel housing military personnel in the center of Saigon with a beautiful view of the city from its top floor. I had been there a few times previously. The entire restaurant was open on the sides with a balcony rail, but with wire fencing around several sides, maybe for security. The restaurant occupied the entire upper floor. I sat alone four tables from the entrance elevator along the Northwest railing contemplating my return to Dak To and finishing up our projects. I was enjoying the smells, the sounds of English language discussions, the round-eyed females, and just enjoying the moments of reprieve in the middle of a war. I was so lucky; I could come and go and enjoy one beautiful moment here and another elsewhere, whereas some soldiers never got to see anything but the trees, the grass, the vines, the mud, the water, the hell of war.

I wasn't expecting anyone to join me, but suddenly out of nowhere Allen Copley appeared. We were both taken aback at seeing each other. He was alone, but even so at first I did not think he was going to join me for dinner, as he seemed a little nervous. Allen looked around, surveyed the tables, and then sat down. Perhaps it was his military intelligence training at work that made him appear so hesitant and suspiciously observant. We had a great dinner. I remember pork chops, mashed potatoes, and corn along with a Coke to drink. I essentially did not drink alcohol at the time most especially when alone anywhere in Vietnam. Allen was particularly interested in the fact that I had played football at Duke University. I was a three-year letterman. We talked football, people we mutually knew, and suddenly Allen blurted out, "My name is not Copley—my real name is Clark. I am Allen Clark." We discussed the fact that he was in military intelligence and working under a *nom de guerre* (false field name). I heard what he said, but it did not really register deep in my memory because, as I had done so many times before in my life, I neglected to realize that tomorrow may not come, and I may never have another chance. I thought I would have more time to discuss it with him later. I felt I would see him again at Dak To, and even if I forgot his name, he could tell me once again later. As we left the beautiful fresh air atop the Rex, one last time I looked over the distant rail onto the Rue de Fleur (Street of Flowers) below, remembering the Buddhist monks setting themselves afire in protest of the war a year or so earlier. It all happened just below us and it seemed so long ago.

I enjoyed this vantage spot, for the cool breeze and the view. Below was the hustle, bustle, of funny-looking tiny French automobiles, bicycles, and mopeds, all scurrying hazardously in all directions without any sense of correctness—no rules of the road, no right-of-ways, just lots of honking horns. From my perch high above the muffled noise of the streets, it reminded me of an anthill having been recently disturbed. Suddenly Allen was gone, but I had discovered Allen Clark.

My trip back to Dak To was the next morning, and this is where my story began. I do not remember whether I spoke with Allen Clark during my last short stay in the Dak To camp, and I do not remember Medic Jimmy Hill.

Upon return to the United States, it seemed surreal to see the orderliness of traffic, the calmness of our everyday way of life, compared to my last year in Southeast Asia.

My residency in ophthalmology began in the sweltering humidity and heat of Washington, D.C. on August 15, 1967, at Walter Reed Army Medical Center. I have always been good with faces, but I have never been good with names. I have often joked that if I did not have my children's names so well memorized, I would forget them. From time to time I looked in the orthopedic wards for Allen. I had heard in the initial report and descriptions of the battle that he had lost both legs. As the time drifted by, I forgot his name. At first I could remember Copley, but I had blanked out completely on the Clark. Then as more time elapsed I even forgot the Copley, but I never forgot the man. I always looked for ex–Special Forces types and asked about Dak To and the captain who lost his legs in June 1967. Over the years, I occasioned to visit many military hospitals and a few VA hospitals. I always looked over the orthopedic wards and asked questions of the staff, but I never was able to find my lost friend. Maybe there is such a thing as divine luck (intervention). Somehow in late March or early April of 2002, while rummaging around on the Internet, I happened upon a Special Forces website overseen by Steve Sherman. At the same time, I asked him about a captain I had known so long ago at Dak To, the one who lost both legs in the battle of June 1967. "Allen Clark was the only person to lose legs on that fateful day," he replied. He gave me Allen's phone number. I called Allen; we talked for a brief period and arranged for a visit. Again, I felt the same exhilarating excitement I had experienced so long ago at times in Vietnam. In the chaotic tragedy and bloodshed of the Vietnam War, in a remote jungle outpost along the border of Cambodia and Laos, I experienced excitement, emotional joy, and satisfaction in delivering a baby; helping to bring forth birth and life into this world. Finding Allen filled me with that same sense of emotional fulfillment and excitement. It was again God's blessing on me.

As it turned out we lived only five hours apart, Allen in Dallas and I in San Antonio. It was within driving distance. How lucky can you be? For me it was a marvelously emotional reunion after almost thirty-eight years. Thank God, my tenacity finally had paid off. Allen did remember me, drove down to San Antonio, and brought photographs he had taken of me treating Montagnards in the Highlands long ago when we were both young. Our paths have since remained close. Why did I persist in looking for him? Why did I like him so much in Vietnam? I have heard that scary situations bring individuals closer together. I don't know why I cared so much. All I can say is what I have said before, Allen was a cut above the rest. Our backgrounds are similar in that we both came from good, loving, Christian homes, with good family backgrounds and family values. Neither of our families was wealthy. We were both taught the virtues of hard work, honesty, the importance of maintaining our good family name, and the need for a quality higher education. Allen, like his father and like my father, ascribed to the high values of patriotism—duty, honor, country. I liked him a lot. Was it divine intervention? Maybe—only time will tell. I do remember long ago the agony and the prayers as I had trouble falling asleep that terrible night, June 17, 1967—prayer can make a difference.

My friend Ron Brown was the master of ceremonies, and Colonel Cottingham read Jimmy Hill's story of saving me. It was a wonderfully fitting occasion to honor this Special Forces medic, Jimmy Hill, with the surprise Purple Heart. We pulled out all the stops with our local Vietnam veteran community to honor this soldier who saved my life.

At the conclusion of the ceremony, my wife, Linda, called to the front of the audience Jimmy Hill, Abe Stice, Andy Cottingham, and myself (in my seldom-used wheelchair after having fallen the previous month and broken my femur). She finished the ceremony proclaiming, "I introduce to you this Band of Brothers."

A picture of my daughter hugging Jimmy was taken and seen by me, but not discussed by Jimmy and me until six months later. He asked me if I had known what she said to him as she hugged him. I said no.

Jimmy said, "She said, 'Thank you for bringing my daddy home.' "

EPILOGUE

Scores of books have been written and many movies made about the war in Vietnam. These books and movies have depicted certain attitudes about and effects of the war, both regarding the American populace and the Vietnam veterans who served in it. The reality of it is that no one book and no one movie speaks for everyone. We are all human, and we all act and react differently to the same situations, the same tragedies, and the same disasters according to our individual upbringings, beliefs, and life experiences.

The one thing that we all do have in common is that no matter what kind of disaster or tragedy strikes, life still goes on. For the brave men and women who fought and served in Vietnam, life has gone on. For those whose emotional wounds and scars won't heal, life may be worse. Some of them have turned to drink, drugs, destitution, and isolation. For others, who also smelled of and tasted death, life today may be sweeter and more precious. Many of them have turned to counseling and support groups to deal with their feelings. Many have melded anonymously into society and are successful spouses, parents, and grandparents engaged in all facets of American life. Vietnam became a learning and maturing experience contributing to the successful business of living, loving, and coping with their lives today. For all of us, Vietnam will forever remain an integral part of our lives. The awful sights, sounds, and events of the war make it impossible for us to lock it away in the closets of our subconscious minds to be forgotten. It will always remain there, where its tapes run over and over and over again in our memories.

Never before had the United States participated in a war like Vietnam. Soldiers of both World Wars I and II were trained together and then sent overseas as a unit. Veterans of those two world wars spent years with the same men, fighting side by side. They were one with one another and experienced a brotherhood, a camaraderie not experienced in Vietnam. Unit reunions have been common for World Wars I and II veterans. Only recently, as veterans reach retirement age, have Vietnam companies and batteries started to reconnect with one another. Because they spent so much time together,

World War II veterans shared their feelings with others who had become their good friends, their "buddies." The military even adopted a "buddy system" where good friends could remain together on future tours.

The men of the two world wars returned to the United States with their respective units and, upon arrival, were debriefed by the military before returning home. The long ship rides home allowed for even more time for them to share their feelings and deal with what they had just experienced together. When they finally reached home, they returned to the welcome arms and support of family and friends who had supported the war through victory gardens, rationing programs, and other expressions of support. Family and friends were willing to listen to their stories, giving them yet another chance to talk about their feelings and experiences to sympathetic listeners. Even so, many of these veterans could not talk much about the specific horrors of the war they had experienced.

On the other hand, the Vietnam soldier experienced something completely different. Combat soldiers were intensively trained how to kill and were then sent to Vietnam as individuals. Sometimes they were not assigned to a specific unit until they arrived in Vietnam, and then many times they did not stay with that unit for their entire tour, but rather were reassigned—sometimes more than once. They performed as they had been trained—hunting down the hated enemy and killing him. When their tours were completed, they came home alone, usually on a plane full of other soldiers who were strangers to them.

The Vietnam combat soldiers were never debriefed, and reached home after quick plane rides on which they sat in stunned silence, still in shock from what they had experienced. In addition, they were never taught how to get rid of the hate that had been so thoroughly instilled in them during training. They never had a chance to talk out their feelings with anyone. They returned home to unrest, protest, and nonsupport and were often confronted by angry citizens who launched verbal assaults against them for their participation in the war. They were expected to blend back into home, family, and community life as if nothing had happened.

Friends and family did not understand, so the men didn't talk about their experiences. They were expected to put the war behind them—to "get over it" and move on—as if it were that easy. Thus, their feelings mounted inside, resulting in inner turmoil and a sense of futility and solitude.

In addition, the soldier fighting in Vietnam did not have the advantage his father had of fighting an organized and uniformed enemy. Although the Viet Cong and North Vietnamese often staged the organized frontal attacks normally expected, the enemy in Vietnam more often than not fought guerilla warfare, launching frequent and unsuspected ambushes from the jungle foliage or the maze of tunnels dug under the jungle floor. He remained unseen and undetected by normal military means and took on various forms. Sometimes he took the form of a village farmer working as a Viet Cong spy or assassin. Sometimes the enemy manifested itself as a village wife on her way to the river to wash clothing while concealing weapons beneath the laundry in her basket—weapons that she might use in a sudden and vicious attack upon unsuspecting and friendly soldiers. Sometimes the enemy even took the form of a small child sent into an American camp by the Viet Cong who had strapped grenades or other explosives onto its frail, young, and innocent body.

Soldiers had to remain on constant alert and not trust anyone young or old, male or female, adult or child. For many soldiers, this was one of the hardest parts of the war with which to deal. This war was up close and personal. Men found themselves faced with the dilemma of defending themselves and their units or sparing the lives of civilians, including women and children, who were forced to take on the role of assassins, used by senseless people with no regard for human life—somewhat like the current conditions facing us in Iraq. The choices were often obvious yet horrible. Such choices often resulted in returning soldiers being spat upon by fellow citizens and hearing "Baby killer" screamed at them from the mouths of angry Americans who could not understand how to condemn a war and its atrocities, but not the warriors who, in obedience to the country that had sent them, were fighting an unorthodox war.

The normal ravages of war take a severe toll on any soldier's emotional well-being. Not only is he separated from his family and home, but he must take the lives of other human beings in the course of combat and self-defense. The fact that we sent our children to fight that war makes the emotional toll even more severe, yet understandable. The average age of a combat soldier in World War II was twenty-six. The average age of the Vietnam combat soldier was *nineteen*! It is no wonder that between one hundred and twenty-five thousand and two hundred thousand (and some reports speculate it could be as high as four hundred and seventy thousand) Vietnam veterans suffer from post-traumatic stress disorder (PTSD) decades after the war's end. Even adults are not emotionally equipped to handle the kinds of experiences witnessed in war. How could our military officials and government leaders expect teenagers going through the emotional and physical turmoil of growing up to do better than our men when we burdened them with the war experience at such a young age?

James Webb, highly decorated Vietnam War Marine, successful author, and dedicated public servant wrote in an article titled "Heroes of the Vietnam Generation" about the young Marines with whom he fought:

> When I remember those days and the very young men who spent them with me, I am continually amazed, for these were mostly recent civilians barely out of high school, called up from the cities and the farms to do their year in hell and then return. Visions haunt me every day, not of the nightmares of war but of the steady consistency with which my Marines faced their responsibilities, and how uncomplaining most of them were in the face of constant danger. The salty, battle-hardened twenty year olds teaching green nineteen year olds the intricate lessons of the hostile battlefield. The unerring skill of the young squad leaders as we moved through unfamiliar villages and weed-choked trails in the black of night. The quick certainty when a fellow Marine was wounded and needed help. Their willingness to risk their lives to save other Marines in peril. To this day it stuns me that their

own countrymen have so completely missed the story of their service, lost in the bitter confusion of the war itself.

Finally, to make matters worse, we soldiers read daily accounts of the unrest at home, which included violent antiwar protests in the streets and vicious editorials in our hometown newspapers. Knowing that many of our own people were not behind us made our jobs that much more difficult. In spite of the blood, in spite of the wounded, in spite of the deaths of friends, in spite of innocent lives lost on both sides, and in spite of the discord at home, most of us believed in what we were fighting for. We believed the war to be necessary to block the spread of communism. We believed in liberating an oppressed people who wanted and had asked for our help. We believed in protecting and preserving the cause of freedom for all people through our sacrifices in Southeast Asia.

Most of us went to Vietnam because we believed in the principles on which this country was founded—the freedoms of life, liberty, and the pursuit of happiness. We believed that other people in other nations deserved those same rights and freedoms. We knew that if we did have to fight for freedom, it would not be purchased cheaply. Necessary sacrifices would have to be made. This is the way that I felt at the time. In reality, though, I recognize that these high and lofty principles may not have been shared or understood by all Americans, especially those of my age bracket at the time who could be termed the *Woodstock generation*.

Between April 1964 and April 1975, 9.2 million men and women served in the military worldwide. Of that number, around one-third, or 3.1 million, were deployed to Southeast Asia where only approximately 1.5 million participated in active combat. Approximately 1.8 million men and women *volunteered* (enlisted and volunteered for Vietnam or asked for that assignment as regular army personnel), meaning that they believed in the cause. Only nine hundred thousand out of the total of 3.1 million were actually drafted, yet these were the people who got the most press and public attention.

I am only one of 153,303 men and women who were physically wounded (75,000 severely) in the line of duty in Vietnam. Only

1,081 of us sustained multiple amputations. I thank God that it was His will not to include me in the 58,148 who lost their lives (47,410 in battle deaths) or the 1,833 who, to this day, are still missing and unaccounted for. I am sure that these people and their families would like to think that their sacrifices were not made in vain. The Vietnam government has admitted that 1.4 million of its NVA soldiers died, not a bad "kill ratio" for our side.

Dave Roever lost half his face when a phosphorous grenade exploded in front of him (*Welcome Home, Davey*). Bob Wieland stepped on a detonated and hidden 82mm mortar round. Both his legs were blown off his body at the hip (Zettersten). Roger Helle suffered fifty-seven shrapnel wounds after he stepped on an M26 fragmentation grenade thrown back by an enemy soldier. After the explosion, the enemy wanted to make certain Helle was dead, so he approached Helle's broken body, pumped two AK-47 rounds into him, and then ran him through with a bayonet. Shrapnel had pierced a phosphorous grenade Helle carried, and it spilled its contents onto his shoulder and arm resulting in severe burns. Helle miraculously survived (*My War Beyond Vietnam*). These stories are not unusual. I also sacrificed my legs in Vietnam. These were the kinds of things that happened in Vietnam every day. My comrades in arms and I would like to think that sacrifices such as these counted for something.

I think that perhaps the most difficult part of the war to accept was its end and how we were treated. Pressured by politics and the tide of public opinion, President Nixon saw fit to pull out of what some believed to be an "unwinnable" war. In so doing, we abandoned an entire country filled with innocent, frightened, and oppressed people, who are not much better off today than the day we left them. They are still enslaved by the communists. For soldiers like me who had been trained to be proud of their country, that day turned into one of embarrassment and sorrow. If we had successfully liberated the South Vietnamese, the sacrifices of more than two hundred and ten thousand men and women would not have seemed so futile. We would have known why we sacrificed so much and would have been proud of it. If we had accomplished our mission and walked away from Vietnam with a victory, perhaps so many veterans would not have struggled with their feelings for so many years, constantly asking themselves if it was really worth it. I know that I have asked myself these same questions over and over.

Regardless of its outcome, the war became a part of all of our lives, and we have each had to learn to deal with it in our own ways. Unlike many other Vietnam veterans who have been unable to cope with the war and its after-effects and who have continued to suffer over the past few decades, I am afflicted with only minor effects of post-traumatic stress disorder. And, like the three men previously mentioned, I have discovered a meaning to it that makes the various after-effects of the war practically inconsequential. For through our shared faith in Jesus Christ, we have found a peace and comfort that surpasses all understanding.

I realize now that if I had not experienced Vietnam, I would not have become the person I am today. If I had not lost my legs, I might not have reached a low enough point in my life where I found it necessary to look up in order to seek the comfort of my Creator. Everything I have experienced has been a necessary part of God's plan for my life, and the rest of my life must grow out of that into whatever God has planned for my future. In light of that, I know my sacrifice was not in vain, and I suspect that Dave Roever, Bob Wieland, and Roger Helle feel the same.

Today, Dave Roever has a successful preaching ministry in which he shares his testimony and shows others that no matter how bad things get, God will always see us through. Roever's story has enabled scores of people to come to know the Lord. His sacrifice was not in vain.

Between 1982 and 1986, Bob Wieland, moved by the hunger he witnessed in Vietnam, literally walked across America on his hands to raise money for the world's hungry, telling people all along the way what God has done for him. During his four-year, three-thousand-mile walk, Wieland also led many Americans to Jesus Christ. He began a new career in acting while continuing his efforts to raise money for the hungry and witness to those he meets along the way. His sacrifice was not in vain, and he continues his "walks" today.

Roger Helle admits to taking a lot of lives in Vietnam. All these years later, he remains a soldier on the spiritual battlefield, where real battles are won and lost. He is the director of Teen Challenge of the Mid-South in Chattanooga, Tennessee, where he battles for the lost souls of runaway teenagers who live on the streets. In his street ministry, he is trying to restore life to the lost. Young men and women have found new life because of Helle's devotion and commitment to his Lord. His sacrifice was not in vain.

Christ healed both the physical and emotional wounds in Dave Roever, Bob Wieland, and Roger Helle and enabled them to see a purpose for their experiences and their suffering. When I discovered His infinite love and grace, I too welcomed the miraculous power of His healing hand and found a new purpose in my life. Perhaps the impact I have on this world may not be on such a spiritual grand scale as that of these fine men, but I strive each day to set such an example that others will notice that I have something different and special. By working at a veteran's medical center, I had daily opportunities to minister to and pray with our warriors who need healing in body, soul, and spirit. Christ's love for me has made me more understanding, definitely more forgiving, and certainly less judgmental. It has been a long journey home from Vietnam, but I am home and at peace in knowing that my God is in charge of my life, the world, and everything in it.

If you have suffered and wondered why, Christ's love can heal your hurt and suffering and turn it into something positive and good just as He has done for me. Without Him, my physical wounds may have healed, but my emotional wounds would not have. Most certainly, my heart would not have healed. Without Him, I would not have become the man I am today. It is only through His sacrifice on the cross because of His unfailing love for me that I am alive and that I have been able to keep my sanity, raise a beautiful family, pursue a career, make a mark in life, develop a forgiving spirit, and put the horrors of Vietnam behind me. His sacrifice for me was not in vain, and this book is as much His story as it is mine.

This is not just another book about the Vietnam War. It is a book about the spiritual war that we all fight on a daily basis—the war between good and evil and the battle for our very souls. I wrote this book for the purpose of telling you that there is victory—victory that brings peace and forgiveness and promise. I hope it has shown you that, no matter what your own personal battle, Christ's love can bring healing and victory.

Allen Clark, 2007

BATTLE PLAN FOR VICTORY

I truly believe that all of us desire healing of body, mind, and spirit, and that is God's desire for us as well. However, in order to achieve this, it takes devotion, attention, commitment, striving, and hard work. Is it worth it? Of course it is, but the tools to acquire these goals often elude us. It took me a long spiritual journey to find these tools—a journey through several churches and denominations, seminars, countless discussions with ministers, the reading of several hundred books, and extensive self-study and even self-ministering. I want to share what I have learned with my readers as I have shared it with countless hurting people in my ministry. I call it "combat faith." I have always been a bottom-line type of person, so I have synthesized, distilled, and summarized where I am at this stage of my journey and share my own personal understanding of what we must do regularly to prosper spiritually, emotionally, mentally, and physically. I do not suggest to others what they should do; I only express what worked for me.

I learned one of the greatest lessons of my life from a friend who taught me that *dis-ease* in life is at the root of all afflictions of body, mind, and spirit. In his book *Healing America's Wounds*, John Dawson refers to Matthew 4:24 when he writes about three categories of afflictions: dis-ease of the body, torment of the mind, and evil spirits that plague the soul (Davidson). Several of the major sources of the dis-eases of our soul are anger, failures, and mistakes that haunt us, and we refuse to accept the consequences that these conditions bring into our lives. When we admit our anger, failures, and mistakes, then we begin to accept responsibility for our own destinies. We have to deal with unhealed hurts, unmet needs, and unresolved issues. As valuable as ministers and other godly people are to us, I finally realized that the responsibility for my own well-being lies within me and no one else. I must be a mature enough Christian to be willing to learn about God's truth for myself and appropriate the weapons and tools He has provided that will enable me to face and fight dis-ease in my life.

It has been my experience that most of us question whether we are ever "good enough" to merit God's healing. We often wonder what we have to do to work our way through a spiritual process to be ready to accept healing. Perhaps it is because we know we are unworthy of such a gift, or perhaps it is because we feel that God doesn't think us worthy of it, or perhaps both. Whatever our inner reasons, God does offer this gift in the same way he offered the gift of salvation. It is freely given because He loves us. We do not have to earn it. It took a long, arduous, and painful journey for me to come to these conclusions. But in my experience, I know them to be true. Because of this, I have committed to help others learn these things too. And it is my hope and prayer that the readers of this book will take these things to heart and perhaps glean hope and healing of their own. If that happens, then in a modest way I will have become a "healing warrior."

1. Confess all sins, thoughts, words, and deeds—both known and unknown. If we confess our sins, "He is faithful and just to forgive us our sins and to cleanse us from all unrighteousness" (I John 1:9). First and foremost, we must invite Jesus Christ into our lives. "If you confess with your mouth the Lord Jesus and believe in your heart that God has raised him from the dead, you will be saved" (Romans 10:9). All sins (thought, word, and deed, known and unknown) must be verbalized as confession (with repentance) so one can receive forgiveness. This is a spiritual truth. Unconfessed sin, no matter how "small" it may be, blocks God's power to work on our behalf. Accept this promise and set yourself some uninterrupted time and ask the Holy Spirit to reveal to you the sins in your life. Confess them to God and then forget them. Once they are forgiven, God no longer sees them, because the blood of Jesus Christ, who spilled His blood on your behalf, covers them. Proverbs 28:13 promises, "He who covers his sins will not prosper, but whoever confesses and forsakes them will have mercy." I *choose* to believe in that teaching.

Next, we must allow Christ to be the Lord of every aspect of our lives and allow Him to heal broken relationships, resolve conflicts, and explore the inner depths of our very souls in order to cleanse all areas of our lives, because we cannot do any of that within our own power. This is one reason Jesus came to earth, but the choice to claim such healing is ours.

2. Engage in prayer every day. Prayer is a way of building a relationship with the Lord. No relationship can survive if only one person is willing to communicate. It all starts with faith and belief that God is who He says He is, that our needs are important to Him, and that He does indeed answer prayers. If we have faith in God, then we must believe in the textbook He gave us, His Word, the Bible. As young people, we studied math, chemistry, and social science texts, believed what we studied, and regurgitated it on tests so that we could obtain good grades and thus an impressive transcript that would get us into college and eventually a prosperous career. However, the most important text for life is the Bible. It teaches us all we ever need to know about living in this world. And most importantly, it teaches us how to pray—how to communicate with our Lord. We learn from Psalm 5:8 that we must "make (our) way straight before (His) face." So when I pray, I ask that God order my day. I ask Him to tell me what and how to pray, what to do and when, whom to call, and what to say. Scripture teaches that God's Word is *alive;* it is a living thing that has power. When all else fails, remember the prayer that never fails: *Thy will be done.*

Use the Lord's Prayer as a model (Matthew 6:9–13). Some Bible scholars prefer to call the Lord's Prayer the Disciples' Prayer or the Model Prayer, because Christ used it to teach His disciples how to pray to the Heavenly *Father*. (This is the first time in Scripture that God is referred to as *Father*.) We don't need to tell God what we need, because He knows our needs before we ever ask (Matthew 6:8). Instead, we need to learn how to talk to Him—to develop a relationship with Him. This prayer shows us that we are to praise and acknowledge God for who He is (v. 9); to ask for His will to be done, not ours (v. 10); to pray for our own daily needs as well as the needs of others (v. 11); and to ask for forgiveness when we fall into temptation (vv. 12–13). In other words, we first look *up* (praising God), then we look *around* (praying for our needs and the needs of others), and finally we look *within* (asking for forgiveness for sin).

Pray in agreement with one another. "Again, I tell you that if two of you on earth agree about anything you ask for, it will be done for you by my Father in Heaven. For where two or three come together in my name, there I am with them" (Matthew 18:19). Find another believer to serve as a prayer partner and exercise community prayer. It is extremely comforting that a prayer partner is not only holding you accountable in your prayer life, but is also praying for and uplifting you to the Father every day.

Speak God's Word back to Him. A variety of formulas for prayer have been published and taught. While they serve as reminders of how we should pray and what we should pray for, God wants our hearts, not a formula. There is wonder-working power in the living Word of God, and I have found that the most powerful prayer a person can pray is to speak God's words back to Him—out loud. Place your name, or a person's name for whom you are praying, in the passage to personalize it to your own prayer needs. God promised in Isaiah that His Word would never return void. "As the rain and the snow come down from heaven, and do not return to it without watering the earth and making it bud and flourish, so that it yields seed for the sower and bread for the eater, so is my word that goes out from my mouth: It will not return to me empty, but will accomplish what I desire and achieve the purpose for which I sent it" (Isaiah 55:10–11). Likewise, if we pray God's Word back to Him, it will not fall on deaf ears because it is a powerful, living thing.

This same principle can be used when one needs healing. Matthew 8 and 9 are called the healing chapters because they contain so many accounts of Christ's healing miracles. Select the passages that can be personalized, insert the appropriate names, and pray them back to the Great Physician who can heal all wounds (Matthew 8:8–9). If you have a troubled child, pray passages Proverbs 1–2 by inserting the child's name, and so forth. God's Word is alive, and it will never return void.

When you want someone to understand a spiritual truth, "Pray ye, therefore, the Lord of the harvest, that he will send forth laborers into His harvest" (Matthew 9:38). Pray for this person to learn truth through another person, through reading Scripture, through seeing a television program (Yes, it can happen!), through music, and so on. This prayer works, because I have experienced its power.

3. **Obey this day to receive answers to prayer.** "And whatever we ask we receive from Him because we keep His commandments and do those things that are pleasing in His sight" (I John 3:22). "For the eyes of the Lord are on the righteous, and His ears are attentive to their prayer, but the face of the Lord is against those who do evil" (I Peter 3:12).

4. **Be loyal to God this day.** God has taught us in I Chronicles 16:9 that the eyes of the Lord run to and fro throughout the whole earth to show Himself strong on behalf of those whose hearts are loyal to Him (i.e., wholeheartedly devoted to Him). That is powerful. In I John 3:22, it is written: "And whatever we ask we receive from Him, because we keep His commandments and do those things which are pleasing in His sight." Continually ask yourself, "Is this action pleasing to God, or does it reflect a wholehearted devotion to God?" If it does not, one lays the groundwork for a torment of the soul.

5. **Watch what you say!** The words we speak are critical. Jesus

Christ said, "But I say to you that for every idle word men may speak, they will give account of it in the Day of Judgment. For by your words you will be justified, and by your words you will be condemned" (Matthew 12:36-37). That's pretty strong! In addition, Proverbs 6:2 teaches, "You are snared by the words of your own mouth; you are taken (have been caught) by the words of your mouth" (Proverbs 6:2) and "My son, give attention to my words; incline your ears to my sayings. Do not let them depart from your eyes; keep them in the midst of your heart; for they are life to those who find them, and *health* to all their flesh" (Proverbs 4:20–22). Our words spoken are powerful. God tells us that. Therefore, all day, each day, I try to keep in mind the importance of everything that I say. James is one of the most practical writers in the New Testament. He puts it very clearly when he says, "With the tongue we praise our Lord and Father, and with it we curse men who have been made in God's likeness. Out of the same mouth come praise and cursing. My brothers, this should not be" (James 3:9–10). It is my desire to begin each day with *positive* words and remember to continue to do so all day.

6. Take every thought captive. Our speech cannot be pure unless our thoughts are pure, "Bringing every thought into captivity to the obedience of Christ" (II Corinthians 10:5). "Finally, brothers, whatever is true, whatever is noble, whatever is right, whatever is pure, whatever is lovely, whatever is admirable—if anything is excellent or praiseworthy—think about such things. Whatever you have learned or received or heard from me, or seen in me—put it into practice" (Philippians 4:8–9).

One night I listened to Nancy Missler who discussed the concept that the secret to success in reducing the torments of the soul is the acronym TECAC. She taught that, if one controls the *T*houghts, then the *E*motions are under control. Our emotions are reflected in *C*hoices of *A*ctions that bring *C*onsequences with which we must live, whether they are good or bad. Therefore, if we analyze every thought, we can sidetrack unhealthy emotions before we start the negative merry-go-around. Paul gives us the tool with which to do this in passages from both Philippians and II Corinthians. Are your thoughts negative or positive? Will the emotions, choices, actions, and consequences of that thought reflect your loyalty to God and be pleasing to Him? The torments of the soul and the disease of daily life for us and for others can all be under control. Discipline and perfect yourself at all costs. Do this, for soon every fleeting thought will be answered, every wish gratified, every deed used (Russell, A. J.: 18).

7. Put on the full armor of God (Ephesians 6:13–17). We must pray daily for faith, because everything that can bring us to complete health relies upon faith. Our prayers will be answered to change us only in the degree to which we exhibit faith in God, His Word, and His promises. Paul writes in Ephesians that, in order to be strong in the Lord, we need to put on the full armor of God—not just the shield of faith, but also the belt of truth, the breastplate of righteousness, the gospel of peace, the helmet of salvation, and the sword of the Spirit, which is the Word of God. These are the weapons with which we fight the evil one. Each day I begin my spiritual preparation for the battles of the day by reciting the Lord's Prayer and putting on the full armor of God as related in Ephesians. This is what we need for protection. It worked for the warriors of old, and it will work for us as modern day warriors in the spiritual battles of life.

8. Forgive all others. For if you forgive men their trespasses, your heavenly Father will also forgive you. But if you do not forgive men their trespasses, neither will your Father forgive your trespasses (Matthew 6:14–15). In order to reduce the torments of the soul, give unconditional love and mercy to everyone you meet. A friend once differentiated between grace and mercy in this way: grace is when we receive something we don't deserve (salvation), and mercy is when we don't get what we do deserve. Mercy is like an acquittal in a courtroom. The sin may have been committed, but we are given a second chance. Forgiveness is very close to mercy. We extend mercy when we forgive others, and we are commanded to forgive others if we desire to be forgiven. Forgiveness for all who have wronged us is imperative. It is a command from the One who first forgave. Do whatever it takes to extend forgiveness—a personal visit, a call, a written card or note, an e-mail—but *forgive* everyone. It is a choice that we must make if we expect to live a healthy spiritual life.

Admittedly, some hurts or wrongs are difficult to forgive and impossible to forget. For example, I have a friend who was repeatedly molested by her grandfather when she was a child. After she became a Christian as a young adult, she knew she had to forgive him *although he had since died.* You see, forgiveness is necessary for the person doing the forgiving in order to get past a wrong and be able to effectively serve God. It was very difficult for her to forgive this man, and she knew she couldn't do it alone. So she prayed for God to forgive him *through her.* Forgiveness did not enter her heart immediately, but through persistent prayer, she slowly realized that she harbored less and less bitterness toward her grandfather as time went on. She could never forget those horrible acts—they are a part of her life experience—but they were no longer dominating her life, and she used them to minister to others who had had similar experiences. We must *choose* to forgive even though we may think we are not able to do so. We can do it only through the power of God.

9. Fear not! Be anxious about nothing, but in everything by prayer and supplication, with thanksgiving let your requests be made known to God (Philippians 4:6). Many of us worry constantly, and most of us worry too much. Worry induces stress and strain, that is, dis-ease. The words *fear not* appear approximately 350 times in God's Word! If He thought it that important to repeat that phrase more than any other in His Word, then we should heed His caution and act in faith by casting all worries upon Him. Next, there is power in *action.* Write the things that worry you on a sheet of paper, pray to turn them over to the Lord, and then burn the paper. Or kneel at the altar at your church during an altar call and symbolically lay them on the altar as you pray to turn them over to the Father. Lay them at His feet, at the foot of His throne, and tell Him that you can't handle them alone. You will be given such a peace that you will know that He is in control and carrying your burden for you. "Come to me, all you who are weary and burdened, and I will give you rest.

Take my yoke upon you and learn from me, for I am gentle and humble in heart, and you will find rest for your souls, for my yoke is easy and my burden is light" (Matthew 11:28–30).

10. Ask for protection and divine help. Are they (angels) not all ministering spirits sent forth to minister to them who are heirs of salvation? (Hebrews 1:14). This is an incredible passage. I take comfort in the idea that God looses and provides these special agents as helpers to protect and help my loved ones and me from the attacks of the evil one. When we feel we are under attack, we must do two things: (1) "Resist the devil and he will flee from you" (James 4:7) and (2) "Whatsoever you shall bind on earth shall be bound in heaven: and whatsoever you shall loose on earth shall be loosed in heaven" (Matthew 18:18). We are not only to resist the devil when we are tempted, but we are also to bind him away in the name of Jesus Christ and ask God to *loose* the power to meet our needs. When we pray to God, we satisfy one side of this equation. To ensure there is no negative spiritual involvement, bind the evil one in the name of Jesus from hindering your prayers. Then ask God in Heaven to loose His power to help you. Both sides of the equation are now covered. Bind yourself to God's will, purpose, timing, truth, righteousness, holiness, integrity, purity, and the mind of Christ and ask for the imparting of wisdom, insight, maturity, discernment, knowledge, and control by the Holy Spirit as well as the ministering angels who are there to protect you (Savard).

11. When you need healing, claim the promise of Peter: "(Christ) who Himself bore our sins in His own body on the tree, that we, having died to sins, might live on for righteousness . . . by whose stripes (wounds) you were healed" (I Peter 2:24). Obviously, there are those who would claim that this relates to the emotional healing of sin only. I choose to believe that there are many Scriptures whose principles can be applied to more than one area of life. Therefore, I choose to apply this particular Scripture to physical healing as well. My thesis is that when the dis-eases of the soul and spirit are addressed and healed, then many dis-eases of the body also disappear or never appear at all. I have personally heard of too many instances of healing not to believe that it is a current gift from God to continue miraculous healings. David Wilkerson's book, *Have You Felt Like Giving Up Lately*, helped me understand my own disappointment when deep faith and fervent prayer did not always lead to healing. He says that sometimes abuses of our body through unhealthy habits, genetics, or just aging preclude miraculous healing. Sometimes these things are difficult for us to accept. However, curtailing dis-eases of our soul and spirit and praying for healing may be able to affect physical healing from bodily dis-ease. Dr. S. I. McMillen writes in *None of These Diseases* that his experiences through his medical practice were replete with examples of bodily disease caused by emotions of "anger, passion, malice and self-centeredness." He goes on to say that "a great variety of resulting neurotic manifestations can produce any of the many psychosomatic diseases." Dr. McMillen believes that "failure to possess His (Holy) Spirit will make us susceptible to many diseases of the body and mind."

It takes a tremendous amount of faith to believe in self-healing (taking Scriptures and claiming them for healing). But God is the Great Physician who can heal whoever and whenever it is within His will to do so. He may, however, have other plans. Sometimes true healing comes only through death. And that is, in the final analysis, perhaps the hardest answer to prayer for most of us to accept.

12. Reflect the fruit of the Spirit in your life. Our soul is made up of our mind, emotions, and will. It is from deep within our souls that we experience the torments of our lives when we don't achieve our goals or desires in life—experiences we often call our failures. Sometimes failures are merely opportunities that have been mislabeled or unrecognized. We must learn to desire what God knows to be best for us and pray to that end. II Timothy 22–25 relates wonderful, achievable guidelines for our lives: "Flee also youthful lusts; but pursue righteousness, faith, love, peace with those who call on the Lord out of a pure heart. But avoid foolish and ignorant pursuits, knowing that they generate strife. And a servant of the Lord must not quarrel but be gentle to all, able to teach, patient, in humility correcting those who are in opposition . . ." However, if the Holy Spirit is in control of our lives, then it only follows that our lives will reflect the fruit of the Spirit, which is love, joy, peace, long-suffering, kindness, goodness, faithfulness, gentleness, self-control (Galatians 5:22). When we do not live in such a way as to reflect the fruit of the Holy Spirit, then we cause dis-ease in our own lives, our relationships go awry, and torments follow.

God does not desire dis-ease in our lives, whether it be emotional, mental, spiritual, or physical. On the contrary, He desires us to be healed. After all, He had a tremendous healing ministry that demonstrated this desire of His heart. In each case, however, it took faith on the part of someone else to bring about that healing, whether it was an intercessor like the Roman centurion or the person who needed the healing. In His Word, God has given us some magnificent weapons to combat the afflictions of the body, mind, and soul. Learn them, commit them to memory, practice them, and use them. Do not be anxious about anything, but in everything, by prayer and petition, with thanksgiving, present your requests to God. And the peace of God, which transcends all understanding, "will guard your hearts and your minds in Christ Jesus" (Philippians 4:7).

In addition, by staying in God's Word and practicing the tools he has given us, we become more like Jesus Christ and more prepared for the battles we must fight until we see Him face to face. After all, that is what we are all preparing for on this earth—to eventually claim our citizenship in Heaven. "This life is not all there is. Life on earth is just the dress rehearsal before the real production. You will spend far more time on the other side of death—in eternity—than you will here. Earth is the staging area, the preschool, the tryout for your life in eternity. It is the practice workout before the actual game; the warm-up lap before the race begins. This life is the preparation for the next. . . . You have an inborn instinct that longs for immortality. This is because God designed you in His image, to live for eternity. Even though we know everyone eventually dies, death always seems unnatural and unfair. The reason we feel we should live forever is that God wired our brains with that desire! (Warren: 36–37).

In a speech to disabled Iraqi and Afghanistan veterans, former Dallas Cowboys quarterback Roger Staubauch said that life is one mortar attack after another. Because I was in a real mortar attack, I can relate to that. I believe that we can remove ourselves from many of the kill zones by making Jesus Lord and Savior of our life.

If life is a workout before the big game, then we need to be in our best condition for that workout. We need to be prepared for battle. We need to have healthy bodies and sound minds in order to face the obstacles that life throws our way. And most importantly, we need to know that God is protecting our paths as long as we obey His commands and trust in His faithfulness to us "For I know whom I have believed, and am convinced that He is able to guard what I have entrusted to Him for that day" (II Timothy 1:12b).

Nick Rowe was captured with Captain Humbert "Rock" Versace on October 29, 1963. As Nick and Rocky were being tied up at elbows and wrists by the Viet Cong ready to be taken into their horrifying captivity in "tiger cages" for the next few years, they both said to each other "God bless you" (Rowe). Rocky was executed in captivity and was eventually honored by the posthumous receipt of the Medal of Honor.

For my fellow veterans, active duty military, and anyone feeling "captive" in their lives, I pray that as you allow yourself to grow spiritually that you will accept my "God bless you."

For more information

I have had the privilege and pleasure of teaching a six-part series to Sunday school classes covering the creation story in Genesis, the First Coming of the Christ, the Holy Spirit, prayer, spiritual warfare, and the Revelation. I've titled this series "The Alpha to the Omega." In addition, I have spoken to combat veterans about healing both the outer and inner wounds of war, based on my own personal experiences as well as teachings of Scripture. More information is available at my ministry website: www.combatfaith.com. My wife, Linda (whose own website is www.voices.name), does dramatic presentations of women of the Bible, some of which I follow with training.

BIBLIOGRAPHY

Billheimer, Paul, *Destined for the Throne.* Minneapolis, MN: Bethany House Publishers, 1975.

Bogle, Eric, *And the Band Played Waltzing Matilda.* Larrikin Music Publishing Pty. Ltd.

Bubeck, Mark I., *The Adversary.* Chicago, IL: Moody Press, 1975.

Collier, Peter and Nick Calzo, *Medal of Honor,* New York, NY: Artisan, 2003.

Davidson, Lieutenant General Garrison (USA), "Lecture to the Class of 1963," 1963.

Dawson, John, *Healing America's Wounds.* Ventura, CA: Regal Books, 1997.

Dearing, Trevor, *Supernatural Healing Today.* Gainesville, FL: Bridge-Logos, 1979.

Helle, Roger, *My War Beyond Vietnam.* Ventura, CA: Regal Books, 1985.

Henry, John C., "Austin's Clark Wanted No Part of Being a 'Token' in VA," *Austin American-Statesman.* Austin, TX, July 22, 1981.

The Holy Bible, Authorized King James Version. Nashville, TN: Broadman Holman Publishers, 1998.

Lemnitzer, Gen. Lyman L. (USA), *Army Information Digest.* Vol. XV, September 1960.

Lewis, C. S., *The Screwtape Letters.* New York Bantam Books, 1982.

Lindsey, Gordon, *Prayer That Moves Mountains.* Dallas, TX: Christ for the Nations, Inc., 1996.

Marshall, S. L. A., *Battle in the Monsoons*, Apollo Edition. New York: William Morrow & Company, 1970.

McMillen, S. I., *None of These Diseases.* Spire Books, second printing, April 1994.

Murphy, Edward F., *Dak To: America's Sky Soldiers in South Vietnam's Central Highlands.* New York, NY: Pocket Book, 1995.

Murray, Andrew, *The Believer's School of Prayer.* Minneapolis, MN: Bethany House Publishers, 1982.

Pentagon Papers. New York, NY: The New York Times Company, 1971.

Redpath, Alan, *Victorious Christian Living.* Old Tappan, NJ: Fleming H. Revell Company, 1955.

Roever, David, *Welcome Home, Davey.* Waco, TX: Word, Inc., c1986.

Rowe, Nick, *Five Years to Freedom.* Boston, MA: Little Brown & Company, 1971.

Russell, A. J., editor. *God Calling.* Old Tappan, NJ: Fleming H. Revell Company. 43rd printing, 1989.

Russell, Dick, *The Man Who Knew Too Much.* Carroll & Graf Publishers, 1992.

Savard, Liberty, *Shattering Your Strongholds.* North Brunswick, NJ: Bridge-Logos, 1992.

Sihanouk, Prince Norodom as related to Wilfred Burchett, *My War with the CIA.* New York, NY: Pantheon Books, a division of Random House, 1972, 1973.

Stanton, Shelby, *Green Berets at War.* New York, NY: Dell Publishing Company, 1985; Martin's Press, 1992.

Stein, Jeff, *A Murder in Wartime.* New York: St. Martin's Press, 1993.

Stilwell, Richard G., *The Army Information Digest.* Vol. XV, September 1960.

Ten Boom, Corrie with John and Elizabeth Sherrill, *The Hiding Place.* Old Tappan, NJ: Fleming H. Revell Company, 1976.

United Press International, "Hagel Resigns VA Post," *Dallas Times-Herald.* Dallas, TX, June 30, 1982.

Warren, Rick, *The Purpose Driven Life.* Grand Rapids, MI: Zondervan Publishing Co., 2002.

Washington Post, February 18, 1991.

White, Thomas B., *A Believer's Guide to Spiritual Warfare.* Ann Arbor, MI: Servant Publications, 1990.

Wilkerson, David, *Have You Felt Like Giving Up Lately?* Grand Rapids, MI: Fleming H. Revell Company, 1980.

Zettersten, Rolf, "A Walk for World Hunger," *Focus on the Family Magazine.* Pomona, CA: Focus on the Family, September 1982.

ACKNOWLEDGMENTS

Without the love, support, encouragement, and assistance from the following, I not only would not have written this book, but I would not be where I am today. I am humbly grateful to each of them:

My Lord and Savior, Jesus Christ, who gave me the gift of eternal life and allowed me to have a second chance in this life; my late parents, Lieutenant Colonel Allen Byron Clark Sr., USA (Ret.), and Amalia De la Fuente Clark, who loved me and taught me to love and serve others; my sister, Betty Chalfont, who was not only my childhood companion, but also my lifelong friend, and to her husband, Lieutenant Colonel Alan, USA (Ret.), and my nephews and nieces, Major (USA) Chuck and Krista Chalfont, Major (USA) Chad and Shannon Chalfont, Major (USA) Jason and Charlene Miseli, and Lieutenant (USN) Chris and Cheryl Jason, all career military families who render me proud; Sergeants Cramer, St. Lawrence, and especially Jim Hill whose battlefield courage protected and saved me; Jackie McAdams Clark, my wife for thirty years, who was my Rock of Gibraltar after the war; the Reverend Andy and Gail Seidel and the Reverend Gene Getz who led me to an understanding of Jesus as Lord; the men and women on Ward 43-A at Brooke Army General Hospital in San Antonio, Texas, who shared my pain, sorrow, and ultimate triumph, especially George Pomerantz, M.D.; Marietta Reed for her invaluable help and expertise in editing and updating my manuscript. She is a talented writer who went the "extra mile" for the book; Andres and Juanita Tijerina, Belinda Theophile, and Paulette Cooper who assisted me in preparing the manuscript; my dear friends Doug and Ginger Simmons, Abe Stice, Mike Eiland, Steve Alpern, and Ron Brown; Colonel Andrew J. Cottingham, USA (Ret.), M.D., for his input on malaria in the Vietnam War and the plague epidemic at Dak To; Gayle Wurst, my literary agent and Richard Kane, my publisher, who believed in my story; Steve Gansen, my editor, and all the other members of the professional team at MBI Publishing in St. Paul, Minnesota, who brought the story to fruition; and Linda, Elizabeth, Christi, and Matthew Bieberich, and Vincent Frost who are the centers of my life.

INDEX

Acers, Maurice, 230
Aleshire, Bill, 245, 246
Alpern, Steve, 123–126
Americans with Disabilities Act, 258, 260
Armogida, Jim, 173
Asturias, Spain, 21
Atwater, Lee, 265

Baker, Jim, 265
Ban Don, 121, 122, 132
Bayoud, George, 222
Ben Het, 136, 143
Benjamin, Ben, 173, 174
Bentsen, Lloyd M., 63, 212, 244
Best, Stephen, 38, 39, 72
Bieberich, Matthew, 277
Bolling, Bud, 280
Boys State, 226
Bradley, Omar, 231
Britcher, John, 53, 54
Brooke Army Medical Center, 47, 51–53, 55, 56, 59–61, 65, 163, 164, 183, 248
Brown, Walter "Ron," 160–162, 292
Bryant, Anita, 95
Bubonic plague, 144–146
Bullock, Bob, 213
Bush, George H. W., 64, 220, 224, 252, 256, 258–260
Bush, George W., 64, 70, 198, 220, 221, 243, 278

Cambodia, 26, 119, 118, 121, 123–125, 128–131, 133, 134, 136, 143, 191–194, 197, 271, 288, 291
Carey, Richard E., 285
Carpenter, Bill, 159, 160
Central Intelligence Agency (CIA), 133, 194–196, 263
Chalfont, Alan, 47, 58, 113, 226
Chalfont, Betty (sister), 47, 48, 56, 58, 113
Chau Doc, 123, 125

Chosin Reservoir, 22
Christensen, Kevin, 248
Chuyen, Thai Khac, 196
Cicconi, James, 228, 248
Clark Air Force Base, Philippines, 45, 46, 50, 51
Clark, Allen Sr. (father), 19, 24, 46, 47, 55, 56, 58, 63, 64, 66, 78, 110, 113 , 247, 248
Clark, Amalia (mother), 20, 24, 47, 56, 58, 112–114, 226, 247
Clark, Christina (daughter), 200, 232, 273, 276
Clark, Jackie (first wife), 12, 35, 37–46, 48–53, 58, 59, 94–96, 98, 99, 101–109, 111–114, 132, 142, 151 153, 170, 171, 176, 184 187, 189, 190, 198, 200, 202, 204, 205, 207, 215, 216, 218, 220, 221, 228, 230–232, 237, 238, 243, 244, 248, 254, 261, 274, 275, 280, 281
Clark, Sharon Elizabeth (daughter), 200, 202, 221, 222, 225, 226, 241, 253, 255, 276
Clements, Bill, 215–225, 227–229, 231, 236, 237, 242, 244, 245, 260, 281
Coe, Doug, 265
Coffman, Thomas D., 80, 242, 243
Collins, Gary, 268
Collins, Jim, 215, 216, 220, 231
Combat Faith Ministry, 267, 279, 313
Connally, John, 220
Cottingham, Andrew J., 143–151, 286 292
Cramer, Sgt., 10–12, 33, 34

Dak Plon, 142
Dak Poko River, 10, 29, 139, 145
Dak To Special Forces, 9, 139
Dallas VA Medical Center, 277, 285
Dart, Justin Jr., 224, 229, 258, 260, 263
Davidson, Garrison, 69, 71

Dawkins, Peter, 71
de la Fuente, Placido, 21
Dean, David, 228, 281, 282
Department of Veteran Affairs, 80, 175, 252, 269, 277, 278
Derwinski, Ed, 253, 254, 256, 261, 266, 267
Desert Storm, 86, 267, 269
Detachment B-24, 132
Detachment B-57, 25, 118, 121, 123, 124, 128–130, 139, 192, 193, 195–197
Detar, Dean E., 286
Dickey, Jim, 232
Disabled American Veterans, 181
Donlon, Roger, 272
Duc Co Special Forces, 128

Eiland, Mike, 131, 132
Eisenhower, Dwight D., 69, 70, 80, 212, 232
Elliott, Bill, 217, 218
Exeter Academy, 63–66, 74, 182, 196

Fellowship Bible Church, 201, 202, 204, 205, 218
Fisers, Arturs, 11, 34
Flook, Bud, 22
Flynn, John, 207
Foley, Bob, 126, 127
Fontenot, Gregory, 86
Fort Bragg, 33, 119, 147, 197, 253
Fort Hood, 36, 40, 42, 101–103, 133, 153, 171, 181, 185
441st Counter Intelligence Corps Group, 23
Frost, Linda (second wife), 249, 279–282, 313

Galloway, Joe, 86
Garn, Harvey, 83
George, Christopher, 95
Gepson, John, 63, 65, 182
Getz, Gene, 202, 203, 218
Gio Linh, 105
Gonzaga Jesuit High School, 61–63, 65, 74, 75
Goodpaster, Andrew J., 257

Gossett, Larry, 14, 15, 26, 139, 146, 158, 159, 197
Grace Episcopal Church, 63
Graves, Howard, 256, 257
Griffeths, Bill, 261
Grover, Hank, 215

Haase, Richard, 262
Hagel, Charles, 240
Harris, Janie, 228
Hawaii, 68, 72, 78, 81, 82, 152, 268
Hays, Brooks, 63, 65
Helle, Roger, 284, 298–300
Hendricks, Howard, 205
Herrington, John, 237
Hickam Field, 268
Higdon, Joseph, 21
Highland Park United Methodist Church, 281
Hill 875, 27, 164
Hill 1338, 50
Hill, Jim, 12–15, 18, 27–30, 33, 34, 164, 270, 282–285, 290, 292
Ho Chi Minh Trail, 10, 118, 135, 149, 151, 196, 209, 288
Ho Ngoc Tau, 118, 193
Holland, Homer, 189
Hollingsworth, James H., 228
Hope, Bob, 131, 208, 238
Hudkins, Dick, 123–126
Hunt, Ray, 231
Hussein, Saddam, 261, 262
Hutchison, Ray, 215, 216, 230
Hyde Park Baptist Church, 277

James, Houston, 278
James, Pen, 234, 237, 238
Johnson & Johnson Pharmaceutical Company, 181, 182
Johnson, Lyndon B., 41, 97, 128, 165, 191, 208, 209
Johnson, Stuart, 254, 255

Kelly, Francis J., 197
Kelly, John E., 102, 181
Kelly, Peter "Bear," 65, 76, 79, 81, 106
Kennedy, John F., 40, 41, 79, 80,

82–84, 119
Kerrey, Bob, 132, 178
KGB, 197
Khmer Serei, 128, 129, 131, 134, 192, 193, 197
Kilgore, Joe, 63, 182
Kilroy, Michael, 105–107, 270
Knaggs, John, 243
Kontum, 28, 120, 132, 133, 135, 141, 145, 155, 159, 197
Korean War Memorial, 257
Krulak, Charles, 269

Ladd, Ernest, 197
Lam, Inchin Hai, 128–131, 192–195
Lamb, Chuck, 204
Landry, Tom, 82, 269
Laos, 26, 119, 124, 131, 135, 151, 271, 291
Lee, Burke, 80, 81
Leghorn radio relay site, 10, 135
Lennon, Frank, 84, 193
Loc Ninh Special Forces, 126
Long Binh, 192

MacArthur, Douglas, 20, 22, 69, 84, 85, 271
Malaria, 148–151
Mann, Ron, 237, 238
Marsh, Jack, 238
McAdams, Jack and Adell, 34, 35, 111, 112, 275
McCarthy, John J. Jr., 192–195
McChristian, Joseph A., 153
McCord, Burt, 101, 270
McLemore, Bill, 278
McNamara, Robert S., 30, 165
McNeil, Tom, 36, 183, 188, 198
McQuarrie, Claude M., 26
Meese, Ed, 87, 238
Meese, Michael, 87
Mike Force, 28, 29, 147, 148, 150, 151, 287
Missler, Nancy, 307
Montagnards, 9, 14, 28, 120–122, 128, 132, 140–144, 146, 148, 154–156, 159, 287, 289, 291
Moore, Demi, 252
Moyers, Bill, 208–210

Murray, Pat, 123, 130, 131, 136

Nandor, George, 25, 34, 130, 159
National Cemetery System, 265
National Debutante Cotillion, 255
Nha Trang, 18, 116–118, 132, 133, 143, 145
Nha Trang Special Forces, 196
Nhia, Le Quang, 15, 157
Nielsen, Elizabeth, 21
Nimmo, Robert, 233, 234, 236–238, 241
North, Oliver ("Ollie"), 254
North Vietnamese Army (NVA), 10, 13, 15, 25, 27–29, 50, 105, 116, 118, 119, 121, 124–126, 133, 135, 140, 148–151, 159, 163, 196, 197, 210, 286–288, 295, 298

Omer, George Jr., 100
173rd Airborne Brigade, 16, 26, 29, 60
Operation Cherry, 131, 133, 136, 137, 192, 194, 195, 197
Operation Desert Storm, 263
Operation Viper, 143

Parfitt, Harold, 198
Parmly, Eleazar, 117, 118
Partain, Edward A., 16, 26, 50, 80
Patrice Lumumba University, 129, 130, 193
Pearl Harbor, 268, 278
Pearl Harbor Survivors Association, 268
Pentagon Papers, The, 30, 31
Perot, Ross, 186–188, 240
Pershing, Dick, 253
Pershing, John, 253
Pickett, David, 207
Pistor, Charles, 213, 228
Pleiku, 10, 16, 18, 26, 27, 33, 52, 117, 120, 128, 199, 287
Pomerantz, George, 60, 61, 95
Powell, Colin, 256
Preston, Marlow, 244
Principi, Anthony J., 272, 278
Project Gamma, 195, 196
Protzman, Bob, 254
Psychiatric Institute of America, 266

Posttraumatic stress disorder
   (PTSD), 26, 94, 175, 176, 266,
   279, 284, 296
Punchbowl Cemetery, 268

Quayle, Dan, 238

Reagan, Ronald, 87, 228–230, 234,
   235, 237, 239, 241, 247, 248
Rex Hotel, 147, 151, 289, 290
Rheault, Robert, 196, 197
Richards, Ann, 243, 244
Roberts, Virginia, 224
Roever, Dave, 284, 298–300
Rove, Karl, 221, 245
Rowe, James N. "Nick," 72, 73, 78,
   212, 253, 313

Santoro, Frank, 61, 62, 65
Sattonstall, William G., 64
Scalia, Antonin, 87
Scalia, Matthew, 87
Second Armored Division, 36, 40, 102
Seidel, Andrew and Gail, 201, 202,
   205, 206, 256, 282
Sendai, Japan, 21
Sihanouk, Prince, 128, 129, 131,
   192, 194, 195
Sill, Lou, 115, 141
Simmons, Doug and Ginger, 190,
   191, 228–231
Singleton, Jerry, 271
Smith, Eldon L., 133
Smyth, Cathy, 190
Snow, Tony, 276
Studies and Observation Group
   (SOG), 9, 10, 13, 135
Sons and Daughters in Touch, 270
Southern Methodist University
   (SMU), 39, 50, 53, 104, 151,
   182–186, 189, 191, 247
St, Luke's Episcopal Church, 40, 41
St. Lawrence, Leslie, 11–13, 34,
   287, 44
Staubauch, Roger, 82, 313
Stephanski, 123–125, 129
Stice, Abe, 164, 292
Stilwell, Richard G., 77, 257
Stockdale, James, 207

Stone, James L., 285
Strake, George W., Jr., 228, 245
Sununu, John, 259, 260
Swindoll, Chuck, 256, 257

Tan Phu Special Forces, 212
Taylor, Maxwell D., 83
Terry, Curtis D., 121, 122
Than, Son Ngoc, 131
Thornton, Michael E., 286
Timperlake, Ed, 256, 263, 267
Tinh Bien, 123–126
Tokyo, 23, 24
Torrey, John Jr., 185
Tower, John, 220, 236, 243
Tri-Border Area, 26, 131

U Minh Forest, 212
Ullam, Madeleine, 261
Urrutia, Henry, 40

Versace, Humbert "Rock," 313
Vesser, Dale, 83, 147
Viet Cong (VC), 85, 116, 117,
   119–121, 124, 140, 141, 151, 158,
   160, 164, 210, 253, 295, 313
Vietnam Veterans Memorial, 266,
   270, 271, 273

Walter Reed Army Institute of
   Research, 11, 139, 143, 146, 150,
   156, 290
Walters, Harry, 267
Webb, James, 240, 296
West Point, 20–23, 36, 38, 40, 43,
   60–63, 66–89, 102–104, 106, 107,
   114, 117, 118, 126, 127, 147, 152,
   160, 173, 182–184, 186, 188, 189,
   193, 196, 198, 201, 205, 212, 232,
   234, 248, 253, 254, 256, 267, 270,
   274, 280, 282, 288
Westmoreland, William C., 29, 76,
   121, 131
White House Fellowship, 213–215
Wieland, Bob, 284, 298–300
Willis, Bruce, 252
Wilson, Drake, 118
Woods, John, 190